Economic Effects of Post-Soci
25 Years from the Outset

Polish Studies in Economics

Edited by Ryszard Kokoszczyński

Volume 7

PL ACADEMIC RESEARCH

Katarzyna Metelska-Szaniawska

Economic Effects of Post-Socialist Constitutions 25 Years from the Outset of Transition

The Constitutional Political Economy Approach

PL ACADEMIC RESEARCH

Bibliographic Information published by the Deutsche Nationalbibliothek
The Deutsche Nationalbibliothek lists this publication in the Deutsche Nationalbibliografie; detailed bibliographic data is available in the internet at http://dnb.d-nb.de.

Library of Congress Cataloging-in-Publication Data
Names: Metelska-Szaniawska, Katarzyna, author.
Title: Economic effects of post-socialist constitutions 25 years from the outset of transition : the constitutional political economy approach / Katarzyna Metelska-Szaniawska.
Description: Frankfurt am Main : PL Academic Research, 2015. | Series: Polish studies in economics ; 7 | Includes bibliographical references.
Identifiers: LCCN 2015039080 | ISBN 9783631669532
Subjects: LCSH: Constitutional law—Europe, Eastern. | Constitutional law—Former communist countries. | Former communist countries—Economic policy—Political aspects. | Law and economic development.
Classification: LCC KJC4445 .M48 2015 | DDC 330.947—dc23 LC record available at http://lccn.loc.gov/2015039080

This research was financed by the Polish National Science Centre (DEC-2011/03/B/HS4/01343).

Reviewed by Jerzy Wilkin

Cover Design: © Olaf Gloeckler, Atelier Platen, Friedberg

ISSN 2191-8848
ISBN 978-3-631-66953-2 (Print)
E-ISBN 978-3-653-06058-4 (E-Book)
DOI 10.3726/978-3-653-06058-4

PL Academic Research is an Imprint of Peter Lang GmbH.

Peter Lang – Frankfurt am Main · Bern · Bruxelles · New York · Oxford · Warszawa · Wien

This publication has been peer reviewed.

www.peterlang.com

Table of Contents

Introduction 7

Chapter 1. Constitutions and economic policy – the theoretical nexus 13

1.1 The Constitutional Economics research program 15

1.2 Persson and Tabellini's (2003) theoretical framework 24

1.3 Future prospects and challenges faced by empirical verification 28

1.4 Constitutions and economic reforms in transition 33

Chapter 2. Post-socialist constitutions in a nutshell 43

2.1 Executive-legislature relations 46

2.2 Constitutional rights and freedoms 50

2.3 Enforcement mechanisms 56

2.4 Summary 60

Chapter 3. Regression analyses of economic effects of post-socialist constitutions 61

3.1 The empirical model 61

3.2 Dependent variable 63

3.3 Constitutional variables 65

3.4 Estimation results 66

3.5 Conclusions 77

Chapter 4. The synthetic control approach to estimating economic effects of post-socialist constitutions 79

4.1 The synthetic control method 79

4.1.1 Advantages of synthetic control 83

4.1.2 Requirements and potential drawbacks 85

4.1.3 Making inferences with the synthetic control method 88

4.1.4 Selected applications of the synthetic control method 90
4.2 Study design 93
4.3 Baseline results (country studies) 98
4.4 Evaluating and explaining the reform gaps 100
4.5 Conclusions 107

Chapter 5. An evolutionary perspective on the role of post-socialist constitutions 109
5.1 The role of the constitution from an evolutionary perspective 110
5.1.1 Crucial rules 111
5.1.2 Stability vs. flexibility of the constitution 114
5.1.3 Imperfect incentives 118
5.2 Empirical tests 120
5.2.1 Introducing direct democracy mechanisms 121
5.2.2 Support for the constitution 128
5.3 Conclusions 134

Conclusions 137

References 143

Appendices 161
Appendix 1. Additional tables 161
Appendix 2. Additional figures 170
Appendix 3. Description of variables and data sources 178
Appendix 4. Unit weights and predictor balance for the synthetic control study 180

List of Tables 191

List of Figures 193

Introduction

During the last ca. 15 years economists provided numerous theoretical and empirical confirmations of a significant role of constitutions for the working of the economy and economic outcomes, in particular with respect to electoral systems, models of government, constitutional rights, and constitutional enforcement mechanisms (see survey by Voigt 2011b). This approach, rooted in Constitutional Economics, views the constitution as a set of "*legal-institutional-constitutional rules that constrain the choices and activities of economic and political agents*" (Buchanan 1987, p. 585). The state constitutional system serves primarily as a mechanism allowing to counteract time-inconsistency problems connected with drafting and implementing economic policy. Containing rules that impose constraints on activity of state authorities, the constitution acts as a mechanism allowing to turn promises made by representatives of state power into credible commitments.

Post-socialist transition taking place since 1989 in countries of Central and Eastern Europe, as well as later in Central and Southwestern Asia, provided a particularly fruitful ground for Constitutional Economics studies. Since 1990 all post-socialist countries of Europe and Asia[1], with the exception of Latvia, adopted new constitutions envisaging varying solutions as regards the structure of government, bill of rights and other issues. This unprecedented time of broad-scale constitutional and, more generally, institutional change has sometimes been called a "*gigantic natural experiment*" (Elster 1991, p. 449), attracting interest of legal scholars, political scientists, sociologists and other social scientists. The contribution of economists concerns, in particular, linking constitutional change with economic policy pursued in these countries and economic performance.

Economic studies relating to post-socialist constitutions conducted to date reveal that several aspects of the constitutional framework laid down in these supreme legal acts, and their practical operation, mattered for economic

1 These are: countries of Central and Eastern Europe (Albania, Bulgaria, Czech Republic, Hungary, Poland, Romania, Slovakia); former Yugoslavian republics (Bosnia and Herzegovina, Croatia, Macedonia, Montenegro, Serbia, Slovenia); and former Soviet republics (Armenia, Azerbaijan, Belarus, Estonia, Georgia, Kazakhstan, Kyrgyzstan, Latvia, Lithuania, Moldova, Russia, Tajikistan, Turkmenistan, Ukraine, Uzbekistan). Acknowledging the differences in the political and economic systems functioning in these countries before 1989, we further refer to all of them as 'post-socialist countries' or 'transition countries'.

performance of these countries during transition (e.g. Hellman 1997, Ahrens and Meurers 2001, Ahrens 2007, Metelska-Szaniawska 2009). In principle, the results of these studies confirm the constitution's main function as a commitment mechanism for policy-making in transition, including the performance in broad-scale post-socialist economic reforms.

Despite their thought-provoking findings and stimulating conclusions, most of the empirical studies in the field of Constitutional Economics, including those pertaining to post-socialist constitutions, struggle with problems of endogeneity and causality, which undermine the validity of the employed empirical models and analytical techniques. The qualitative nature and country-specificity of various aspects examined in such analyses can also significantly limit the explicability of quantitative large-sample studies conducted within this field, as well as the reliability of the results and conclusions stemming from them. In this situation it comes as no surprise that authors active in this field often call for case study analyses, allowing to focus on country specificity and institutional detail, to support the large sample econometric analyses. Comparative case study research however suffers from its own problems and shortcomings, including in particular the lack of formalization in selecting the comparison units.

With such a list of caveats and challenges relating to empirical studies in Constitutional Economics it is not surprising that the current generalization level of the theory in this field is insufficient and its further development rests on the ability of empirical researchers to surmount these obstacles. Paraphrasing Douglass North (North 1990), we know that 'constitutions matter', however 'which sets of constitutional rules' and via which channels of influence, remains largely unclear, primarily as empirical studies conducted to date have delivered a wide range of incomparable results, which are questionable on several grounds for reasons mentioned in the previous paragraph. In this book we aim to contribute to surmounting these obstacles for further development of Constitutional Economics.

We base our empirical studies on the experiences of post-socialist countries in the period of (nearly) 25 years from the outset of transition in 1989. The central claim (thesis statement) of this book is that constitutional solutions, adopted by post-socialist countries after 1989, which enhanced the credibility and commitment of decision makers in the field of economic reforms conducted by these countries during the transition period, constituted a framework conducive to such reforms. In particular, we focus in this respect on the significance of structural provisions, bills of rights, as well as constitutional enforcement mechanisms. This claim builds up on consequent and systematic exploration of the link between constitutional rules and performance in the area of economic reforms by post-socialist countries, conducted by the author for the last several years, [initiated by Metelska-Szaniawska (2008)], and allows to organize the presented theoretical and empirical considerations. Several arguments justify refocus on the link between constitutions and economic reforms in post-socialist countries. The current account, presented in this book, is not only significantly enriched in several dimensions – by encompassing a notably longer time-period of nearly 25 years from the outset of transition, new constitutional rules, and broader and much more reliable data. The main contributions are: firstly, introducing a novel empirical approach allowing to respond to several of the caveats mentioned earlier, including the endogeneity allegation, and secondly, enriching the currently existing theoretical and empirical framework with elements suggested by Evolutionary Political Economy.

In order to circumvent the problems of endogeneity and causality in comparative studies with relatively small sample sizes, a new statistical approach has recently been developed, called the synthetic control method. It focuses on comparing the evolution of a studied outcome variable for a unit (e.g. country or region), where a particular intervention or event took place, with its evolution for a 'synthetic counterfactual' (i.e. 'synthetic' unit of interest, where the studied intervention or event did not occur) constructed based on a data-driven procedure of selecting comparison units that approximate the characteristics of the unit exposed to the intervention. Recently, the method has been successfully applied in several studies of economic consequences of large-scale events such as natural catastrophes (e.g. Cavallo et al. 2010, Barone and Mocetti 2014), political conflicts (e.g. Bove et al. 2014 and Costalli et al. 2014 – on civil wars; or Acemoglu et al. 2014a – on Egypt's Arab Spring), as well as in studies focusing on effects of legal and policy interventions (e.g. Abadie et al. 2010, Bohn et al. 2014, Heim and Lurie 2014, Baum and Ruhn 2013, Doerrenberg and Peichl 2014). We apply this method to reassess the conclusions regarding the role of constitutional rules for economic reforms in post-socialist countries and contrast the obtained findings with results of studies conducted using regression estimation techniques.

In addition to the above contribution to empirical Constitutional Economics and, thereby, potentially to further development of the theory, we also attempt to enrich the latter with this book by opening the research on economic effects of constitutions to insights from the evolutionary approach to politics, as proposed by Evolutionary Political Economy. While interest in the topic of constitutions can be traced as far back as to the works of the predecessors of this approach, such as Friedrich August von Hayek (e.g. Hayek 1979) or Joseph Schumpeter

(1942/1987), none of these studies, nor works of their followers, identify factors that a comprehensive account of economic effects of constitutions should incorporate, in an attempt to reconcile this view with the Constitutional Economics approach. We take up this challenge, present the potential channels, as well as offer empirical tests of preliminary predictions stemming from the theory and conclusions regarding the future development of this promising strand of research.

The book is structured as follows.

In Chapter 1 we elaborate on the theoretical nexus between constitutional rules and economic policy-making. We draw on the core components of the Constitutional Economics research program, as well as the recent 'standard' – Persson and Tabellini's (2003) theoretical framework. We also discuss the obstacles and challenges that further development of such research on constitutions faces, as well as lay down the theoretical grounds for our empirical studies of economic effects of constitutions on post-socialist economic reforms, presented in the subsequent chapters.

As economic transition in post-socialist countries is a topic that has received ample attention of economists, also within political economy (for most recent collections see Hare and Turley 2013, Aslund and Djankov 2014) and new institutional economics (e.g. North 1997, Fischer and Sahay 2004, Lissowska 2006, Opper 2008 and others), we refrain from presenting in this book another survey of this literature and focus directly on the presentation of the constitutional framework that emerged in these countries after 1989. Chapter 2 provides, therefore, the relevant background information about post-socialist constitutions, relating in particular to their provisions establishing the systems of government, constitutional bills of rights, as well as enforcement mechanisms.

Chapter 3 is devoted to a first verification of the theory underlying the relationship between constitutions and economic reforms in post-socialist countries after 1989 based on an empirical model developed earlier in Metelska-Szaniawska (2008, 2009). In a panel data regression setting we attempt to identify constitutional rules composing the rule framework conducive to successful performance in the area of post-socialist economic reforms such as privatization, liberalization, enterprise restructuring, etc. While this study delivers a handful of stimulating results, we also reflect on its potential caveats.

Based on the latter reflections, in Chapter 4 we introduce and apply the synthetic control method to reassess the effect of constitution-making in post-socialist countries on their performance in the field of economic reforms during transition. We proceed in two steps: Firstly, we verify whether the adoption of a constitution had any effect on economic reforms in each of the post-socialist countries (and if so, then was this effect positive or negative, and what was its magnitude). Secondly we study in what way these effects depend on the actual constitutional solutions adopted within these legal acts. Thanks to employing this novel approach we are able to avoid several technical caveats that have arisen in earlier studies and verify the validity of their conclusions. In addition, it allows us to obtain country-specific results for each individual post-socialist state, as well as formulate valuable insights regarding the actual mechanisms or channels of influence of the constitutional framework on economic reforms.

Finally, in Chapter 5 we enrich the view at the role of the constitutional framework for economic policy by incorporating into the analysis insights offered by an evolutionary perspective on politics and policy making. We discuss the potential theoretical channels of influence and provide two empirical tests relating to the constitutional rules providing for direct democracy mechanisms, as well as to popular support for the constitution. The results that we obtain allow not only to broaden the understanding of the relation between constitutions and economic reforms in post-socialist transition but also to bring a modest contribution to the theoretical background underlying the economic effects of constitutions.

The book finishes with conclusions, where we reflect on the significance of our findings for development of empirical and theoretical Constitutional Economics, as well as transform the main implications into potential policy-recommendations.

Bearing in mind the cross-disciplinary nature of Constitutional Economics, we would like to emphasize that the book is addressed in particular to economists. While we hope that it will also be of interest to other social scientists interested in studying consequences of legal and constitutional systems, as well as other problems at the nexus of constitutional law, political science and economics, the principal target on economists affects the terminology, structure and content of the book.

This book is an outcome of the author's interest in the constitutional political economy approach to post-socialist transition and expertise in this field accumulated over the past ca. decade. However, its publication in this form would not be possible had it not been for the invaluable support of several persons and institutions. We are particularly grateful to professor Jerzy Wilkin, who agreed to review this work before its publication and provided numerous helpful remarks, in particular pertaining to the theoretical underpinnings of the presented study. We would also like to thank professor Ryszard Kokoszczyński, editor of the Polish Studies in Economics series, for having proposed the opportunity to publish this work within the series. Parts of this book have earlier been presented by the author at various international conferences and seminars. We would like to thank, in particular, participants of the 2013 'How Constitutions Matter' workshop at the University of Oxford, SIDE-ISLE 2013 Annual Meeting in Lugano, 2014 Law and Economics Workshop in Bologna, 2014 European Public Choice Society (EPCS) Annual Meeting in Cambridge, 2014 Annual Meeting of the European Association of Law and Economics in Aix-en-Provence, and 2015 Annual Meeting of the European Association of Law and Economics in Vienna for valuable and helpful comments. The usual disclaimer applies. This research was funded by the Polish National Science Centre (DEC-2011/03/B/HS4/01343).

Last but certainly not least, I would like to thank my husband Michał, daughter Karolina, and son Mikołaj – for their constant support for my work and understanding at times when the consequences of the scarcity of time resources were most difficult to bear.

Chapter 1. Constitutions and economic policy – the theoretical nexus

Economic studies view the constitution from different angles. The common feature of these approaches is, however, the treatment of constitutions as certain meta-rules defining the fundamental constraints within which political, economic and social actors make their choices and take their actions (Buchanan 1987). In this context the constitution is viewed as a crucial element of the institutional order within the state and thereby also an important factor shaping the functioning of the society. Based on such general approach economists have developed arguments emphasizing the constitution's role in, inter alia, conflict-solving and coordinating collective action (e.g. North et al. 2009, Weingast 1993), improving efficiency of resource allocation by establishing property rights protection (e.g. Acemoglu and Robinson 2006), as well as in the distribution of political and economic rents (e.g. Greif 2008).

Taking as a starting point the view of the constitution as a kind of social contract, economists approach its analysis through the lens of: contract theory, treating it as an incomplete contract; agency theory, focusing on principal-agent relationships connected with its functioning; or (evolutionary) institutional economics, viewing it as the result of cultural evolution or a 'bundle' of conventions. Notwithstanding many significant differences between these perspectives, their common feature is the attempt to approach the constitution with the use of dynamic models of human behavior.

In this chapter we provide the theoretical background for those economic studies of constitutions which strive to explain the relevance of constitutional rules for policy-making in the state and thereby – economic outcomes. Systematic research focusing on economic effects of constitutions began in the 1990's and has been developing intensively during the recent years. The starting point for many such analyses is the model of the democratic policy-making process proposed by Persson and Tabellini (2003). Constitutional rules, functioning as 'rules of the game' for political and economic actors in a state, determine the institutional setting for policy-making and influence political outcomes. By doing so these rules participate in transforming citizens' preferences regarding policy into policy decisions. The latter influence the functioning of markets and economic performance of countries.

Several constitutional rules and their economic effects have so far been analyzed theoretically and empirically, e.g.: electoral rules and electoral systems, including differences between proportional and majoritarian voting rules or district size (e.g. Persson and Tabellini 2003); rules regarding structure of power within the state, in particular different models of government and separation of powers (e.g. Persson and Tabellini 2003, Treisman 2007, Blume et al. 2009b); rules introducing direct democracy mechanisms, e.g. mandatory referenda (e.g. Matsusaka 1995, Blume et al. 2009a); constitutional bills of rights (e.g. Blume and Voigt 2007); constitutional enforcement mechanisms, in particular rules determining the position and functioning of the constitutional judiciary (e.g. Feld and Voigt 2003); rules regarding constitutional change (e.g. Rasch and Congleton 2006). Among economic variables explained by reference to, inter alia, these constitutional rules are macroeconomic outcomes (economic growth, per capita income, labor productivity, total factor productivity), fiscal policy variables (government revenue, government expenditures, budget deficits, composition of government spending), governance variables (corruption, government efficiency), as well as other variables describing individual behavior (e.g. the propensity to cheat on taxes) or entire societies (e.g. reported life satisfaction).

Studies of economic effects of constitutions, though, as mentioned above, mainly based on Persson and Tabellini's (2003) formal model of the democratic policy-making process, reach down in their fundaments to the research program of Constitutional Economics, as introduced and developed in particular by the Nobel Prize laureate James M. Buchanan[2]. Therefore, we begin this chapter with a presentation of the Constitutional Economics research program with particular emphasis on these aspects which make it not only useful, but fundamental, for studies of economic effects of constitutions. Secondly, we describe the formal framework for studying economic effects of constitutions as proposed by Persson and Tabellini (2003) and applied by their numerous followers. Thirdly, we reflect on the future development prospects for the theory regarding economic effects of constitutions and on challenges that its verification faces. Finally, we relate the sketched theoretical background to the specific topic of our study, i.e. the potential significance of constitutional rules for performance in the area of post-socialist economic reforms.

The matter under consideration in this book is obviously also strongly linked to the literature on factors explaining successful performance in economic reforms during post-socialist transition from the centrally-planned economy to

2 The Nobel Prize in Economics (or, to be precise, the Sveriges Riksbank Prize in Economic Sciences in Memory of Alfred Nobel) was awarded to James M. Buchanan in 1986 "*for his development of the contractual and constitutional bases for the theory of economic and political decision-making*".

the market system, in particular as regards political and institutional determinants influencing this process. This literature underwent particularly intensive development at the turn of the century and is very rich (e.g. Roland 1994; Balcerowicz 1996; Dewatripont and Roland 1997; Amsden et al. 1998; Fish 1998; Kołodko 2000, 2001; Raiser et. al 2001; Roland 2000, 2002; Hare 2001; Winiecki 2001; Aslund 2002; Campos and Coricelli 2002; Dąbrowski and Gortat 2002a,b; Milczarek 2002; Fidrmuc 2003; Havrylyshyn and van Roode 2003; Godoy and Stiglitz 2006; Lissowska 2006; recently Hartwell 2013; Aslund and Djankov 2014, including Treisman 2014; works mentioned therein and many others[3]) but also to a significant degree matured. This book, in its theoretical dimension, is aimed, in particular, as a contribution to the development of a much less matured field of Constitutional Economics. Therefore in this chapter we present the theoretical underpinnings of our study originating from the constitutional economics literature, refraining at the same time from devoting a separate section to the literature on economic reforms in transition and directing an interested reader to one or more of the sources listed above (Hare and Turley 2013 is also a recent compendium of the works on economics and political economy of transition). The results and implications from this study can of course also be treated as an enrichment and extension of this literature.

1.1 The Constitutional Economics research program[4]

Economics is essentially a social science concerned with the conditions and principles of making choices. Until mid-20th century economic theory focused on making choices within certain operative institutional structures. It was assumed that such structures constitute constant exogenous constraints on the choices that were made. In the 1950s a new research program developed – later known as Constitutional Economics – which allowed for broadening the research field of economics by introducing analysis of the choice of these constraints, i.e. the so-called 'rules of the game', with the use of standard tools of economic analysis – rational choice theory.

---

3 We limit the list to works published in English. However, there also exists considerable literature published by authors from post-socialist countries in their national languages.

4 Parts of this section borrow from the author's earlier Polish-language published works, in particular Metelska-Szaniawska (2008, 2012), as well as Fałkowski and Metelska-Szaniawska (2015).

The research program of Constitutional Economics, also known as Constitutional Political Economy, originally emerged on the basis of Public Choice[5]. James M. Buchanan, as mentioned earlier – the most outstanding scholar in Constitutional Economics, defined this field as an attempt to "*explain the working properties of alternative sets of legal-institutional-constitutional rules that constrain the choices and activities of economic and political agents, the rules that define the framework within which the ordinary choices of economic and political agents are made*" (Buchanan 1987; p. 585).

Constitutional Economics is, naturally, concerned with constitutions. Buchanan defined the notion of constitution in the simplest way as a "*set of rules which constrain the activities of persons and agents in the pursuits of their ends and objectives*" (Buchanan 1977; p. 292). With such a definition many systems of rules could be regarded as constitutions. To illustrate we could mention the constitution of a firm (the firm's partnership agreement) or a statute of a church[6]. The sense of the economic approach to constitutions is reflected in the reference, which is often made in the literature, to the mythological story of Ulysses[7] and the Sirens. During his long journey in the seas, Ulysses, the mythological ruler of the kingdom of Ithaca, desired to hear the voices of singing Sirens. He was, however, aware of the unavoidable consequences – the ship of the one, who listened to these sounds, was pushed onto the rocks and destroyed. Formally, at this moment Ulysses faced the time-inconsistency problem. His optimal plan would be to listen to the singing Sirens and, subsequently, continue his journey. Had he, however, fulfilled the first part of his plan, he would no longer be capable of fulfilling the other one. This problem arises because Sirens affect Ulysses' preferences during the fulfillment of his plan. According to the mythological story, Ulysses decided to constrain his freedom and ordered his men to tie him to the mast of the ship, plug their ears, and row in the earlier determined direction. In this manner Ulysses created the so-called private constitution for himself, i.e. a set of rules which operate to limit one's possibilities of making future choices. Thanks to this he was able to fight certain propensities of his future self which, he knew, will destructively influence his holistically construed interests.

The theory of private constitutions, sometimes also called 'individualistic constitutional economics' (Buchanan 1990, p. 5) occupies merely a narrow segment

5 As a matter of fact, many scholars consider Constitutional Economics as part of Public Choice. Mueller (1997) refers to Constitutional Economics as Constitutional Public Choice.

6 Interesting studies in these fields are, inter alia, Gifford (1991) and Vanberg (1992).

7 In Greek mythology Odysseus.

of the Constitutional Economics domain. The main topic of analysis in this field remains the study of constitutions based on mutual agreement of human communities. Ulysses should in this case be treated not only as an individual actor but as a representative of the society as a whole. The mast and ropes are symbols of the rules whereon the social order is based[8]. Accordingly, Constitutional Economics should not be regarded as a research program concerned with a specific subject-matter but rather as a certain approach to the analysis of many different sets of institutional constraints.

The term 'constitution' may, therefore, stand for one of four categories:

- constraints that individuals place on themselves in order to accomplish their own goals (private constitutions);
- constraints that individuals voluntarily place on each other in various social situations, e.g. in marriage, family, housing communes, sport clubs, trade unions, churches, firms, etc.;
- constraints placed by citizens on representatives of state power;
- constraints placed by the state power on citizens.

Most analyses within Constitutional Economics concern the third and fourth category – rules composing the constitutional systems of states. The constitution, being the supreme legal act in any country, is in these cases treated as a mechanism allowing for counteracting the time-inconsistency problem connected with pursuing public policy. Containing a catalogue of fundamental rights and freedoms, as well as other constraints on the activity of state power, the constitution primarily allows to turn promises made by representatives of state power into credible commitments. Since constitutional rules formulated within the operative provisions of law may differ in some countries from the principles functioning there factually (while other countries do not have written constitutions), a differentiation is introduced between *de iure* constitutions (sets of rules contained within the enacted law) and *de facto* constitutions (sets of factually operative rules).

The Constitutional Economics literature can be subdivided into two branches – the normative and the positive one. The normative branch is concerned with the legitimization of actions undertaken by the state power and its representatives.

---

8 It is no coincidence that Ulysses tied to a mast constitutes the logo of the main scientific journal in the field of Constitutional Economics – *Constitutional Political Economy*. In its first issue Brennan and Kliemt (1990) provide a detailed justification for the choice of this very logo and indicate some limitations on the analysis of the time-inconsistency problem.

In other words, it aims to indicate the conditions that must be fulfilled for the effects of collective choice to be regarded as fair or efficient. The positive branch is interested, on the one hand, in studying the creation and modification of constitutional rules and, on the other hand – in analysis of the effects of introducing and existence of various constitutional rules. A similar distinction is introduced by Mueller (1997). According to this author, there are two possible approaches to the most fundamental question of Constitutional Economics concerning the origins of institutions constraining actions of self-interested actors. The first one is normative in nature: which political institutions should the society choose in order to foster the interests of individual citizens? The second one is of positive nature: why do we have different political institutions in different countries?

A considerable part of the Constitutional Economics literature represents the normative branch. The hard core of this program, as required by the Lakatosian classification, is composed by three elements: methodological individualism, rational choice, and generalization of the individualistic and rationality postulates to all persons within the political community, as laid down in Buchanan (1990). The fundamental concepts originate from Buchanan and Tullock's seminal work *The Calculus of Consent* (Buchanan and Tullock 1962). It is here that Buchanan draws the critical distinction between 'constitutional' and 'postconstitutional' levels of choice, which define two stages in his model of the political process. The constitutional stage is where self-interested individuals establish the constitutional contract, i.e. a kind of social contract based on unanimous consent, following Buchanan's re-discovery of Wicksell's (1896) procedural norm. As Wagner (1987, p. 14) rightly summarizes: "*Constitutional choice is analogous to choosing the rules by which we are to play a game, whereas postconstitutional choice is analogous to choosing a strategy for playing the game in light of the rules already chosen. Just as the characteristics of a game are shaped by its rules, so too are the characteristic outcomes of legislative and regulatory processes*". According to this approach policy outcomes are treated as natural results of people's pursuit of their interests through the political process, with their actions being shaped and constrained by constitutional rules. These rules, in turn, govern the costs and gains to legislators of alternative policy decisions. When policy outcomes are recognized as following an economic logic, better outcomes (or 'good' policies) are rather the matter of constitutional reform than of "*getting better politicians elected to Congress*" (Wagner 1987, p. 14). In this way the constitutional contract provides a framework for the conduct of economic and political life.

The view of politics as a two-stage process comes back in many subsequent works of Buchanan as a certain normative benchmark, by relation to which assessments of the quality of real-world political institutions are made. Treating the constitution as a social contract, as described above, guarantees each individual equal treatment at the constitutional stage, while the unanimity requirement provides for protection of individuals' rights and ensures that rules and institutions envisaged by the constitution will apply equal treatment to all. Such approach to political order also implies that actions taken at the postconstitutional stage are effectively constrained by rules created at the first (constitutional) stage. This concerns not only individuals as citizens but also their elected representatives and bureaucrats, as well as others in charge of administering the state system. Constitutional rules may, obviously, be only established at the constitutional stage of the political process. If actual institutional solutions in a country fulfil the criteria spelled out by Buchanan, he calls its political system 'constitutional democracy'.

According to Buchanan's approach the state has two particular functions. On the one hand, it ensures enforcement of rules contained within the constitutional contract, while on the other hand – it is responsible for the provisions of public goods. Therefore, it is at the same time a protective and a productive state. The minimum 'constitutional mix' should then comprise: constraints on human behavior vis-à-vis other individuals, including well-defined property rights, provisions concerning the enforcement of these rights, as well as rules concerning the production and financing of public goods.

Recently, the interest in positive constitutional economics studies has significantly increased. This literature, both theoretical and empirical, may be subdivided into two parts: The first one treats constitutional rules as *explananda* and aims to identify forces and factors determining the adoption and change of constitutions. The second one is interested in effects of different constitutional rules, i.e. treats constitutions as *explanans*. Although these two directions of interactions are highly interconnected, composing thereby a challenge for empirical researchers that we will return to in several of the subsequent sections and chapters of this book, here we will focus primarily on the theoretical background of studies relating to economic effects of constitutions.

As explained earlier, the main function of the constitution for the economy, as seen by Buchanan and proponents of his Constitutional Economics, is to serve as a commitment mechanism. Therefore, in studying economic effects of constitutions, proponents of this approach devote particular attention to constraints which the constitution places on those in power in the state in order to ensure that the promises that they make do not remain mere empty declarations. Three main types of such constraints can be identified in the existing literature of the field: constraints stemming from separation of power, constraints stemming from rights and freedoms granted to individuals and their groups, as well as constraints originating from other constitutional rules. We present the reasoning behind each type of constraints, with relation to selected literature, below.

Constraints connected with separation of power stem directly from the fact that the constitution provides the basis for splitting the primary functions, responsibilities, prerogatives, competences and obligations between the different organs of the state, as well as introduces checks and balances. In theoretical economic studies the problem of separation of powers is viewed from various perspectives. Firstly, it is approached as a certain type of specialization, where the legislature constitutes a forum for political bargaining at relatively low transaction costs, the hierarchically-constructed executive allows for mitigating the costs of implementation of law, and the judiciary supplies neutral interpretation of law ensuring that commitments of members of the legislature made during the bargaining process gain credibility. Secondly, separation of powers is treated as separation of a political cartel. This classical approach of economists to the analysis of the structure of power within the state stems from the assumption that from an economic point of view the state is a monopolist as regards the exercise of institutionalized coercion. Separation of powers causes destabilization of the political cartel that could emerge in the event, whenever a certain group (e.g. political party) took control over this monopoly[9]. To identify the particular effects of introducing separation of power for various actors within the state it is, however, crucial to distinguish whether this separation resembles horizontal or vertical (functional) separation of a monopoly (this important observation is particularly attributed to Brennan and Hamlin 1994). Economists typically agree that while executive-legislature relations, bicameralism, and independence of the judiciary are mainly expressions of horizontal separation, federalism and decentralization are considered primarily as forms of vertical separation of powers (see more in Voigt 2011b).

Thirdly, separation of powers is analyzed in relation to the model of demand and supply of legislation and the role of interest groups in this setting. Two conflicting views emerge in this respect from an old debate on the constitution-making

9 The fact that we contemporarily have three or four branches of power in most countries of the world also has its justification within economic theory. Industrial Organization studies indicate that when four suppliers operate in a market, the latter functions nearly as a competitive market. Any reduction in the number of suppliers results in an increase of the likeliness of monopolistic practices. This reasoning regarding market structure may also be applied with respect to the structure of power within the state.

in the United States (see e.g. on the one hand Beard 1913/1986, Posner 1986, Tollison 1988, and on the other hand – Macey 1987). The first one sees separation of powers as the cornerstone of interest group bargains that the constitution is thought to represent. The effects of this are that the constitution slows the pace of progressive change and stifles political expression of the general society's will (Beard 1913/1986), increases durability of special interest legislation (e.g. Crain and Tollison 1979), and ultimately facilitates transfer of wealth from the general population to well-organized special-interest groups. According to an alternative view, separation of powers constitutes the basis for a credible constitutional method of constraining rent-seeking activity undertaken by special-interest groups (Macey 1987). Constitutions, establishing the structure of power, lay down the meta-rules that interest groups must follow in order to obtain the enactment of laws that they favor. These rules, including in particular the separation of powers, determine the level of transaction costs that interest groups face when attempting to achieve the enactment of desired legislation. The higher the level of these costs at the constitutional level, i.e. the more costly it is for an interest group or coalition to obtain favorable legislation, the lower the supply of special-interest legislation in a society and the less detrimental their activity to the working of the economy overall.

Fourthly, separation of powers also affects policy-making by exerting influence upon the manner of exercising power within the state. Instead of hierarchical relationships it introduces equivalency of actors and the necessity to bargain in order to implement new solutions. The need for cooperation between branches of power causes that they begin to act strategically vis-à-vis each other. The view at separation of powers from the perspective of bargaining models, describing strategic interactions between veto-players (organs, powers, actors) influencing policy-decisions, shows in what way these decisions depend on preferences of branches of power participating in the enactment of laws and the structural rules of these interactions defined in the constitution[10].

Finally, the existing (as a matter of fact, mainly political-science) literature on the significance of the number of veto-players for policy making and its effects is naturally closely bound with the discussion presented here relating to constitutional separation of powers[11]. The conventional understanding is that reform is more difficult when there exist numerous veto players. Each additional veto player,

10 For a detailed overview see Cooter (2000).

11 Voigt (2011b, p. 234) refers to the number of veto players in the state as 'the new separation of powers'.

understood as a political actor with the ability to block policy change, either shrinks the set of policies that can defeat the status quo or leaves it unchanged (Gehlbach and Malesky 2010). Therefore, policy stability is expected to be higher when the number of veto players increases (Tsebelis 1995, 2002). One should however bear in mind, as Gehlbach and Malesky (2010) emphasize, that such stability may be desirable when there is a need to commit to established policy (Keefer and Stasavage 2003), but it can be detrimental when policy change is necessary (Cox and McCubbins 2001). Gehlbach and Malesky (2010) contribute significantly to the understanding of the theoretical nexus between the number of veto players (as a constraint on policy makers' discretion) and decision making in the field of (economic) policy. They introduce an actor not emphasized in conventional veto-player theory but 'natural' to Constitutional Economics – special interest groups. Such groups do not have formal veto power but may lobby veto players in an attempt to convince them to implement particular policies. In their formal model Gehlbach and Malesky (2010) show that, under certain conditions, the power of special-interest groups is more constrained in the case when there are numerous veto players. In particular, if these groups must compensate each veto player to choose policy change instead of preserving the *status quo*, then such policy change becomes less attractive as veto players increase in number. This has the effect of making it less likely that the *status quo* will be overturned in favor of policies that bring benefits to narrow but organized groups. In certain contexts, this implies that changes in policy (or, in particular, economic reforms) will be greater when veto players are numerous than when their number is not large[12].

These theoretical perspectives are often allowed to interpenetrate themselves as fundamental frameworks for more detailed empirical studies of the economic effects of the constitutional separation of powers. Such studies have been conducted both in relation to horizontal separation (based mainly on the presidential-parliamentary distinction but also relating to such issues as bicameralism in the legislature), as well as to problems of federalism and decentralization regarded as expressions of vertical separation (for a survey of these studies see Voigt 2011b). We will return to these examples in the next section.

An important place in the considerations of separation of powers from an economic perspective is devoted to the problem of independence of the judiciary and its position within the structure of power in a state and, to a lesser

12 Henisz (2000) and literature that developed based on his approach argue that higher numbers of veto-players correspond to better economic performance in terms of investment (more veto players result in stronger political constraints and less discretion in political decision making) and, ultimately, also economic growth.

degree, direct democracy mechanisms implemented in constitutions of various states. Both an independent judiciary, as well as the society as such in direct democracy, can play the role of additional veto-players in the structure of power and therefore may constitute further constraints on this power enforcing credibility of policy-makers' commitments. In this context an independent (constitutional) judiciary is often regarded as the final stage in turning promises made by representatives of state power into credible commitments or a solution to the 'dilemma of the strong state', i.e. protection of citizens from the discretionary infringement of their rights by the state (Feld and Voigt 2003, Voigt et al. 2015). As regards direct democracy mechanisms, an important role may also be attributed to this element of the constitution if one approaches it from the point of view of evolutionary theories. This has, however, not been studied extensively by the literature to date and will be further elaborated on in Chapter 5.

The second type of constraints that the constitution places on those in power in the state to enhance credibility of their commitments stem from rights and freedoms granted by constitution-drafters to individuals and their groups[13]. Their influence on the discretion of those in power is twofold. The so-called negative rights, also called veto rights (Voigt 2011b), provide protection to minorities from the majority in power. One may indicate two categories of such rights – those establishing a freedom from state or third party interference (e.g. prohibition of torture) and those establishing freedom to undertake a certain activity (e.g. freedom of association or freedom of expression, allowing for public critique of representatives of state power). The so-called positive rights, in turn, place an obligation on those in power to undertake certain actions for the sake of individuals and their groups (e.g the right to healthcare, the right to remuneration) and in this way, if they are enforced, they can enhance credibility of commitments made by representatives of state power to the citizens. Rights and freedoms have been considered from an economic perspective by, inter alia, Hayek (1976), Knack and Keefer (1995), Sen (1999), Barro (2000), Farber (2002), and Blume and Voigt (2007), with the latter confirming several channels of their direct and indirect effect on economic outcomes in an empirical study.

---

13 One should notice the close relation between the structural rules connected with separation of powers in the state and the scope of rights and freedoms that the constitution of the state grants. This interdependence is one of the foundations of separation of powers á la Montesquieu. In economic studies it has already been argued by North and Weingast (1989) that establishing separation of powers allows for more effective enforcement of property rights (in their case for 17th century Britain).

Finally, as mentioned above, economists identify commitment-enhancing constraints imposed on state power also within other elements of the constitution. In this regard they study e.g. fiscal rules (e.g. Blume and Voigt 2013), rules governing organization and functioning of various national supervisory bodies (e.g. Blume and Voigt 2011), as well as constitutionally-safeguarded central bank independence (e.g. Acemoglu et al. 2008). In general, results of empirical studies in this area confirm the suggestions of the theory.

A seminal contribution to the development of positive studies of the role of constitutional rules for policy making and economic outcomes has been made by Persson and Tabellini (2003). We devote the next section to presentating it in more detail.

1.2 Persson and Tabellini's (2003) theoretical framework

Before presenting the issue announced in the section heading, we first justify why Persson and Tabellini's (2003) approach deserves a separate section in this work. We have already mentioned that their contribution has been seminal to the development of the research agenda interested in economic effects of constitutions, both as regards empirical studies and the corresponding theory. While this is one reason, the other one is that Persson and Tabellini (2003) do not ascribe their work to the Constitutional Economics research program, preferring to allocate it under the heading Political Economics (see also Persson and Tabellini 2000) or Comparative Political Economy, as Acemoglu (2005) calls it. The issue raised loudly pronounced disagreement about the relationship between Political Economics and Constitutional Economics, or more broadly – Public Choice (see Blankart and Koester 2006, 2007, as well as a reply by Alesina et al. 2006). We agree with the view that the two approaches should not be seen as competing, as well as that Political Economics is certainly rooted in the Public Choice and Constitutional Economics tradition. However, we do not want to go too far and therefore elaborate on Persson and Tabellini's (2003) work separately.

The starting point for Persson and Tabellini's (2003) account of economic effects of constitutions, from the perspective of a democratic policy making process, is that citizens and groups in a country have conflicting preferences over economic policy. Such assumption is not new in economic studies relating to politics and can be indeed said to reach back to the fundamental public choice literature (e.g. Black 1948; Arrow 1951; Downs 1957; Stigler 1970, 1972). It is there that various agents – voters, lobbyists, politicians – are assumed to have induced preferences over policies, i.e. they understand that different policy choices will map into different outcomes, and consequently their preferences over policies are shaped by their preferences over the outcomes that will be induced by the policies (Acemoglu 2005). The role of political institutions in such setting is to aggregate these preferences into specific political outcomes. The latter in turn induce policy decisions. Constitutional rules determine political institutions in a state, therefore the role of the constitution in this setting is that it participates in the process of transforming citizens' preferences regarding economic policy into policy decisions.

Persson and Tabellini (2003) distinguish between three types of economic policy based on its beneficiary: policy benefiting many citizens, policy benefiting a narrow group of citizens, and policy benefiting only a specific group of politicians. Each of these types of policy is connected with a different type of economic conflict. Policy benefiting many citizens (of a public good type), such as for example broad redistributive programs or even more national defense, is evaluated similarly by large groups of beneficiaries. Policy benefiting narrow groups of citizens (often of a local public good type), such as specific redistributive programs (e.g. support to farmers or government enterprises), based on discretionary decisions of politicians, involves a higher degree of citizens' (voters') conflict over policy. This type of policy is often referred to as 'pork barrel'. The third type of policy generates rents for politicians (in legal form of salaries and financing of political parties, or illegal corruption) and, therefore, turns on a conflict between the citizens (voters) and politicians (or other government officials). How these conflicts are resolved and what policy we observe depends on the constitutional framework within which policy decisions are made in a country.

At the general level the role of political institutions shaped by constitutional rules in resolving conflict between different groups of voters, different groups of politicians, as well as voters and politicians, is similar to the role of market institutions resolving conflicts between consumers and producers over price and product quality and between different producers over profit. The equilibrium that will prevail in the market will be influenced by regulation determining the barriers to entry and scope of competition, as well as other legislation concerning accountability of producers vis-à-vis consumers for bad product quality or collusive behavior. In the analogy concerning political institutions economic policy is the equilibrium outcome of a delegation game between rational voters and politicians. The voters (multiple principals) elect politicians (agents) who choose policy to further their objectives. The relationship is based on the rewards from the voters to the politicians in form of election or re-election. But, as Persson and Tabellini (2003) emphasize, these rewards are mostly implicit leaving the politicians a certain degree of power in the form of residual control rights. The constitution, perceived in this approach as an incomplete contract, sets the rules for the discussed delegation game and, thereby, establishes the crucial framework for policy making.

Persson and Tabellini (2003) focus on two constitutional rules – electoral rules and systems of government. From the point of view of our study the second issue is of particular relevance. Although the main focus of Persson and Tabellini (2003) in this respect is to compare the presidential and parliamentary systems of government, in their theoretical approach they relate to the broader constitutional concept of separation of powers. Presidential systems are regarded as leading to stronger separation of powers than in parliamentary systems, as most presidents do not depend on the support of the majority of parliament to remain in power, while in most parliamentary systems the chief executive does. As in their earlier studies (Persson et al. 1997, 2000), the authors argue that checks and balances associated with a stronger separation of powers constrain politicians from abusing their powers by increasing their accountability vis-à-vis the citizens. With a weaker separation of powers in parliamentary systems it is argued that collusion of politicians with each other at the voters' expense is facilitated. Weaker accountability of politicians vis-à-vis voters in equilibrium in such setting leads to higher rents and taxes than in the case of stronger separation of powers, where higher accountability of politicians counteracts their abuse of power taking here the form of diverting tax revenues for private gains (Persson and Tabellini 2003). They also argue that in parliamentary systems the majority of both voters and politicians in power can enact redistributive programs with benefits clearly targeted at themselves. This implies that these groups are able to improve their situation to the detriment of other groups in the state constituting the minority. Combining their theoretical approach with other relevant accounts in the literature of political science, political sociology and political economy, Persson and Tabellini (2003) come up with a list of theoretical predictions regarding the significance of the parliamentary system – presidential system distinction for various aspects of policy making in the state, such as the size of the government, scope of rent extraction, government deficits and others.

This brings us to the final stages of Persson and Tabellini's (2003) general model of the democratic policy-making process that we started the description of their theoretical approach with. According to this model, as we discussed in more detail above, constitutional rules, influencing political outcomes, transform citizens' preferences regarding policy into policy decisions. The next stage of the process is that the latter then influence the behavior of markets as well as economic outcomes such as prices of different goods, employment and wage levels in different sectors of the economy, etc. In this way Persson and Tabellini (2003) justify the link between constitutional rules and economic outcomes. These outcomes later feed back into citizens' policy preferences giving potential impulse for policy change. As one can see, the account of the democratic policy-making process that these authors propose links the domain of traditional comparative politics (interested primarily in how political institutions affect political outcomes) with the domain of traditional economics (studying the behavior of market participants and economic outcomes).

While Persson and Tabellini's (2003) work has received significant recognition in the field[14], it has also been criticized on several grounds with the most important line of allegations relating to the assumed exogeneity of the constitutional rules in their theoretical (and empirical) framework. The problem is expounded bluntly in a review by Acemoglu (2005). The core of the problem is that just as agents are assumed by Persson and Tabellini (2003) to have induced preferences over policies because they recognize the implications of these policies for their well-being, agents should also have induced preferences over political institutions as different institutions will generate different policies and thus lead to different economic outcomes. This logic forces one to think of constitutional rules establishing political institutions as endogenous. This point is also raised with regard to Persson and Tabellini's (2003) approach by Blume et al. (2009b) and it corresponds to the newest contributions in the research on endogenizing constitutions (e.g. Ticchi and Vindigni 2010, Hayo and Voigt 2013). According to this approach constitutions are not necessarily just 'predetermined' by history and exogenous, but are likely to be determined by the same factors that influence policy change. We will return to this issue in the next section and in Chapter 5.

Persson and Tabellini (2003) also offer stimulating empirical results stemming from econometric tests of the predictions of their theory. They relate, in

---

14 Acemoglu (2005, p. 1047) praises their work in the following way: "*Bearing in mind the difficulties of estimating causal effects in social sciences, especially in cross-country data, the book is a tremendous success.* [...] *Few political economy papers can be written from now on that do not take this book, both its methodological and empirical contributions, seriously*". Blume et al. (2009b, p. 199) also admit: "*Although* [Persson and Tabellini (2003)] *have many predecessors, their book is still remarkable for at least two reasons: First, it represents the broadest cross-country analysis of the effects of two basic rules to date and, secondly, they were able to elicit many scholarly responses within a very short period of time*". In his survey of the positive strand of the Constitutional Economics research program Voigt (2011b, p. 213) relates to Persson and Tabellini's (2003) work as "*becom*[*ing*] *almost a standard for analyzing economic effects of constitutions*".

particular, to consequences of various electoral rules (district magnitude, electoral formula, and ballot structure), as well as forms of government (parliamentary/presidential classification). These results have been thoroughly discussed, criticized and replicated by several authors in the recent literature (e.g. Acemoglu 2005, Blume et al. 2009b, Voigt 2011b) so we refrain from presenting them here in greater detail[15]. To conclude with, we emphasize that from the point of view of the focus of our study in this book, Persson and Tabellini's (2003) framework is of vital importance as it attributes particular attention to policy decisions as a crucial intermediate step in the relation between constitutional rules and the working of the economy. This step is the primary focus of our study linking constitutions to economic reforms in post-socialist countries.

1.3 Future prospects and challenges faced by empirical verification

As we showed in the preceding two sections, economic theory explaining potential links between constitutional frameworks and policy making in the state is already considerably rich. It falls primarily under the label of Constitutional Economics but can also be found under other headings such as Political Economics, Comparative Political Economy, (Constitutional) Public Choice, Constitutional Law and Economics and more generally – New Political Economy or even New Institutional Economics[16]. However, there are still several areas of disagreement (e.g. regarding the consequences of introducing the separation of powers – between the proponents of the private-interest serving view of the constitution and the public-regarding view of the constitution), while other areas remain underdeveloped (e.g. regarding the distinction between the *de iure* and *de facto* constitutional rules and the role of *de iure* provisions in influencing, perhaps indirectly, policy decisions and outcomes)[17]. Further development of this body of theory, as well as increasing its degree of generalization, requires more empirical work. Until barely ca. 15 years ago empirical studies in the field of positive Constitutional Economics were extremely rare. However, as mentioned in the introduction to this book, empirical studies of economic effects of constitutions have flourished

15 As a matter of fact, they will be included in Table 1 in the subsequent section.

16 On how Constitutional Economics relates to these other approaches within Economics and on the junctions of Economics with other social sciences see e.g. Buchanan 1990, Van den Hauwe 2000, Blankart and Koester 2006, 2007, as well as Metelska-Szaniawska 2012 (in Polish).

17 See more on both examples in the preceding sections.

in the recent years. Table 1, located in Appendix 1, presents a selective overview of such works basing on the application of econometric techniques (quantitative studies), together with their primary results. The studies have been organized in the table according to the constitutional rule that they examine. A more extensive survey of studies published up to 2010 is provided by Voigt (2011b).

A brief view at Table 1 (in Attachment 1) indicates that a whole range of constitutional rules have already been studied in recent years with the focus on their potential effects on various economic policy and economic outcome variables. A more detailed examination, however, reveals that the results stemming from these studies, as listed in Column 4 of the discussed table, often do not allow to formulate unambiguous conclusions regarding verification or falsification of a given prediction stemming from the theory. In some cases the results of two or more studies stand in contradiction (e.g. Persson and Tabellini 2003 and Blume et al. 2009b with regard to the significance or insignificance, respectively, of presidential form of government for total factor productivity or broadly construed government expenditure). For others a more detailed account raises several doubts as to the reliability and completeness of these results. The allegations are, in principle, of twofold nature. On the one hand, they concern methodological (and technical) issues, and on the other – limited accessibility or reliability of data.

Without any doubt we can admit that the availability of data, which is inevitable for quantitative studies of constitution-related problems, has increased tremendously over the most recent years. One important development has been the release of an enormous database resulting from the Comparative Constitutions Project (Elkins et al. 2014, ver. 2.0), which contains year-by-year information on hundreds of formal (i.e. *de iure*) characteristics of written constitutions, both current and historical, for most independent states from 1789 to 2013. The *de facto* indicators relating to constitutions have exhibited less spectacular but still significant development over the recent years. Two examples from this area are the publication of a substantially updated version of Feld and Voigt's (2003) judicial independence indicators by Voigt et al. (2015), as well as the construction of constitutional under- and overperformance scores for enforcing various categories of rights by Law and Versteeg (2013) that will be presented in Chapter 2 of this book. While one may always criticize quantitative measures on the ground of failing to capture important nuances of constitutional settings and specificity, it should be observed that measures made recently available present constantly increasing levels of sophistication, creativity, and scientific scrutiny, contributing considerably to improvements in this field.

While the above suggests that studies under development at the moment and in near future have the potential to significantly advance in terms of more data and *more reliable* data, overcoming methodological and technical problems raised with regard to these studies will be much more difficult. This is for several reasons which we now briefly discuss.

Firstly, economic effects of constitutions have mainly been studied on a rule-by-rule basis, i.e. the potential significance of a given rule has been analyzed in isolation from the remaining constitutional framework operative in the state. Given such approach it was impossible to account for potential interactions between rules and solutions, which could in fact be complements, substitutes, antagonists or neither. The conjecture that there exist relations between the operation of such various rules seems to stem, inter alia, from the results of several recent works devoted to the study of the significance of political institutions on economic outcomes (e.g. Acemoglu and Robinson 2005, Giavazzi and Tabellini 2005, Persson and Tabellini 2006, Wacziarg and Welch 2009).

Secondly, a vast majority of studies of economic effects of constitutions conducted to date treat constitutional rules as exogenous. As a matter of fact, as mentioned above, this was the main criticism of Acemoglu (2005) and Blume et al. (2009b) with regard to the seminal work of Persson and Tabellini (2003). Constitutional change is, however, an indisputable fact. In their study of endurance of national constitutions, covering a worldwide sample of constitutions starting from 1789, Elkins et al. (2009) find that constitutions survive on average 19 years. Obviously, constitutional change does not take place in isolation from the socio-economic environment of countries and, therefore, empirical studies analyzing the impact of constitutional frameworks on the economy should also account for potential reverse causation and common factors that could affect both the choice of constitutional rules as well as policy making within the state and economic outcomes. Research on determinants of constitutional change has, however, recently only begun and is far from sufficient in its development to allow for formulating a coherent theory and unambiguous predictions. This is one of the reasons why studies aimed at searching for economic effects of endogenous constitutions remain so far limited and not infrequently superficial. The other reason for an unsatisfactory state of research on economic effects of endogenous constitutions is the problem of finding empirical techniques which would allow to conduct such meaningful analyses.

Indeed, and this is our third point here, many criticisms of the discussed research agenda are directed at the empirical techniques employed by authors in this field. Most of their research is based on cross-country econometric studies, which are criticized in particular for the questionable 'one model fits all' assumption that underlies them. Potential problems of simultaneity, reverse causality, and omitted variable bias are among other important allegations. The use of panel data studies is relatively rare. While in some cases, when the constitutional framework under examination is relatively stable, this may be justified, as argued above the long endurance of constitutions can generally not be taken for granted. Involving the time dimension can give way for studies of the effects of constitutional dynamics, including, in particular, potential lagged effects of constitutions on policy making and economic outcomes. This, however, raises once again the most substantial line of critique concerning treatment of constitutional rules as exogenous variables. From the technical point of view this is a particularly difficult problem to solve as meaningful instruments are usually not available.

Given the above caveats and shortcomings it is not surprising that proponents of Constitutional Economics call for intensifying the application of other empirical approaches in studies of the nexus between constitutions and policy making, as well as economic outcomes (see, in particular, Voigt 2011a). This concerns, first of all, case studies. Several examples are already available: Beard (1913/1986) analyzing the making of the United States Constitution; Elster (2000) comparing this process to that of the revolutionary constitutions in France; or more recently Raudla (2010) examining the case of Estonia. While case studies can certainly enrich and broaden our understanding of the working of constitutions and their effects given country-specific settings, this approach also bears its own problems (concerning, in particular, the choice of comparison units) and, in our opinion, can only be treated as a supplement, not a substitute, for studies described earlier.

The other possible avenue of developing further empirical research within Constitutional Economics is through experiments. Experimental Economics is interested in studying human behavior in an empirical manner, on the basis of experiments conducted in laboratories[18]. Such analysis may, for example, be applied in experiments aimed at testing new institutional solutions or studying fundamental rules, which individuals are willing to accept in laboratory conditions. In the first case, such analysis supplements the Comparative Institutional Analysis approach and allows for formulating better predictions concerning the potential consequences of different institutional, or in our case constitutional, solutions. It may also point to the existence of important but unexpected side-effects of introducing certain changes in the constitutional framework. While

18 Experimental economics and its methodology is broadly presented by, inter alia, Kager and Roth (1995).

some first attempts to study 'constitutional' choice in an experimental setting have already been made (e.g. by Sutter et al. (2010), who propose a game, where individuals decide on the kind of institution under which they want to play the game before actually playing it[19]), it seems that this avenue is particularly promising from the point of view of future development of normative Constitutional Economics referring to fundamental rules, which individuals would be willing to accept given certain conditions. If one succeeds in creating similar conditions in a laboratory, hypotheses concerning these rules become testable.

Finding solutions to the long list of problems connected with studies of economic effects of constitutions conducted to date is a major challenge for proponents of the Constitutional Economics approach and, at the moment, a significant obstacle to further development of the theory regarding the nexus of constitutions and economic policy (and outcomes). In this book we propose several contributions to this research agenda, both in terms of introducing a new empirical technique allowing to mitigate or avoid several important caveats discussed above, including the endogeneity problem and unjustified cross-country comparisons, as well as in terms of supplementing the analysis with two new variables stemming from a distinct view at the studied problem from the perspective of evolutionary theories. We also study the potential significance of several elements of the constitutional framework at the same time, not on a rule-by-rule basis. Obviously, this is not sufficient to identify the nature of potential relationship between the included rules (i.e. whether they are e.g. complements, substitutes etc.), however allows to avoid the allegation of providing partial, unjustified results about individual rules because of omitting other important components of the constitutional framework[20]. Before we seriously engage on this endeavor we complete this chapter by referring the theoretical framework presented so far and predictions stemming from it to the (broadly-conceived) case of post-socialist constitutional change and economic transition.

---

19 Another example is Kocher et al. (2006), who incorporate the choice between individual and collective decision-making in their game, what can be interpreted as the choice between direct and representative democracy (see Voigt 2011a).

20 A more detailed examination of the potential interactions between these rules remains on the agenda for future research.

1.4 Constitutions and economic reforms in transition[21]

Based on the central claim of Constitutional Economics, according to which the constitution acts as a commitment device for the state in its policy-making activity, one can propose the following approach to the argument concerning the role of constitutional rules for performance in the area of economic reforms. The constitution, allowing for counteracting the time-inconsistency problem connected with pursuing public policy, containing a catalogue of fundamental rights and freedoms, as well as other constraints on the activity of state authority, allows for turning promises made by representatives of state power into credible commitments. Economic reforms require investments from non-state actors and may be costly, especially in the short run. If promises made by the state authority to enforce property rights are credible, then these actors will adopt a longer time horizon and will be more willing to make investments. Hence the role of the constitution for economic reforms in transition. It is primarily fulfilled by the constraints imposed by the constitution on the activity of the state authority (low concentration of political power) and by the functioning of a relatively broad bill of rights. The latter can be regarded as an indispensable precondition for secure property rights and thus a guarantee of a minimum amount of certainty that is required for higher investment rates (Blume and Voigt 2007). Having their basic rights and freedoms envisaged by the constitution, individuals will be less reluctant to undertake pro-reform activity that could require short-run sacrifices. This regards both the socio-economic rights (e.g. the willingness of different groups of employees to accept the uncertainty connected with engaging in reforms will be higher when the constitution envisages relatively broad guarantees regarding employment), as well as political rights and civil liberties (e.g. violation of basic human rights may lead to citizens' protest and instability that are likely to have a negative effect on the readiness to invest in reforms)[22]. A broad bill of rights also contributes to the emergence of the loci of independent economic power, stimulating the reforms process and facilitating the sustainment of reforms (see e.g. Fish 1998). To complete the picture, constitutional provisions have little meaning when their enforcement is not guaranteed. This role

---

21 Paragraphs 1–2, 4, and 6 of this section borrow from Metelska-Szaniawska (2008, 2009).

22 In addition, some studies suggest that different types of rights may be regarded as complements, where respect for basic human rights cannot be substituted by anything else (Blume and Voigt 2007). Other authors argue that respect for basic human rights may be treated as a signal regarding government credibility in promising economic (property) rights (Farber 2002).

is fulfilled by an independent constitutional judiciary. Such courts constitute the final stage in turning promises of the state authority into credible commitments. Finally, since (as will be shown in Chapter 2) constitutional rules formulated within the operative provisions of law differ in many countries from the principles functioning there factually, the differentiation between *de iure* constitutions (sets of rules contained within the enacted law) and *de facto* constitutions (sets of factually operative rules) should also be accounted for when undertaking a study of economic effects of post-socialist constitutions.

In the mid-1990's a debate emerged on the role of the constitution in the process of economic transition between the so-called negative and positive constitutionalists. The first view (based on North 1990, Weingast 1993, and much of the Constitutional Economics literature) argues that constitutions, being crucial mechanisms for establishing credible commitments, give economic actors the confidence required for entering into contracts and making long-term investments, which are necessary for the adoption and success of economic reforms. Such reforms, just as any policy-making activity of the state, are affected by the time-inconsistency problem. The constitution allows for counteracting this problem by enhancing stability of the political system and restraining the discretionary power of the state. Positive constitutionalists, however, question whether such constrained state authority is capable of pursuing economic reforms. Przeworski (1991) notes that since output is expected to follow a 'J-curve' during the transition period, with short-term declines balanced against long-term growth, successful implementation of economic reform requires isolating the government from electoral pressure that is likely to arise together with the difficulties and pains of the transition process. In a similar vein Holmes (1995) argues that the magnitude of tasks associated with simultaneous political and economic transition requires sufficient capacity and flexibility of the state authority to push through difficult policy choices. This is also regarded as an argument in favor of postponing of the constitution-making process until the goals of economic transition have been achieved or, alternatively, suggests adopting interim constitutions – a process called 'stopgap constitutionalism' (Holmes 1995)[23].

Several years later, Ahrens (2007) proposed a market-enhancing governance structure for post-socialist countries, emphasizing the role of an institutional framework guaranteeing state strength, which at the same time places effective

23 Hellman's (1997) basic econometric tests suggest that postponing the adoption of new post-socialist constitutions did not advance the process of economic reforms. See more on this in Chapter 5.

limits on this strength (inter alia through checks and balances). According to this view, it is inevitable for successful transition that the state is sufficiently strong to implement policies, protect property rights and counteract state capture by well-organized special interest groups. In such a strong state policy makers are characterized by a relatively high degree of autonomy (understood as the capability to avoid the influence of those special interest groups), what allows for making policy in a stable, transparent and predictable way. However, the state in transition must also be constrained so as not to abuse its powers. This requires various checks on the state's powers in order to counteract predatory behavior, political rent seeking and corruption, which could otherwise take place to the detriment of the citizens. Potential solutions that Ahrens (2007) puts forth in this respect are establishing the separation of powers and implementing the rule of law[24]. The approach proposed by Ahrens (2007) can certainly be viewed as an indication that the two seemingly contradictory approaches of negative and positive constitutionalism are reconcilable. For the 'rules of the game' to function effectively as a commitment mechanism in a state undertaking economic reforms is not only inevitable to establish constraints on state power to prevent its abuse but also to ensure the strength and capacity of the state so that its organs and representatives can implement policies as they were designed, not succumbing to political rent seeking and other pressures. This governance-related literature also indicates the relevance of the perspective of accession to the European Union for strengthening commitment of the states involved in this process to implementation of market-enhancing reforms.

The theoretical framework proposed by Persson and Tabellini (2003) also corresponds well to the setup under examination in post-socialist countries and additionally allows to refine the focus of such study as regards the 'economic effects' of interest. As Persson and Tabellini (2003) argue, constitutional rules, influencing political outcomes, participate in transforming policy preferences of citizens into policy decisions. This approach can also be applied to policy decisions in the area of post-socialist economic reforms. In the final stage of Persson and Tabellini's (2003) model those policy choices influence the behavior of markets and economic outcomes. Many studies (e.g. Hellman 1997; Falcetti et al. 2002; Radulescu and Barlow 2002; Babetskii and Campos 2007) argue that economic reforms implemented by post-socialist countries did not translate automatically

24 The remaining crucial pillars of the market-enhancing governance structure proposed by Ahrens (2007) are building state capacity through public administration reforms and establishing vital economic institutions.

to higher growth rates (at least not in the short run). Therefore, post-socialist transition provided a particular motivation for the analysis of the link between constitutional rules and economic policy (economic reforms) – an intermediate step in Persson and Tabellini's (2003) approach.

To summarize, the central claim (thesis statement) of this book is that constitutional solutions, adopted by post-socialist countries after 1989, which enhanced the credibility and commitment of decision makers in the field of economic reforms conducted by these countries during the transition period, constituted a framework conducive to such reforms. While, as discussed earlier, studies rooted in Constitutional Economics, focusing on economic effects of constitutions, usually emphasize the role of the constitution as a commitment mechanism for economic performance of countries (economic growth and other macro-economic outcomes), we shift the focus to the role of the constitution as a commitment-enhancing device for decisions taken within the political sphere concerning economic reforms in transition. As the broad scale and multidimensional character of post-socialist transition, regarded as large-scale institutional change, required reforms transcending the level of ordinary policy making, we further extend the focus to also encompass some changes in these countries' economic institutional framework (as e.g. in the case of privatization). The building blocks of a general model explaining the role of the constitution for economic reforms in transition, constituting the fundament for the empirical studies conducted further in this book, is presented in Figure 1[25]. In this model constitutional rules, such as structural provisions, bills of rights, and enforcement mechanisms, participate in transforming voters' preferences regarding economic reforms into decisions on these reforms (understood as policy decisions, as well as decisions on the economic institutional framework), where these reforms subsequently influence the behavior of markets and economic outcomes. The latter feed back into voters' preferences. The proposed model refines and extends Persson and Tabellini's (2003) approach in two crucial dimensions: firstly, by identifying the specific constitutional rules which matter in the studied context; secondly, by introducing two specific transmission channels contributing to the commitment-enhancing

25 As the model is intended to capture the role of the constitutional-rule framework for economic reforms in post-socialist countries, we focus here on the transmission channels between constitutions and economic reforms and, therefore, deliberately refrain from including other non-constitution-related determinants of economic reforms and economic outcomes in transition, as well as their potential interrelationships. References to literature on these topics are provided in other parts of this book and will be included in the empirical studies.

feature of the constitution in the studied context (via restraints on discretionary power, as argued by negative constitutionalists, and via capacity-building, as argued by positive constitutionalists). The presented framework allows to situate the considerations presented in this book at the nexus of political economy of transition (also called political economy of reform) and Constitutional Economics (or Political Economics relating to constitutions). Viewed in this way, the suggested model could be considered the theoretical fundament for what could be named 'constitutional political economy of reform' or 'constitutional political economy of transition'.

Figure 1: Constitutional rules and post-socialist economic reforms – the theoretical nexus

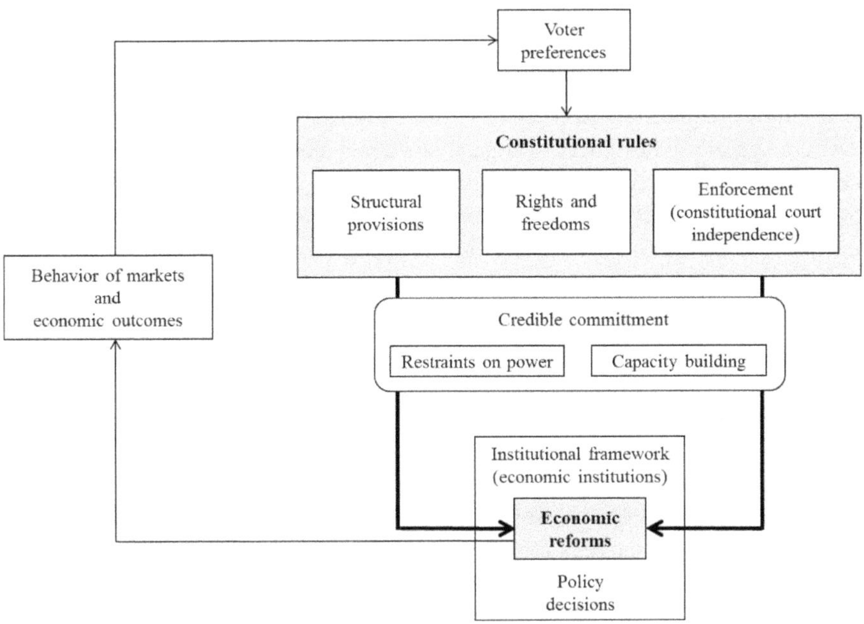

Source: Author's graph.

A handful of empirical studies have been devoted so far to testing some of the hypotheses that stem from this theoretical background. Several of them looked at the influence of the concentration of political power on progress in economic reforms in transition. EBRD (1999) studies the relationship between the power of political executives (as measured by a standardized index of formal presidential power[26], applied, per analogiam, to prime ministers in countries with parliamentary systems of government) and progress in economic reforms, as measured by EBRD's aggregated transition indicator[27]. A simple bivariate analysis reveals a strongly negative correlation between the two. Hellman (1997) obtains a confirmation of these results using an slightly more enhanced econometric methodology. He employs an index of formal presidential power based on earlier research of Shugart and Carey (1992), Geddes (1994), and McGregor (1994), taking account of the appointment procedure and legislative powers of the president, and finds that stronger presidency is associated with less economic reforms and that these consequences are even stronger in countries, which opted for stopgap constitutionalism. Kitschelt (2001a) proposes a revision of these results and argues that the effect of strong presidential powers on post-socialist economic reforms is contingent upon the social and political contextual conditions that are more or less favorable to the aggregation of interests through parties engaged in programmatic competition. In countries, where such programmatic parties emerged early, the greater willingness to engage in market-liberalizing economic reforms coincides with the tendency to choose parliamentary systems of government and for presidents – to counteract economic reforms. Conversely, in countries with unfavorable conditions for the formation of programmatic parties (e.g. Romania, Russia, or even stronger – Armenia, Kyrgyzstan, or Moldova), it may be that the powerful president pushes for economic reforms and the provision of public goods against rent-seeking special interests. Kitschelt (2001a) also suggests that this conclusion may even stronger apply to countries with authoritarian regimes as they are characterized by generally unfavorable conditions for mobilization of political interest and economic reforms.

Although primarily a political science study, Gehlbach and Malesky (2010) offer a very relevant for the topic of this book account of the significance of the number of veto-players for performance in the area of economic reforms by post-socialist countries after 1989. As mentioned briefly in Section 1.1, with their formal model they show that the existence of numerous veto players may weaken the power of special interest groups, making in this way advancement in policy (or, more specifically, economic reform) more likely when the number of veto players increases. As the experience of various post-socialist countries shows, special interest groups often prefer partial to full reform. Partial

26 Based on a slightly modified version of the scale introduced by Shugart and Carey (1992).

27 See Section 3.2 for more details concerning the indicator.

economic reforms, however, frequently generate rents for the 'chosen few' while leaving the majority worse off than in the case of *status quo*[28]. If one assumes that veto players trade off welfare-enhancing policies and contributions from organized interests (as advocated e.g. by Bates 1981, Grossman and Helpman 1994, Olson 1965), then when partial reform is inefficient and there exist numerous veto players, special interest groups may find that the rents generated by partial reform are outweighed by the cost of compensating each veto player for choosing it (Gehlbach and Malesky 2010). If, in turn, the political demand for full reform outweighs the preference for the *status quo*, then movement toward full reform may be greater when the number of veto players is large. This is why Gehlbach and Malesky (2010) predict that veto players may facilitate economic reform when the status quo is no reform. At the same time, they also expect that reform reversals should be less likely when the approval of many actors is needed to overturn the status quo (i.e. also when the number for veto players is relatively high). Consistent with the predictions of their theoretical model, they find that the number of veto players is positively associated with performance in economic reform of post-socialist countries after 1989, but only when the *status quo* was associated with little or no reform. They also confirm that reform reversals in these countries were less likely when veto players are numerous.

Metelska-Szaniawska (2008, 2009) provided the most comprehensive studies of constitutional determinants of economic reforms in post-socialist countries to date. The focus is extended to three main elements of contemporary constitutions – the structure of power, constitutional rights and freedoms, as well as the constitutional enforcement mechanism. The main finding of that panel data analysis, covering up to 23 post-socialist countries for the period 1989–2001 or up to 20 post-socialist countries for the period 1989–2004, respectively, is a confirmation of the link between the constitutional framework and performance in economic reforms. In particular, countries with a lower concentration of state power (implied inter alia by a deeper separation of powers and therefore more veto-players) experience more successful performance in the field of economic reform, just as countries with a relatively broader scope of factually functioning catalogue of political rights and civil liberties. Noteworthy exceptions (with regard to concentration of state power) are countries committed to European integration (those that became member states in 2004) and countries lacking

28 As Gehlbach and Malesky (2010) argue, the idea that partial reform may be suboptimal is present in the economic theory of the second best, when satisfying one optimality constraint while leaving others unsatisfied may be worse than doing nothing at all.

democratic transitions (Central Asia). *De iure* constitutional court independence seems another significant feature of the post-socialist countries' constitutional framework conducive to successful economic reforms. In principle, therefore, the obtained results confirm the main function of the constitution as a commitment mechanism (with some non-uniformity in the influence of constitutional variables on economic reforms in different groups of countries, at different periods of transition and for different categories of reform). Though the results prove their robustness to various modifications of the model specification, constraints in data availability limit the conclusions considerably, in particular with regard to the role of the constitutional enforcement mechanism. The described studies also fall short of solving the potential problem of endogeneity of constitutional rules.

As elucidated in the introduction to this book, the contribution of this work to the existing empirical literature is at least threefold. Firstly, we replicate the general model developed in Metelska-Szaniawska (2009) and apply it to study a much larger dataset including the most recent years of transition (beyond 2004), which could not be analyzed earlier due to unavailability of data. As a result, this book covers the period of nearly 25 years from the outset of transition, i.e. between 1989 and 2012 and allows to formulate assessments regarding a more long-term relationship between constitutions and economic reforms in transition. Thanks to including the most recent measure of constitutional court independence developed by Voigt et al. (2015), we also nearly double the number of post-socialist countries covered by the study focusing on the effects of constitutional court independence, revealing new and more reliable conclusions in this area. Secondly, we propose a different empirical approach based on a recently developed method allowing to avoid the potential endogeneity bias in an attempt to re-assess the conclusions regarding the relevance of constitutional rules for post-socialist economic reforms. Thirdly, we extend the framework of analysis to include additional aspects of the relationship between constitutions and economic reforms in transition that can be drawn from works on Evolutionary Political Economy. Given that the studied transition period is now considerably longer, we include two additional variables: the first one relating to mechanisms of direct democracy and their contribution to building commitment of post-socialist governments to economic reforms during the transition process, and the second one connected to popular support for the constitution affecting the strength of such commitment. Taken together, these contributions, presented in chapters 3–5 of the book, provide empirical results expanding and enriching the existing theory in an attempt to allow for better understanding of the constitutional framework's relevance for performance in economic reforms in post-socialist countries from 1989 on. As an introduction to these considerations, in Chapter 2 we provide the Reader with the essentials on post-socialist constitutions with a particular focus on the variety of solutions adopted by transition countries as regards those constitutional rules which could contribute to a meta-rule framework conducive to performance in post-socialist economic reforms.

Chapter 2. Post-socialist constitutions in a nutshell

Following the fall of socialism (or communism), it became impossible for countries referred to in this book as post-socialist to function on the basis of their socialist (communist) constitutions. The adoption of new legal acts providing fundaments for creating new constitutional systems – the rule of law, separation of powers, civil society or nation's sovereignty – became a necessity. As already mentioned, this period of post-socialist constitution-drafting has sometimes been referred to as a "*gigantic natural experiment*" (Elster 1991, p. 449).

The adoption of post-socialist constitutions took place in the period 1990–2011, with greatest intensity between 1990 and 1996. Details of this process are presented in Table 2, which provides not only the dates when these constitutions were adopted but also when they were further amended in the period until 2013. Serbia and Croatia adopted new constitutions in 1990 although at that time they still constituted components of the Socialist Federal Republic of Yugoslavia[29]. The last country to adopt its first post-socialist constitution during the 1990's was Ukraine (in 1996)[30]. Hungary operated on the basis of its numerously amended 1949 constitution throughout most of the transition period, adopting a new constitution as late as in 2011. One country of the region – Latvia – did not adopt a new constitution after 1989, returning to its 1922 constitution (with several significant amendments).

Table 2: Constitutions in post-socialist countries of Europe and Asia

Country	Last pre-1989 constitution	Post-socialist constitution(s)	Post-1989 constitutional amendments
Albania	1976	(1991), 1998	1992, 1993, 2008
Armenia	1977 [a]	1995	1991, 2005
Azerbaijan	1977 [a]	(1991), 1995	2002, 2009

29 The Croatian Constitution of 1990, forming the basis for the sovereign existence of this state, remains in force. Serbia has a new constitution adopted in 2007 (in the period 1992–2003 the Federal Constitution of FR Yugoslavia was in force, in 2003 the Constitutional Charter of Serbia and Montenegro was adopted, the union between these states dissolved in 2006).

30 In the second half of the 1990's several countries adopted their second post-socialist constitutions (e.g. Albania in 1991 and 1998, Poland in 1992 and 1997).

Country	Last pre-1989 constitution	Post-socialist constitution(s)	Post-1989 constitutional amendments
Belarus	1977 [a]	1994	1996, 2004
Bosnia and Hercegovina	1974 [b]	1995	2009
Bulgaria	1971	1991	1990, 2003, 2005, 2006, 2007
Croatia	1974 [b]	1990	1997, 2000, 2001, 2010
Czech Republic	1960 [c]	1993	1989, 1990, 1991, 1992, 1998, 2000, 2001, 2002
Estonia	1977 [a]	1992	2003
Georgia	1977 [a]	(1992 reinstated), 1995	every year in the period 1999–2013 except 2007
Hungary	1949	2011	1989, 1990, 1993, 1994, 1995, 1997, 2000, 2001, 2002, 2003, 2007
Kazakhstan	1977 [a]	(1993), 1995	1998, 2007
Kyrgyzstan	1977 [a]	1993, 2006, 2007, 2010	1996, 1997, 2003
Latvia	1977 [a]	1922 (reinstated in 1991)	1994, 1996, 1997, 1998, 2002, 2003, 2004, 2005, 2007
Lithuania	1977 [a]	(1990), 1992	1996, 2002, 2003, 2004, 2006
Macedonia	1974 [b]	1991	1992, 1998, 2001, 2003, 2005, 2009, 2011
Moldova	1977 [a]	1994	1991, 1993, 1996, 2000, 2001, 2002, 2003, 2006
Montenegro	1974 [b]	1992, 2007	
Poland	1952	(1992), 1997	2006, 2009
Romania	1965	1991	2003
Russia	1977 [a]	1993	1989, 1990, 1991, 1992, 1996, 2001, 2008
Serbia	1974 [b]	1990, 2006	
Slovakia	1960 [c]	1992	1998, 1999, 2001, 2003
Slovenia	1974 [b]	1991	1997, 2000, 2003, 2004, 2006
Tajikistan	1977 [a]	1994	1999, 2003
Turkmenistan	1977 [a]	1992, 2008	1995, 1999, 2003, 2006
Ukraine	1977 [a]	1996	1991, 1992, 1995, 2004
Uzbekistan	1977 [a]	1992	1993, 2003, 2007, 2011

Notes: Provisional/interim constitutions in brackets.

[a] Constitution of the Soviet Union. In most of the republics there also operated 'republican' constitutions.

[b] Constitution of the Socialist Federal Republic of Yugoslavia.

[c] Constitution of the Czechoslovak Socialist Republic.

Source: Own elaboration on the basis of Elkins et al. (2014).

The main common feature of post-socialist constitutions is the attempt, reflected in their content, to break away from the socialist (communist) past, by giving priority to provisions declaring the democratic nature and sovereignty of these states. All currently operative post-socialist constitutions refer to 'democracy' or 'democratic' (some of them even as many as 11–13 times – e.g. in the constitutions of Serbia and Slovakia), while only one – the constitution of Croatia, mentions 'socialism' and this in the chapter on 'Historical Foundations'.

Nevertheless, constitutions of post-socialist countries have not been drafted according to a single model[31]. They differ in basic characteristics such as their length (from less than 5000 words for Latvia to more than 19000 words for Poland, Serbia and Ukraine) and in whether the constitution is composed by a single legal document or more (two – for the Czech Republic, three – for Lithuania). However, more importantly, the specific constitutional solutions encompassed by these acts vary significantly.

Studies of constitutional systems of post-socialist countries fall within the domain of comparative legal scholarship[32]. In this book, devoted to economic effects of post-socialist constitutions, we limit our discussion of this matter to a short, but (hopefully) convincing account of the significant differences of these systems, focusing on those aspects which will further be studied in the empirical parts of the book – the structure of government (in particular, the relationship between government powers involved in policy-decision decision-making, i.e. the executive and the legislature), the catalogues of constitutional rights and freedoms, and the constitutional enforcement mechanisms. Bearing in mind that this book is primarily addressed to economists, we provide the comparisons, in so far as it is possible, in quantitative form, using various sources of constitutional data that have been recently made available.

31 For a discussion of the potential influence of foreign models on constitution-drafting in post-socialist countries see e.g. Ludwikowski (1998), who calls the latter process 'gardening' (where constitutional solutions "*are like seedlings carefully chosen from different gardens and implanted, piece by piece, into living, constantly changing vegetation composed of rules, norms, and institutions*", p. 64), Ludwikowski (2000), Ordeshook (2002), Osiatynski (2003), or Dupre (2003).

32 Polish-speaking readers may refer to our earlier work – Metelska-Szaniawska (2008) – for more detailed descriptions of constitutional systems of post-socialist countries in the period 1989–2006.

2.1 Executive-legislature relations

With respect to the relationship between executives and legislatures, usually referred to as 'form of government' or 'system of government', comparative politics distinguishes between presidential, semi-presidential and parliamentary systems. Three influential classifications based on this distinction (with some additional variants) have been published in the recent years and used extensively by researchers working at the nexus of political science, law and economics. They are: Cheibub (2007), Norris (2009), and the World Bank Database of Political Institutions (DPI – most recent version published in 2013) based on Beck et al. (2001)[33]. Table 3 (in Appendix 1) presents the post-socialist systems of government as specified within these classifications and supplements them by a classification devoted to this part of the world proposed earlier, based on country-sources, by Metelska-Szaniawska (2009). A first look at the table reveals a mixed picture, in particular because of significant differences in the classification of countries between the included sources. Only with respect to Latvia (parliamentary system) and Georgia (presidential system) all classifications converge. A general tendency that one can observe is 'more parliamentarism' in countries such as Albania, the Czech Republic, Hungary (under the 1949 constitution, with post-1989 amendments), Latvia, Slovakia, and 'more presidentialism' in countries, which emerged after the dissolution of Soviet Union in Central and Southwestern Asia.

Drawing on the recent increasingly pronounced critique of such classifications, emphasizing their archaic and non-systemic character (see e.g. Cheibub et al. 2013), we further focus on specific constitutional solutions defining the relationship between the executives and the legislatures in post-socialist countries. A 'core set' of six such attributes, stemming directly from formal constitutional provisions, has been proposed by Cheibub et al. (2013). It includes: (1) whether the executive has the power to veto legislation; (2) whether the executive has decree power; (3) whether the executive has emergency powers; (4) whether the executive can initiate (ordinary) legislation; (5) whether the legislature has oversight powers with respect to the executive; (6) whether the executive (unilaterally) appoints the cabinet. Positive answers to questions (1)-(4) and (6), as well as a negative answer to (5) indicate a stronger position of the executive vis-à-vis the legislature. To broaden the picture, we supplement this list of attributes by (7) whether the executive can dissolve the assembly.

33 See the cited sources for specific definitions employed by the various authors.

The respective information about attributes (1)-(7) for constitutions of post-socialist countries is presented in Table 4. One should bear in mind that 'the executive' encompasses both the head of state and the head of government, so it should not raise concern that systems characterized earlier as parliamentary or mixed are receiving many positive answers in Table 4. The general picture that the table delivers confirms considerable variety between formal constitutional provisions in post-socialist countries, indicating 13 different sets of attributes among the 31 constitutions included in Table 4 [34]. While the largest group, composed of 14 constitutions, is characterized by presence of all seven attributes (7 positive answers represented by the '+' sign), one can also find seven unique sets of attributes (combinations present only in a single constitution). Based on Table 4 one could attempt to argue that the executive has the strongest position vis-à-vis the legislature in Kazahkstan and Russia [positive answers for attributes (1)-(4) and (6)–(7)], while the opposite holds for Bosnia and Hercegovina, Macedonia, as well as Montenegro's 1992 Constitution (no longer in force).

One should, however, bear in mind the preliminary character of such conclusion and that a more nuanced assessment should include distribution of other powers, e.g. regarding constitutional amendment proposals, budgetary powers, powers relating to declarations of war and peace, as well as immunity provisions for each of the two powers. For our argument, we need not reach so far. The main lesson for us is that post-socialist constitutions differ significantly in their solutions as regards systems of government (executive-legislature relations).

34 For two countries – Poland and Serbia (former-Yugoslavia), more than one post-1989 constitution is included in Table 4, as detailed data for them are available.

Table 4: Formal constitutional attributes determining the executive-legislature relationship in post-socialist constitutions

Country	**Consti-tution adoption year**	**(1) Executive veto power**	**(2) Executive decree powers**	**(3) Executive emergency powers**	**(4) Legislative initiative of the executive**	**(5) Legislative oversight of the executive**	**(6) Executive power to appoint cabinet**	**(7) Executive power to dissolve assembly**
Albania	1998	+	+	+	+	+	+	+
Armenia	1995	+	+	+	+	+	+	+
Azerbaijan	1991	+	+	+	+	no	+	no
Belarus	1994	+	+	+	+	+	+	+
Bosnia and Hercegovina	1995	no	no	no	+	no	+	+
Bulgaria	1991	no	+	+	+	+	+	+
Croatia	1991	+	+	+	+	+	+	+
Czech Republic	1993	+	+	no	+	+	+	+
Estonia	1992	+	+	+	+	+	+	+
Georgia	1995	+	+	+	+	+	+	+
Hungary	1949	+	+	+	+	+	+	+
Kazakhstan	1995	+	+	+	+	no	+	+
Kyrgyzstan	1993	+	+	+	+	+	no	+
Latvia	1922	+	+	+	+	+	+	+
Lithuania	1992	+	+	+	+	+	+	+
Macedonia	1991	+	no	+	+	+	+	no
Moldova	1994	+	+	+	+	+	+	+
Montenegro	1992	no	+	no	+	no	+	no

Country	Constitution adoption year	(1) Executive veto power	(2) Executive decree powers	(3) Executive emergency powers	(4) Legislative initiative of the executive	(5) Legislative oversight of the executive	(6) Executive power to appoint cabinet	(7) Executive power to dissolve assembly
Poland	1992	+	+	+	+	+	+	+
	1997	+	no	+	+	+	+	+
Romania	1991	+	+	+	+	+	+	+
Russia	1993	+	+	+	+	no	+	+
Serbia	1992	no	no	+	+	no	+	+
	2003	no	+	+	no	no	+	+
	2006	+	no	+	+	+	+	+
Slovakia	1992	+	+	+	+	+	+	+
Slovenia	1991	no	+	+	+	+	+	+
Tajikistan	1994	+	+	+	+	no	+	no
Turkmenistan	1992	+	+	+	+	+	+	+
Ukraine	1996	+	+	+	+	+	+	+
Uzbekistan	1992	+	+	+	+	+	+	+

Source: Own elaboration on the basis of Cheibub et al. (2013) and their online appendix with data from Elkins et al. (2014).

2.2 Constitutional rights and freedoms

Concerning catalogues of rights and freedoms, post-socialist countries did not develop a common constitutional model either. Breaking with their pre-1989 past, they envisaged broad, unambiguously worded catalogues of human rights that are directly enforceable and binding upon all state institutions and ensured their supremacy over legislation by a system of judicial (constitutional) review (Sadurski 2002). To this end all currently operative post-socialist constitutions contain a separate section devoted to rights and freedoms provisions, however even with regard to such crude indication as the length of this section they vary considerably. One will find Bosnia and Hercegovina (549 words), Latvia (965 words), and Lithuania (1233 words) on one extreme, and Romania (4082 words), Ukraine (4192 words) and Serbia's 2006 Constitution (5580 words) on the other extreme (Elkins et al. 2014). A special case in this respect is the Czech Republic, where rights and freedoms are encompassed by a separate document (the Charter of Fundamental Rights and Basic Freedoms) attached to the constitution.

Data gathered by Elkins et al. (2014) allow to identify 117 different constitutional rights present in constitutions of the world since 1789 (35 civil and political rights, 22 legal process rights, 32 social and economic rights, 28 minority rights)[35]. Based on a subset of their data for post-socialist countries, in Table 5 we present a very general picture of the formal (*de iure*) protection of rights and freedoms in constitutions of these countries[36]. The differences between countries in this respect are not as discernible as for legislature-executive relations. The smallest variation is encountered for the category of political rights and

35 According to calculations by Ginsburg and Melton (2015), five of these rights and freedoms were present in more than 90% constitutions of the world in 2010: the general guarantee of equality, freedom of expression, freedom of assembly, freedom of association, and freedom of religion.

36 The numbers that we obtain for different types of rights for post-socialist countries based on the Elkins et al. (2014) database, which are discussed in this section and presented in Table 5, differ from the overall numbers of rights for these countries published recently in the 'CCP Rankings' on the website of Elkins et al.'s Comparative Constitutions Project (http://comparativeconstitutionsproject.org/ccp-rankings/). These discrepancies are due to different approaches taken to the classification of certain constitutional provisions as rights. Even with the specific numbers diverging, the main lines of conclusions from the discussion presented in this section and in Table 5 remain valid for both approaches.

civil liberties, where nearly all countries score between 14 and 19 (mean = 16.7, standard deviation = 1.7), with the sole exception of Bosnia and Hercegovina with 12 protected rights mentioned in the constitution. More differences are observed for the remaining categories. Legal process rights (mean = 7.9, standard deviation = 2.8) are formally most broadly protected by the relatively young constitutions of Montenegro (12 rights) and Serbia (14 rights)[37], while on the other extreme we have Bosnia and Hercegovina (1 right), Uzbekistan (2 rights), and Latvia (3 rights). Minority rights (mean = 7.5, standard deviation = 2.8), together with anti-discrimination measures contained by the discussed constitutions, are most pronounced for such countries as Armenia (12 rights), Serbia and Slovakia (11 rights), while in a few other constitutions they are hardly mentioned – Belarus (2 rights), Poland (1 right), Kyrgyzstan (0). The largest differences between countries, if one considers the simple measure of standard deviation, are visible with regard to social and economic rights (mean = 19.6, standard deviation = 4.2). While some constitutions list comprehensive rights regarding social security, education, healthcare, work protection, etc. (e.g. Armenia – 27 rights, Serbia – 25 rights, Ukraine – 24 rights), others provide only for a limited number of such rights (Bosnia and Herzegovina – 5 rights, the Czech Republic, Kazakhstan, and Latvia – 15 rights). Overall post-socialist countries constitutionalize ca. 50 rights in their constitutions, with the constitutions of Serbia (69 rights) and Armenia (67 rights) being most protective in this respect and constitutions of Bosnia and Herzegovina (25 rights) and Latvia (32 rights) on the other extreme. The variation between constitutions, as measured roughly by the standard deviation, is noticeable (8.5), however drops below 4 when one removes the 4 extreme cases mentioned above from the sample.

The practical operation of provisions regarding constitutional rights differs more significantly amongst the discussed countries. This topic has recently been thoroughly studied in the global perspective by Law and Versteeg (2013). They propose several measures of constitutional compliance in the area of bills and rights and distinguish between four types of constitutions as regards the protection of rights and freedoms: (1) strong constitutions, i.e. ones with high *de iure*, as well as *de facto* protection (constitutions which promise much and deliver much in

37 One hypothesis why these relatively young constitutions contain the broadest formal protection of legal process rights is that they follow the global increasing trend present in this respect over the recent years (see Ginsburg and Melton 2015).

Table 5: Formal protection of rights and freedoms in post-socialist constitutions (as of 2013[a])

Country	Overall Rights and Freedoms	Political Rights and Civil Liberties	Legal Process Rights	Social and Economic Rights	Minority Rights and Anti-Discrimination
Albania	58	17	10	21	10
Armenia	67	18	10	27	12
Azerbaijan	56	17	8	23	8
Belarus	47	17	5	23	2
Bosnia and Herc.	25	10	1	5	9
Bulgaria	53	17	6	23	7
Croatia (2009)	51	16	10	16	9
Czech Rep.(2008)	48	16	8	15	9
Estonia	53	17	9	17	10
Georgia (2004)	53	17	9	18	9
Hungary	51	15	7	20	9
Kazakhstan (2006)	46	15	7	15	9
Kyrgyzstan	52	17	9	20	6
Latvia	32	14	3	15	0
Lithuania	52	17	7	21	7
Macedonia	51	16	9	16	10
Moldova	52	17	5	23	7
Montenegro	59	17	12	23	7
Poland	49	19	8	21	1
Romania	52	18	9	20	5
Russia	54	18	10	20	6
Serbia	59	18	10	20	11
Slovakia (2003)	57	18	10	20	9
Slovenia	52	17	7	21	7
Tajikistan	47	15	6	19	7
Turkmenistan (2005)	57	18	9	24	6
Ukraine	45	18	2	18	7
Uzbekistan (1992)	69	19	14	25	11
Mean	51.7	16.7	7.9	19.6	7.5
Median	52	17	8.5	20	7.5
Max	69	19	14	27	12
Min	25	10	1	5	0
Standard deviation	8.5	1.7	2.8	4.2	2.8

Note: [a] For countries, for which data for 2013 were not available, the most recent year is taken into account and reported in brackets next to the country name.

Source: Own elaboration on the basis of Elkins et al. (2014).

practice); (2) sham constitutions, i.e. ones with high *de iure* protection and low *de facto* protection (constitutions which promise much and deliver little in practice); (3) weak constitutions, i.e. ones with low *de iure*, as well as *de facto* protection (constitutions which promise little and deliver little in practice); (4) modest constitutions, i.e. ones with low *de iure* protection and high *de facto* protection (constitutions which promise little but deliver much in practice). Table 6 (in Appendix 1) presents a subset of this data for post-socialist countries of Europe and Asia.

Data in Table 6 relate to two dimensions – 'constitutional underperformance' and 'constitutional overperformance', with four columns for each of them, reporting performance in the area of personal integrity rights, civil and political freedoms, socio-economic and group rights, as well as overall scores[38]. The constitutional underperformance scores measure the extent to which countries promising a relatively generous catalogue of rights *de iure* in their constitutions succeed at upholding those rights in practice. Each country's underperformance score provides the proportion of the total number of rights in its constitution that was actually respected, i.e. 0 indicates that the country seriously violated all of the rights included its constitution, while 1 indicates perfect respect of all the rights included in the constitution. These scores allow to distinguish between countries with strong constitutions and those with sham constitutions[39]. Table 6 reveals

38 Law and Versteeg's (2013) analysis involves a representative sample from each of the three categories constrained by the necessity of choosing *de iure* rights for which corresponding *de facto* compliance data could be found. As a result their study includes the following 15 rights: prohibition of arbitrary arrest and/or detention, prohibition of torture, right to habeas corpus, fair trial rights, prohibition of death penalty (falling within the category of personal integrity rights); freedom of assembly and/or association, freedom of movement, freedom of religion, right to vote, freedom of the press and/or expression (civil and political freedoms); right to health, right to education, gender equality in marriage, gender equality in labor relations, general protection of minority rights or right of minorities to be represented in government (socio-economic and group rights).

39 To be specific, a country is identified as having a strong constitution if its constitution contains at least 10 of the 15 rights listed in the preceding footnote and it respects more than half of the promised rights. Conversely, a country is classified as having a sham constitution if it promises at least 10 of those 15 rights but respects half or fewer of these promised rights (Law and Versteeg 2013, p. 885).

that of the 26 post-socialist constitutions for which data are available[40] 18 are strong constitutions, while 6 are sham constitutions. Countries with the highest underperformance scores (i.e. most respect for rights in their constitutions) are Slovenia (#3 'strongest' constitution of the world according to Law and Versteeg 2013[41]), the Czech Republic (#4 in the above classification) and Estonia. On the other extreme one will find Russia (#5 'worst sham' constitution in the world according to Law and Versteeg 2013), as well as the remaining post-socialist countries with sham constitutions: Uzbekistan, Tajikistan, Turkmenistan, Belarus, and Azerbaijan. It is noticeable that most 'disrespect' for the constitution is found in the area of civil and political freedoms, where countries with sham constitutions such as Russia, Uzbekistan and Turkmenistan score 0.

Two post-socialist constitutions fall short of the classification of strong and sham constitutions[42]. Their type can be determined based on the constitutional overperformance scores reported in the remaining columns of Table 6. Overperformance scores measure the extent to which countries respect rights that are *not* found in their constitutions. This measure enables to distinguish between countries with modest constitutions (which promise few rights *de iure* but respect many *de facto*), and countries with weak constitutions (where protection for rights is low both on paper and in practice)[43]. As with the constitutional underperformance scores, each country receives a constitutional overperformance score between zero and one which is equal to the proportion

40 Data for Serbia and Montenegro have not been assembled by Law and Versteeg (2013).

41 This classification ranks all countries according to their underperformance scores, taking also into account the scope of their success or failure. As the authors explain, "[*t*]*he more rights that a country promises in its constitution, the more impressive it becomes to fulfill every promise; conversely, the more promises that a country breaks, the more sweeping its failure*" (Law and Versteeg 2013, p. 898). Therefore, in case of identical underperformance scores countries are ranked according to the number of rights promised in their constitutions. This is the reason why Slovenia is ranked #3 and the Czech Republic #4, even though the underperformance scores are 0.962 for both (Slovenia, however, includes 14 of the 15 studied rights in its constitution, while for the Czech Republic it is 13 rights).

42 I.e. they include less than 10 of the 15 rights enumerated in footnote 38 in their constitutions.

43 To be specific, a country is classified as having a weak constitution if its constitution contains 8 or fewer of the 15 rights enumerated in footnote 38 and respects less than half of the rights that are omitted from the constitution. A country is defined as having a modest constitution if its constitution contains 8 or fewer of these 15 rights but it actually respects half or more of the omitted rights (Law and Versteeg 2013, p. 885).

of omitted rights that were nevertheless respected in practice. Table 6 allows to identify one modest constitution among the studied countries – for Bosnia and Herzegovina (in fact, the #5 'most modest' constitution in the world according to Law and Versteeg 2013), as well as one weak constitution – for Kazakhstan (#3 weakest constitution in the world according to Law and Versteeg 2013). It also reveals some level of overperformance for strong and sham constitutions, however one must bear in mind that the number of rights that are not included in the constitution *de iure* is in these cases very small (amounting to not more than 3). Overperformance is more common for socioeconomic and group rights, as well as personal integrity rights, while for civil and political freedoms this phenomenon fails to materialize at all in post-socialist countries.

The problem of the relationship between *de iure* and *de facto* constitutional rights protection has become a lively debated issue in the most recent literature (see e.g. Melton 2013 and literature cited therein; as well as Bjoernskov 2015 for property rights in post-socialist countries). As such, this discussion also falls within a broader debate about the significance of formal constitutional rules for their factual operation. As Melton (2013, p. 1) puts it, "*[t]he critique of constitutions as mere parchment barriers is as old as the practice of writing them down*". The main question here is whether the constitution imposes significant constraints on those in power and establishes rules, according to which the political game is played within states, or simply composes *parchment barriers* (as James Madison, the 4th US President put it – see more Levinson 2011). More and more often researchers interested in the economic approach to constitutions also enter the debate[44]. However, from the point of view of our argument it is most crucial to observe that in the case of rights and freedoms, it is not that much *de iure*

44 On the one hand, they acknowledge that gaps between the constitution text and its functioning in practice are inevitable, both because of imperfectness of actors drafting the constitution (in particular, bounded rationality), as well as the need identified in legal literature to apply 'workarounds' allowing for a more pragmatic approach to situations, when the constitution text is a source of institutional tensions (see e.g. Tushnet 2009). The literature advocating the relevance of *de iure* rules (constitution text) argues, however, that constitutional solutions work provided that they are self-enforcing, what means that it is not necessary that an external actor supervises the execution of a bargain (see e.g. Ordeshook 1992, Weingast 1997). Constitutional provisions written on paper and publicly available contribute to the constitutional self-enforcement mechanism thanks to providing a focal point, around which various actors may concentrate their enforcement efforts (Carey 2000, Elkins et al. 2009).

constitutional provisions but rather their *de facto* operation that testifies to the differences in this area in post-socialist countries after 1989.

2.3 Enforcement mechanisms

Constitutional provisions have little meaning when their enforcement has not been guaranteed. All post-socialist countries examined in this study, except Turkmenistan, established constitutional courts for this purpose[45]. However, as with systems of government and constitutional rights and freedoms, they differ significantly as regards, inter alia, the constitutional courts' position vis-à-vis other state organs, guarantees of the independence of judges and internal autonomy of the courts, as well as the legal effects of courts' judgments. As discussed in the previous chapter of this book, it is, in particular, the broadly conceived independence of constitutional courts that determines their efficacy in fulfilling the crucial role of neutral constitutional enforcers within the policy-making process in the state. Therefore, in this section we focus on such features of the constitutional courts established in post-socialist countries which determine their scope of (*de iure* and *de facto*) independence.

Defining judicial independence is not an easy task. Becker (1970, p. 144) proposes the following useful definition: "*Judicial independence is (a) the degree to which judges believe they can decide and do decide consistent with their own personal attitudes, values and conceptions of judicial role (in their interpretation of the law), (b) in opposition to what others, who have or are believed to have political or judicial power, think about or desire in like matters, and (c) particularly when a decision adverse to the beliefs or desires of those with political or judicial power may bring some retribution on the judges personally or on the power of the court*". One could not speak of judicial independence and, in particular, constitutional court independence under the socialist (or communist) rule when the state was considered the 'embodiment of the people' and a formal division of powers was deemed unnecessary. In line with this approach in most post-socialist countries constitutional courts did not exist before 1989. The only exceptions were the then existent Yugoslavia (with a constitutional court since 1963) and Poland (*de iure* since 1982, *de facto* since 1986). Notwithstanding the formal provisions determining their existence, the genuine powers of both of these courts were inevitably subject to the restrictions stemming from the communist party rule at

45 In case of Estonia the Supreme Court includes a Constitutional Review Chamber which decides questions of constitutionality. Therefore we focus on Estonia's Supreme Court in this study.

that time (Sadurski 2001). As a matter of fact, the legal framework defining their functioning also changed significantly after 1989.

Drafters of new post-socialist constitutions envisaged clauses guaranteeing judicial independence for most of these states, as well as provided various safeguards of this independence. As mentioned earlier, constitutional review was established in constitutions of all of these countries, except for Turkmenistan, and for some of them this actually preceded the adoption of the new constitution (e.g. for Hungary – in 1989). As Herron and Randazzo (2003) indicate, the judiciary's willingness to demonstrate its independence has, however, not always been accepted by other political actors. In particular, conflicts between the judiciary and the executive have occasionally arisen, e.g. in Russia where the constitutional court was suspended in 1993 and reinstated two years later with a significantly weaker position vis-à-vis other branches of power and limited scope of competences.

As in previous sections, we refrain here from discussing in detail the legal frameworks provided for the functioning of constitutional courts in post-socialist countries and their independence (for a thorough account see e.g. Sadurski 2014). Instead, we focus on providing a brief account of the differences between countries in this respect, using measures of constitutional court independence that have been developed in the recent literature for the purpose of application in constitutional-law-and-economics empirical studies.

Smithey and Ishiyama (2000) introduced the first index of judicial power and independence (*de iure*) for a group of post-socialist countries of Europe and Asia. Its construction takes account of the courts' scope of competences concerning constitutional review and the extent of independence granted by the constitution to such courts vis-à-vis other institutional actors in the state. A more comprehensive indicator, available in two variants – the *de iure* judicial independence indicator and the *de facto* judicial independence indicator[46], has been constructed by Feld and Voigt (2003) and very recently updated in Voigt et al. (2015). The *de iure* indicator takes into account formal rules regarding the following issues: institutional stability of the environment for the constitutional court's activity (including the constitutional amendment process); the procedure of appointing judges; their term of office and remuneration; the accessibility of

46 To be precise, given the differences in the structure and organization of the judiciary, as well as constitutional enforcement mechanisms as such, between countries of the world, their focus is on each country's highest court, regardless of whether it deals exclusively with constitutional issues or whether it is the Supreme Court for all areas of law.

the court; the division of cases between the judges of the court; the court's scope of competences; and the public announcement of the court's decisions. The *de facto* indicator reflects the practical operation of constitutional courts (e.g. the factual duration of judges' terms of office, their factual remuneration levels and the financial situation of the courts, the stability of legal rules governing the operation of the courts, etc.).

In Table 7 we present the values of these indicators for post-socialist countries[47]. In all cases they range from 0 to 1, where higher numbers correspond to more independent courts. All three columns provide a similar observation: there is considerable heterogeneity between post-socialist countries as regards both their *de iure*, as well as *de facto* constitutional court independence. Concentrating first on the more recent data from Voigt et al. (2015), *de iure* independence ranges from 0.462 for Russia and Kazakhstan to 0.919 for Romania (with the mean of 0.642 and standard deviation 0.155). Even more variation is observed for *de facto* independence ranging from 0.3 for Belarus to 1 for Armenia[48] and 0.875 for Lithuania (mean = 0.61, standard deviation = 0.178). Taking a peak even deeper into the construction of these indicators one will find considerable variation also as regards the individual components of both of them. Only for four out of 18 such individual components post-socialist countries score within the range, which is smaller than the maximum possible interval [0,1][49]. Interestingly, a certain aspect

---

47 Other measures of judicial independence are also used in the literature (e.g. Cingranelli et al. 2014, Melton and Ginsburg 2014, Linzer and Staton 2012). We do not report them here because: either they are not available for many post-socialist countries, or they do not relate to the constitutional judiciary, or they are less inclusive in their coverage of independence than indicators mentioned above, or for a combination of these reasons. Rios-Figueroa and Staton (2014) provide an evaluation of the content, construct, and convergent validity of 13 cross-national measures of judicial independence, however this study does not cover the most recent developments in this field.

48 The unexpectedly high values of this indicator for Armenia and Azerbaijan (0.867) are attributed by Voigt et al. (2015) to the fact that their construction is based solely on three components due to data availability constraints. One should bear in mind the limited reliability of this indicator for these countries.

49 These are: mention of the constitutional court in the constitution (scores for post-socialist countries between 0.5 and 1), term length of judges (score between 0.2 and 1) – both for the *de iure* indicator, as well as effective average term length of judges (between 0.15 and 1) and frequency of changes of the legal framework for the operation of the court (between 0.2 and 0.8) – both for the *de facto* indicator. We would like to thank Jerg Gutmann for sharing the Voigt et al. (2015) data on individual components of the indicators.

of 'overperformance' (understood here as a higher level of *de facto* than *de iure* independence) is observable in a significant number of countries, e.g. Lithuania, Poland and many (non-Baltic) former soviet republics (including e.g. Georgia, Kyrgyzstan, Russia, Tajikistan)[50]. Smithey and Ishiyama's (2000) data confirm the general picture by revealing additionally noticeable differences in the *de iure* courts' power[51].

Table 7: Constitutional court independence in post-socialist countries

Country	Smithey and Ishiyama (2000)	Voigt et al. (2015)	
		de iure	*de facto*
Albania	–	0.828	0.508
Armenia	0.83	0.584	1.000
Azerbaijan	0.50	0.638	0.867
Belarus	0.45	0.452	0.300
Bosnia and Herzegovina	–	0.844	0.480
Bulgaria	0.70	0.762	0.667
Croatia	0.47	0.671	0.350
Czech Republic	0.56	0.739	0.717
Estonia	0.39	0.842	0.731
Georgia	0.56	0.754	0.850
Hungary	0.58	0.688	0.594
Kazakhstan	–	0.362	–
Kyrgyzstan	–	0.599	0.669
Latvia	0.58	0.658	0.600
Lithuania	0.70	0.619	0.875
Macedonia	0.61	0.714	0.536

50 As the brief description of the two indicators shows, the *de facto* indicator is not limited to reflecting the factual operation of the legal rules composing the formal indicator. The relationship between *de iure* and *de facto* judicial independence is a topic of recent disputes (see in particular Hayo and Voigt 2007, as well as Melton and Ginsburg 2014 and the sources mentioned therein).

51 The surprising value of 0.00 of this indicator for Poland can be explained by the fact that its construction is based on the 1992 provisional constitution and fails to include sub-constitutional legislation of that time.

Country	Smithey and Ishiyama (2000)	Voigt et al. (2015)	
		de iure	*de facto*
Moldova	0.72	0.549	0.550
Montenegro	–	0.750	0.536
Poland	0.00	0.538	0.880
Romania	0.42	0.919	0.571
Russia	0.95	0.362	0.686
Serbia	–	0.522	0.533
Slovakia	0.31	0.691	0.621
Slovenia	0.56	0.869	0.431
Tajikistan	–	0.407	0.588
Turkmenistan	–	–	–
Ukraine	0.53	0.439	0.371
Uzbekistan	–	0.527	0.350

Source: Own elaboration on the basis of the sources mentioned in the table.

2.4 Summary

The discussion of solutions envisaged by post-socialist countries in their new post-1989 constitutions, pertaining to structure of power, the protection of constitutional rights and freedoms, as well as constitutional court independence, provided in this section, was aimed to be illustrative but we are aware that a comparative constitutional-legal scholar will not be satisfied by its generality. Certainly, the presented quantitative measures fall short of capturing many nuances connected with the discussed sophisticated matters. However, even at this level of generality one can notice several differences between post-socialist countries in formal constitutional solutions adopted in these areas after 1989, which are considerably strengthened if one additionally accounts for heterogeneous compliance levels. *De iure* and *de facto* differences examined together give an overall picture of significant variety as regards these crucial components of the constitutions in the post-socialist world, which we further relate to performance in economic reforms in these countries. We present three studies of the link, as justified by the underlying theory discussed in Chapter 1, in the next and subsequent parts of the book.

Chapter 3. Regression analyses of economic effects of post-socialist constitutions

In this chapter we undertake an empirical study aiming to confirm the significance of constitutional frameworks for performance in the field of economic reforms in post-socialist countries of Europe and Asia from 1989 to 2012. To this end we re-estimate the model first introduced in Metelska-Szaniawska (2008, 2009) and applied for the time periods 1989–2001 and 1989–2004, respectively. The main question that we ask the data is whether given the now considerably longer transition time period under analysis and much more reliable data, the main findings of those earlier studies, summarized in Section 1.4, hold.

We begin by presenting the design of the empirical model, as well as descriptions of the dependent and crucial independent variables (together with their data sources). For more details on these issues we direct the reader to the sources mentioned above. We then report and discuss the results. In the last section we put forth the most important conclusions and reflections.

3.1 The empirical model

The empirical model that we construct takes constitutional rules adopted by post-socialist countries as explanans and aims to identify their economic effects, understood as performance in post-socialist economic reforms. In other words, the dependent variable in our econometric model, measuring the advancement in reforming the economy, is explained by independent variables representing the potential constitutional factors and a set of control variables.

Among the constitutional variables we take into account the main components of modern constitutions, which we introduced and discussed from the point of view of their potential relevance for economic reforms in transition in Chapters 1 and 2. They are the structure (concentration) of power in the state, the bills of rights, and the enforcement mechanism (independence of the constitutional judiciary). As for the control variables, the existing literature regarding post-socialist economic reforms indicates the following determinants: 'initial conditions' for reform (e.g. de Melo et al. 2001; Falcetti et al. 2002; Falcetti et al. 2005); foreign financial aid received during transition (Fish 1998); outcome of the initial post-socialist elections, i.e. elite turnover (Fish 1998; EBRD 1999); duration of the economic reforms process (Hellman 1997); power of interest groups in a state (EBRD 1999; IMF 2000); various social and cultural factors (Fish 1998; EBRD 1999).

The starting point for our analysis is the following basic model specification:

$$econ\_reform_{it} = \alpha_1 concentration_{it} + \alpha_2 rights_{it} + \alpha_3 CCI\_deiure_i + \\ +\alpha_4 CCI\_defacto_i + \alpha_5 trtime_{it} + \alpha_6 trtime_{it}^2 + \alpha_7 (IC \times trtime)_{it} + \\ +\alpha_8 (IC \times trtime^2)_{it} + \alpha_9 elections_i + \alpha_{10} trust_i + \varepsilon_{it}, \quad (1)$$

where ε_{it} is the error term and the complete list of employed variables and data sources is provided in Appendix 3[52]. We present the dependent variable and constitutional variables in more detail shortly.

The study consists of panel data analyses. The discussion of employed estimation techniques is presented alongside the results. The sample includes post-socialist countries enumerated in footnote 1, except for Bosnia and Herzegovina, Montenegro, and Serbia (due to unavailable data for some control variables). By construction or due to limited availability of data some specifications encompass slightly smaller groups of countries. We focus on the time period beginning in 1989, i.e. when, following the fall of socialism, the first group of the discussed countries engaged in post-socialist economic reforms. Following Falcetti et al. (2002), as well as Falcetti et al. (2005), we propose to operate in 'transition time' rather than calendar time. Transition time is defined as beginning in 1989 for Poland and Hungary, 1990 for other Central and Southeastern European countries (except Albania), 1991 for Albania and the Baltic states, and 1992 for the former Soviet republics. This allows for accounting for the fact that transition started at different times in different countries[53]. The upper limit of the time period under analysis is 2012, as determined by the availability of data.

52 Measures of the influence of various forms of state capture by interest groups (including corruption) on the functioning of enterprises, as well as foreign aid and different geographical/cultural variables proved insignificant in all specifications, while not being available for the entire sample, therefore we withdrew them from further analysis.

53 It was shown in Chapter 2 that the first post-socialist constitutions were adopted primarily in the period 1990–1996, i.e. usually slightly later than the initiation of the economic reforms process. Including the early years of transition, however, allows to study the influence of the adoption of new constitutions on economic reforms (as compared to the preceding situation), while also rendering the empirical study more reliable thanks to a considerably larger number of included observations. We return to the issue of causality and simultaneity in subsequent sections and Chapter 4.

3.2 Dependent variable

The dependent variable in the estimated model is an aggregated transition indicator, also called the index of economic reforms (*econ_reform*), constituting an average of a set of indicators of structural economic reforms, published annually by the European Bank for Reconstruction and Development in subsequent issues of *Transition Report* (EBRD, 1994–2013). The following categories of reforms are included: privatization and enterprise restructuring (three indicators: large-scale privatization; small-scale privatization; governance and enterprise restructuring), as well as market liberalization and competition (three indicators: price liberalization; trade and foreign exchange system; competition policy)[54]. Data for these six indicators are available for all post-socialist countries for the period 1989–2012.

EBRD's indicators of structural economic reforms are intended to provide a basis for systematic comparison of the course of market-oriented reforms amongst post-socialist countries. Based on a survey of EBRD analysts, each country is given a rating in each of the aforementioned areas, ranging from 1 (little or no reform) to 4+ (standards and performance typical of advanced industrial economies)[55]. Figure 2 presents the evolution of the aggregate indicator based on a simple average of the above six indicators for the period 1989–2012. Whilst the starting value of the indicator was for most countries identical (or very similar), the further progress in economic reforms varies greatly[56].

Employing progress in economic reforms, not indicators of economic performance such as GDP growth, as the dependent variable in the study allows us to focus on the influence of constitutional variables directly on the decision-making by governments in the field of (economic) policy, as suggested by the theory[57].

---

54 Data on financial sector reforms are only available up to 2010, therefore these reforms have not been included. Conclusions from estimations conducted for the period up to 2010 including these reforms are generally in line with the results presented here.

55 Detailed methodological issues regarding the construction of these indicators are discussed by EBRD (1995).

56 The discussed measure reflects factual achievements so there is no risk that the similarity of the starting point for all countries is explained by the fact that they undertook reforms at a similar moment in time.

57 Several criticisms have been raised as to the reliability of EBRD's transition indicators. Subjectivity, bounded and ordinal nature, focus only on end results (not dynamics), equal weights for all components of the aggregate indicator, and relative nature are some examples. In response to these allegations alternative measures have been proposed (see examples in Metelska-Szaniawska 2009). However, most of them fail to account for many components of reforms (focusing most often on liberalization and privatization) or are based on not fully reliable data.

Figure 2: Economic reforms in post-socialist countries as measured by EBRD's aggregated transition indicator, 1989–2012

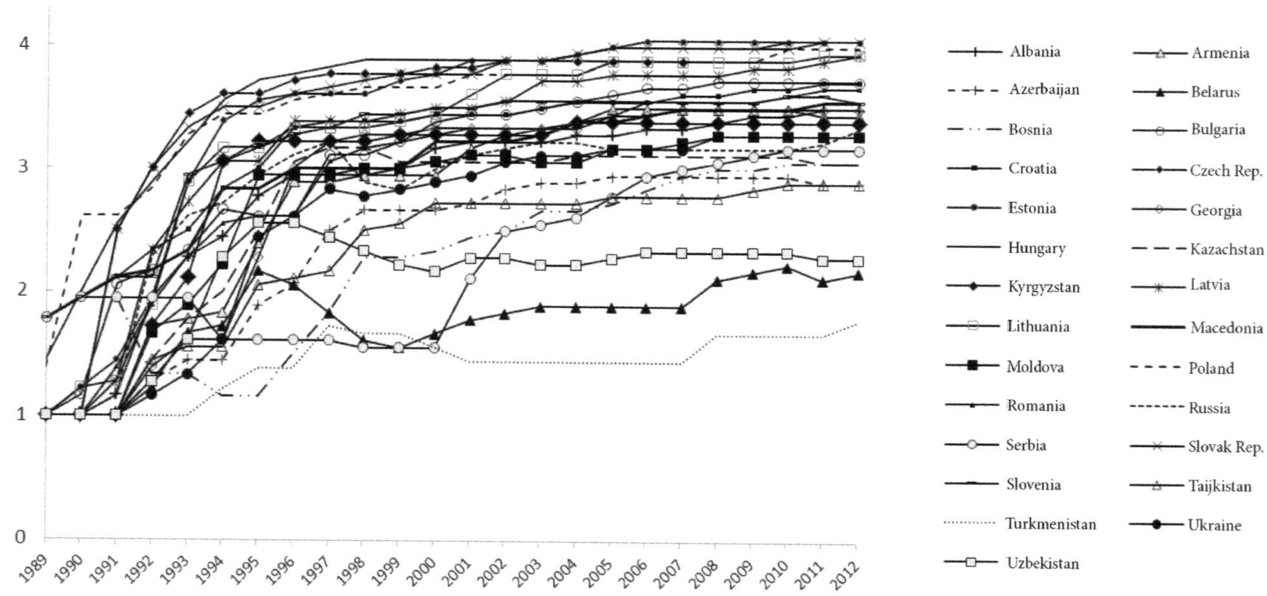

Source: Author's calculations and graph on the basis of EBRD (1994–2013).

3.3 Constitutional variables

This subsection presents in short the indicators applied as proxies for the constitutional elements included in the study – the structure of government (*concentration*), bill of rights (*rights*), the constitutional enforcement mechanism (*CCI*). Further details are provided in Metelska-Szaniawska (2009).

For the structure of power we use a measure of the concentration of political power in the state based on a spatial model of political interaction in the process of drafting state policy (number of veto-players), called here the *concentration of power index*. It is based on an index of political constraints developed by Henisz (2000, 2013) and calculated in the following way: *concentration* = 1 – *political constraints index* (Henisz 2013). This measure includes the following aspects: formal separation of powers within the state (the number of branches of power capable of vetoing a proposed policy amendment); party composition (alignment across branches of power); and preference heterogeneity within each of the legislative chambers. Given the above it is the most comprehensive of the available indicators concerning structure of power in the state and its concentration, suitable for application in the context of the presented study.

Bearing in mind that, as explained in Section 2.2, post-socialist countries demonstrate considerable levels of constitutional underperformance in the field of rights and freedoms (while some exhibit overperformance) and that it is *de facto* protection of rights and freedoms that has been identified by the literature to matter for policy making and economic outcomes, with the relationship between *de iure* and *de facto* protection largely still an open question[58], for the scope of the constitutional system of rights and freedoms we use a measure of the factual functioning of political rights and civil liberties in a country, called here the *rights index*. It is based on data on political rights and civil liberties published by Freedom House (1990–2013). The following form is used: $rights = 7 - (PR + CL)/2$, where: *PR* – the Freedom House political rights rating, *CL* – the Freedom House civil liberties rating. The political rights ranking is based on a checklist including the electoral process, political pluralism and participation, while the civil liberties indicator encompasses freedom of expression and belief, associational and organizational rights, the rule of law, personal autonomy, and individual rights[59].

58 See e.g. Melton (2013) and literature discussed therein.

59 Our account of constitutional rights and freedoms does not capture the protection of socio-economic rights, which, as we revealed in Section 2.2, demonstrates significant variation between post-socialist countries. The available *de facto* indicators

For the constitutional enforcement mechanism we use the *de iure* and *de facto* constitutional court independence indicators, discussed in Section 2.3 and called for the sake of the empirical study the *CCI indicators*. The *de iure* indicator takes into account formal rules regarding: institutional stability of the environment for constitutional courts' activity (including the constitutional amendment process); the procedure of appointing judges; their term of office and remuneration; accessibility of the court; division of cases between judges of the court; the court's scope of competences; and public announcement of the court's decisions. The *de facto* indicator reflects the practical operation of constitutional courts (e.g. factual duration of judges' terms of office, their factual remuneration levels and financial situation of the courts, stability of legal rules governing the operation of the courts, etc.). Both indicators have been introduced by Feld and Voigt (2003) and recently recalculated by Voigt et al. (2015)[60].

3.4 Estimation results

The primary interest of the study is to obtain statistically significant coefficients associated with variables representing the potential constitutional determinants of economic reforms in transition. Whilst it will not be possible to interpret the specific values obtained, we will draw conclusions about the significance, direction and, in some cases, intensity of the relationship. If we obtain a negative coefficient associated with the concentration index and a positive coefficient for constitutional rights, this will be a confirmation of the negative constitutionalists' view on the role of the constitution in post-socialist transition. A positive coefficient for the concentration index will be evidence in favor of positive constitutionalism. Positive significant coefficients for constitutional court independence variables will confirm the role of these courts as a final stage in turning promises of the state authority into credible commitments.

---

corresponding to these rights are, however, in large part based on post-constitutional issues (e.g. regarding trade tariffs, restrictions on capital flow, tax rates, price controls etc.) and therefore are of little value for this study.

60 We emphasize that the *de iure* and *de facto* indicators are by construction based on different components (see details in section 2.3), i.e. they concern different dimensions of constitutional court independence and the *de facto* indicator is not limited to reflecting the factual operation of the legal rules composing the formal indicator (the simple correlation between these indicators for our panel of transition countries is 0.022). Accordingly, they should be regarded as complementary measures. This justifies including both indicators in the econometric analyses.

Table 8 presents the estimation results for the basic specification. Columns 1–3 report them for a limited version that does not include the *CCI* and *trust* variables allowing for the largest possible sample size (25 countries). In all three estimated models (OLS, fixed effects, and random effects[61]) we find negative coefficients on concentration of power and positive coefficients on constitutional rights. These variables are also significant at a 1% level. This suggests a first confirmation of the arguments of negative constitutionalists. The results obtained for the remaining variables included in the model are generally in line with the expectations[62].

Columns 4–5 of Table 8 extend the specification to include the *CCI* variables (decreasing the sample to 23 countries[63]), while Columns 6–7 present the results obtained for the model including both the *CCI* variables and the *trust* variable (20 countries[64])[65]. All of these results confirm the earlier conclusions regarding the *concentration* and *rights* variables. At the same time they point to the importance of the constitutional enforcement mechanism for economic reforms

---

61 The result of the Hausman test allows for the use of random effects estimators. Such result was also obtained for further analyzed specifications. Due to identified problems of heteroskedasticity, autocorrelation and cross-sectional dependence, Driscoll-Kraay standard errors are reported in this and subsequent tables (where relevant).

62 Both variables regarding transition time are significant showing continuous reform advancement throughout the period (a positive coefficient on *trtime*) with some tapering off (a negative coefficient on $trtime^2$). The coefficient corresponding to the interaction of initial conditions and transition time is negative suggesting that the influence of initial conditions on economic reforms in transition has been falling over time. This effect is slightly attenuated by the positive coefficient on the interaction between *IC* and $trtime^2$. Not all results confirm the significance of the initial conditions for reforms given the more-than-20-year-long period under analysis. The remaining variables – *elections* and *trust* (where included) are significant and their coefficients positive, what is consistent with the theory. Some tested specifications of the model revealed the significance of the first and second lag of the dependent variable (path dependence of economic reforms), however with no alteration of the principal conclusions regarding the constitutional variables.

63 Kazakhstan and Turkmenistan are not included due to unavailability of data (in the latter case due to nonexistence of the constitutional court).

64 Kyrgyzstan, Tajikistan, and Uzbekistan are further excluded due to unavailability of data.

65 The results for the fixed effects model are not presented since both the *CCI* indicators and the *trust* variable are time-invariant and would be omitted.

Table 8: Estimation results for specification (1), 1989–2012 (dependent variable: $econ\_reform_{it}$)

	Coefficients						
	without *CCI* and *trust*			with *CCI*, without *trust*		with *CCI* and *trust*	
Independent variables	**I OLS**	**II Fixed effects**	**III Random effects**	**IV OLS**	**V Random effects**	**VI OLS**	**VII Random effects**
$concentration_{it}$	−0.31*** (−2.27)	−0.55*** (−6.08)	−0.53*** (−5.96)	−0.35*** (−3.08)	−0.50*** (−5.67)	−0.53*** (−5.21)	−0.55*** (−6.26)
$rights_{it}$	0.15*** (8.51)	0.12*** (5.85)	0.12*** (6.26)	0.11*** (8.64)	0.12*** (6.57)	0.11*** (9.79)	0.13*** (6.76)
CCI_deiure_i	–	–	–	−0.27*** (−2.37)	−0.46*** (−2.05)	−0.23*** (−2.27)	−0.25 (−1.14)
$CCI\_defacto_i$	–	–	–	0.31*** (2.80)	0.42*** (2.28)	0.37*** (3.57)	0.33* (1.85)
$trtime_{it}$	0.20*** (5.95)	0.19*** (25.48)	0.19*** (25.62)	0.20*** (6.21)	0.20*** (25.18)	0.20*** (6.55)	0.20*** (24.21)
$trtime^2_{it}$	-6.1×10^{-3}*** (−4.81)	-5.7×10^{-3}*** (−18.47)	-5.8×10^{-3}*** (−18.59)	−0.01*** (−4.98)	−0.01*** (−18.09)	−0.01*** (−5.23)	-6×10^{-3}*** (−17.00)
$(IC\times trtime)_{it}$	-8.9×10^{-3}*** (−3.80)	-5.2×10^{-3}* (1.68)	2.1×10^{-3} (0.74)	−0.01* (−2.00)	1.3×10^{-4} (0.04)	-6.9×10^{-4} (−0.28)	-1.5×10^{-3} (−0.49)
$(IC\times trtime^2)_{it}$	4.6×10^{-4}*** (3.15)	-4.9×10^{-5} (0.36)	6.4×10^{-5} (0.52)	3.1×10^{-4}*** (2.24)	1.1×10^{-4} (0.90)	1×10^{-4} (0.74)	1.2×10^{-4} (0.86)

	Coefficients						
	without *CCI* and *trust*			with *CCI*, without *trust*		with *CCI* and *trust*	
Independent variables	**I OLS**	**II Fixed effects**	**III Random effects**	**IV OLS**	**V Random effects**	**VI OLS**	**VII Random effects**
$elections_i$	0.13*** (8.99)	–	0.08*** (2.40)	0.13*** (7.91)	0.09*** (3.52)	0.13*** (12.76)	0.12*** (4.58)
$trust_i$	–	–	–	–	–	1.13*** (3.67)	1.07* (1.90)
constant	1.03*** (10.91)	1.75*** (16.69)	1.47*** (9.82)	1.15*** (10.11)	1.44*** (6.61)	0.89*** (5.58)	0.91*** (3.17)
R^2	0.815	0.766	0.797	0.857	0.852	0.878	0.877
F-stat. / χ^2-stat.	1003.88	378.50	2339.37	1870.07	2425.06	9002.05	2494.04
Number of observations	544	544	544	502	502	439	439
Number of countries	25	25	25	23	23	20	20

Note: Values of the t-statistic in brackets. * Significant at a 10% level, *** Significant at a 5% level.

Source: Author's calculations.

in transition. Consistent with Voigt et al. (2015), as well as several earlier studies of economic effects of judicial independence that they mention, we find that *de facto CCI* has positive economic effects – in this case on post-socialist countries' performance in economic reforms. This conclusion also conforms with the negative constitutionalists' arguments interpreting constitutional court independence as an important final stage in the constitutional commitment mechanism. *De iure CCI* is found not to contribute to successful economic reforms in these countries, which is also in line with conclusions of the more general studies on economic effects of *de iure* judicial independence. Interestingly, this variable is found significant with a negative coefficient in Columns 4–6 of Table 8. Before embarking on a search for potential explanations of this result[66] we present the next results, which put in question the strength of this conclusion[67].

Table 9 presents the results of more refined estimations based on the systems approach. The latter allows to study potential simultaneous effects between variables included in the study and may therefore allow to tackle a limited part of the potential endogeneity problem.

Column 1 of Table 9 presents the results of estimations taking into account the effects between economic reforms and economic growth of post-socialist countries, as suggested by some of the literature on transition (e.g. Falcetti et al. 2005). We supplement the basic specification with a new control variable accounting for economic growth and analyze this equation in the following system with a supplementing growth equation:

$$\begin{aligned} econ\_reform_{it} = {} & \alpha_1 concentration_{it} + \alpha_2 rights_{it} + \alpha_3 CCI\_deiure_i + \alpha_4 CCI\_defacto_i + \\ & + \alpha_5 trtime_{it} + \alpha_6 trtime_{it}^2 + \alpha_7 (IC \times trtime)_{it} + \alpha_8 (IC \times trtime^2)_{it} + \\ & + \alpha_9 elections_i + \alpha_{10} trust_i + \alpha_{11} growth_{it} + \varepsilon_{it} \end{aligned} \qquad (2)$$

$$\begin{aligned} growth_{it} = {} & \beta_1 (IC \times trtime)_{it} + \beta_2 (IC \times trtime^2)_{it} + \beta_3 trtime_{it} + \beta_4 trtime_{it}^2 + \\ & + \beta_5 econ\_reform_{i,t-1} + \beta_6 CCI\_defacto_i + \beta_7 fiscal_{it} + \\ & + \beta_8 recovery_{i,t-2} + \eta_{it}, \end{aligned}$$

66 Potential explanations could relate to the recent debate on the importance of the formal provisions governing *de iure* judicial independence for countries' *de facto* performance in this field (e.g. Melton and Ginsburg 2014), as well as literature on the potential adverse economic effects of the functioning of strong formal institutions in postsocialist transition (e.g. Bjoernskov 2015 – in relation to property rights protection).

67 It is also noticeable that in most specifications the positive effect of *de facto* constitutional court independence offsets the negative effect of *de iure CCI*.

where η is the error term in the growth equation[68,69].

Column 1 of Table 9 reports the results of the Three-Stage Least Squares (3SLS) estimation of specification (2) without the *trust* variable (23 countries), while Column 2 – with the *trust* variable (20 countries). We indeed find an effect of growth on economic reforms, while the feedback effects from economic reforms to growth are less certain (insignificance or marginal significance). Columns 3–4 of Table 9 relate to an extended systems estimation accounting additionally for potential feedback effects between economic reforms and constitutional solutions. Obviously, constitutions result from a certain design process involving various factors. In order to account for this we estimate systems consisting of equation (1), with economic reforms as the dependent variable, and equations treating constitutional variables as explananda[70].

As we are most interested in conclusions regarding constitutional variables in this setting, we shall make three important observations based on the results presented in Table 9. Firstly, the *concentration* variable is marginally significant only in one specification, while otherwise it is insignificant and its coefficient takes different signs. Secondly, the *rights* variable remains significant with a positive

68 The growth equation follows from a detailed study of the determinants of economic growth in transition, and the influence of economic reforms thereon, by Falcetti et al. (2005). Some variables are not included due to unavailability of data. Introducing *trust* in the growth equation did not alter the presented conclusions for the constitutional variables.

69 We include *rights* as a potential determinant of economic reforms, and not economic growth, following Fidrmuc's (2003) finding that democracy is highly correlated with liberalization (an important component of economic reforms) but has an ambiguous effect on growth. We also observe that in our data simple partial correlation between *rights* and *econ_reform* is 0.69, whilst for *growth* it is only 0.03. We proceed similarly with the concentration of power variable (correlation with *econ_reform* -0.63, whereas with *growth* only -0.09). Based on the findings of recent literature (e.g. Feld and Voigt 2003; Voigt et al. 2015) we include *de facto CCI* in the growth equation.

70 Except for *econ_reform* we do not include any explanatory variables of constitutional choice, since the remaining factors are to a large extent immeasurable (but see more on this in Chapter 5). This could be the reason for the rather low R^2 for equations, where constitutional variables are *explananda*. We attempted to include the *trust* variable to reflect the influence of civil society on the constitutional design process, however it did not prove significant. For methodological reasons we include lagged constitutional variables in the reform equation. We do not expect a direct connection between progress in economic reforms and constitutional court independence.

Table 9: Results of system estimations, 1989–2012

Independent variables	**Coefficients**			
	I **3SLS,** **specification (3)** **without *trust***	**II** **3SLS,** **specification (3)** **with *trust***	**III** **3SLS,** **extended system** **without *trust***	**IV** **3SLS,** **extended system** **with *trust***
REFORMS (dependent variable: $econ\_reform_{it}$):				
$concentration_{it}$	0.02	−0.12*	−0.01	−0.10
$rights_{it}$	0.11***	0.10***	0.14***	0.12***
CCI_deiure_i	−0.03	−0.07	−0.01	−0.05
$CCI\_defacto_i$	0.30***	0.25***	0.28***	0.24***
$trtime_{it}$	0.13***	0.14***	0.12***	0.13***
$trtime^2_{it}$	-3.8×10^{-3}***	-3.7×10^{-3}***	-3.3×10^{-3}***	-3.5×10^{-3}***
$(IC\times trtime)_{it}$	-2.2×10^{-3}	2.1×10^{-3}	-1.8×10^{-3}	2×10^{-3}
$(IC\times trtime^2)_{it}$	1.6×10^{-4}	-7.5×10^{-5}	1.4×10^{-4}	-7.3×10^{-5}
$elections_i$	0.13***	0.13***	0.12***	0.13***
$trust_i$	–	0.98***	–	0.95***
$growth_{i,t-1}$	3×10^{-3}*	3.6×10^{-3}***	2.6×10^{-3}	3.4×10^{-3}***
constant	1.23***	1.06***	1.30***	1.04***
R^2	0.850	0.870	0.842	0.866
χ^2-stat.	2198.09	2225.83	2333.54	2289.02
GROWTH (dependent variable: $growth_{it}$):				
$trtime_{it}$	2.31***	2.35***	2.22***	2.20***
$trtime^2_{it}$	−0.09***	−0.09***	−0.08***	−0.09***
$(IC\times trtime)_{it}$	−0.06	−0.08	−0.05	−0.07
$(IC\times trtime^2)_{it}$	2.2×10^{-3}	4.2×10^{-3}	1.4×10^{-3}	3.7×10^{-3}
$econ\_reform_{i,t-1}$	1.52	1.05	1.62*	1.31
$fiscal_{it}$	0.35***	0.35***	0.35***	0.35***
$recovery_{i,t-2}$	0.76	0.33	0.91	0.36
$CCI\_defacto_i$	4.12***	5.62***	3.99***	5.26***
constant	−15.41***	−14.75***	−15.11***	−14.41***

Independent variables	Coefficients			
	I 3SLS, specification (3) without *trust*	II 3SLS, specification (3) with *trust*	III 3SLS, extended system without *trust*	IV 3SLS, extended system with *trust*
R^2	0.354	0.352	0.353	0.351
χ^2-stat.	211.91	180.63	201.94	167.50
CONCENTRATION (dependent variable: $concentration_{it}$):				
$econ\_reform_{i,t-1}$	–	–	−0.16***	−0.11***
constant	–	–	1.13***	0.94***
R^2	–	–	0.202	0.123
χ^2-stat.	–	–	119.39	51.58
RIGHTS (dependent variable: $rights_{it}$):				
$econ\_reform_{i,t-1}$	–	–	2.05***	1.51***
constant	–	–	−2.60***	−0.56
R^2	–	–	0.399	0.316
χ^2-stat.	–	–	315.35	178.43
Number of observations	388	334	388	334
Number of countries	23	20	23	20

Note: * Significant at a 10% level, *** Significant at a 5% level.

Source: Author's calculations.

coefficient throughout the various system estimations. Thirdly, while *de facto* constitutional court independence also remains significant throughout the system estimations, *de iure CCI* is not even marginally significant in any of them. These findings suggest that in general the scope of the functioning bill of rights was a more important element of the constitutional framework for post-socialist economic reforms than the factual structure of power within the state, with an exception of *de facto* constitutional court independence (which can be viewed as the final stage of the commitment mechanism in relation to economic reforms but also as a crucial mechanism for constitutional rights enforcement). While, due to highly limited availability of data, studies conducted to-date could not confirm the relevance of *de facto CCI* for economic reforms in post-socialist countries, in this study such result is among the most robust and convincing.

Given the finding in Metelska-Szaniawska (2009) that (de)concentration of state power is more influential at the outset of transition, while bills of rights are particularly important for sustaining reforms in the long run (their influence becomes stronger, the longer the duration of transition), the general result obtained in this section is not surprising. It additionally motivates a more detailed study of the relation between constitutional variables and economic reforms for different groups of countries included in the sample[71].

In order to shed more light on the country-specific aspects of the analyzed question, we conduct estimations including interactions of constitutional variables and dummy variables representing particular groups of countries[72]. Various country groups have been analyzed. Table 10 presents the most interesting findings. It reports the coefficients on the constitutional variables (i.e. *concentration* and *rights* variables; we did not find a convincing motivation for the study of country-specific effects with regard to constitutional court independence), the remaining variables in these regressions behave as in earlier specifications[73].

The first three rows of Table 10, pertaining to the country group-specific influence of *concentration*, reveal the following noteworthy observation. Countries which became Member States of the European Union during the studied time period (denoted *EU* in the table) experienced a less negative influence of the concentration of state power on economic reforms than other countries included in the sample (based on the positive coefficient obtained for the relevant interaction variable in all estimation included in the table). As a matter of fact, the size of this coefficient reveals an altogether positive effect of *concentration* on economic reforms in these countries. As argued in Metelska-Szaniawska (2009), such result could be explained by the fact that preparations for EU membership constituted an alternative constraining mechanism against the potential abuse of concentrated state power in these countries (see also e.g. Ahrens 2007), demonstrating

71 In the reform equation the control variables behave as in the single-equation framework, while in the growth equation they all have the expected signs, with initial conditions marginally (in)significant and recovery insignificant. *De facto* constitutional court independence is a significant determinant of economic growth.

72 Following the explication in Brambor et al. (2006), next to the interaction term we include in each specification the relevant constitutive terms, i.e. constitutional variables and country-group dummies under examination.

73 Since data on *trust* are not available for Central Asian countries, this control variable is not included in estimations aiming at identifying country-specific effects for this group of countries.

Table 10: Estimation results for country groups, 1989–2012
Dependent variable: $econ\_reform_{it}$

	OLS	RE	3SLS (basic)	3SLS (extended)
$(concentration \times EU)_{it}$	1.09*** [-0.62***]	0.99*** [-0.65***]	0.42* [-0.15***]	0.42* [-0.12]
$(concentration \times FSU)_{it}$	0.72*** [-1.02***]	0.65*** [-0.97***]	0.12 [-0.18***]	0.15 [-0.15*]
$(concentration \times CA)_{it}$	0.50 [-0.45***]	0.74*** [-0.58***]	-0.14 [-0.01]	-0.18 [-0.03]
$(rights \times EU)_{it}$	-0.10*** [0.13***]	-0.11*** [0.14***]	-0.03 [0.11***]	-0.03 [0.13***]
$(rights \times FSU)_{it}$	0.02 [0.10***]	0.09*** [0.07***]	-0.03 [0.12***]	-0.02 [0.13***]
$(rights \times CA)_{it}$	0.10*** [0.12***]	0.01 [0.12***]	0.18*** [0.11***]	0.18*** [0.13***]
Number of observations	439 / 502†	439 / 502†	334 / 388†	334 / 388†
Number of countries	20 / 23†	20 / 23†	20 / 23†	20 / 23†

Notes: Values of the coefficient on the relevant constitutional variable in brackets.
* Significant at a 10% level, *** Significant at a 5% level.
† For estimations involving *CA* (see footnote 73).

Source: Author's calculations.

the relevance of positive constitutionalists' arguments for this group of countries[74]. Commitment could have been enhanced in this setting via three channels. Firstly, the specific roadmap of actions and requirements for accession forced the establishing of a mechanism in these countries, whereby representatives of the state power provided signals to economic actors indicating their credibility (concerning the subsequent targets that had to be met in terms of reforms, as well as the consequences of failing to achieve them). Secondly, the existence of such mechanism led to limiting the discretion in politics. Thirdly, it also led to a change in the incentive structures in the public sector, including a significant dilution in the effectiveness of special interest group pressure on policy makers' decisions. Additionally, as Ahrens (2007) argues, the close and relatively clear perspective of accession to the EU could have constituted an external 'anchor' mechanism for reforms in the economic,

74 Many of these countries also score relatively lowest on the concentration index within the sample.

political, and administrative spheres. To sum up, the results obtained for this group of countries clearly indicate the relevance of the 'strong but constrained state' argument, as presented in particular by Ahrens (2007) and discussed in section 1.4.

We cannot speak of any other convincing country-group effect based on the results reported in the first three rows of Table 10 pertaining to concentration of state power. According to the results of the random effects estimation, there seem to be more effects identified for former Soviet republics (excluding the Baltics, which are EU member states since 2004), as well as, and in particular, for Central Asian republics, however on the basis of the discussions presented so far in this chapter we treat the system estimation results (two last columns of Table 10) as more reliable than RE (and OLS) and, therefore, refrain from such conclusions. The fact that we do not find a positive effect of *concentration* on economic reform performance in Central Asian former Soviet republics (Kyrgyzstan, Tajikistan and Uzbekistan – denoted *CA* in the table) is a particularly interesting result, as it seems to repudiate the earlier finding of such significant effect in Metelska-Szaniawska (2009). The latter study claimed that the fact that positive constitutionalists' argumentation was found more relevant for explaining the effect of concentration of power on economic reforms in the former Soviet republics located in Central Asia could be explained by reference to studies from the field of political science (e.g. Antoszewski and Herbut 1998), which observed strongly concentrated state power arising in countries, where the democratization process was obstructed and delayed by the lack of democratic tradition. From the group of post-socialist countries in Europe and Asia this was most strongly the case for Central Asia. Due to the lack of democratic traditions, these countries could embark on any economic reforms only with the state power relatively strongly concentrated. Otherwise further destabilization of government would follow, likely to constitute a serious obstacle to implementing broadly-construed economic reforms. Based on the results presented in Table 10 we can now say that such effect is sustainable only for a limited time and does not find its confirmation when one studies the (nearly) 25-year period from the outset of transition.

The country-group-specific results discussed above are valuable verifications of preliminary results obtained in Metelska-Szaniawska (2008, 2009). Another confirmed result of that study concerns the relatively stronger role of constitutional rights and freedoms in Central Asia than in the remaining post-socialist countries (sixth row of Table 10). The reform-'friendly' constitutional setting in these countries would require not highly concentrated political power, which is relevant only for a limited period of transition, but broad and effectively enforced constitutional rights and freedoms. With regard to other former Soviet republics (excluding Central Asia and the Baltics), denoted *FSU*, Table 10 yields no particular insights about the role of *concentration* nor *rights*, suggesting the potential significance of other non-constitutional factors in these countries, which remain beyond the focus of this study. A negative coefficient is obtained for the *rights* variable for post-socialist countries that have applied for EU membership, however it was not confirmed by the results of the more reliable system estimations.

3.5 Conclusions

In this chapter we studied the effects of constitutional change on economic policy in the area of post-socialist economic reforms, involving privatization, liberalization, enterprise restructuring, competition policy and so forth. We found a confirmation of the link, based primarily on the role of the constitution in building credible commitment of political actors vis-à-vis economic actors and the entire society. Noteworthy exceptions (in particular, with regard to concentration of state power) were countries committed to European integration, which experienced a strong 'external' commitment-enhancing mechanism[75]. The crucial element of the credibility-enhancing constitutional framework that emerged from the results obtained in this chapter for all of the studied countries[76] was *de facto* independence of their constitutional courts.

While many findings of earlier studies by Metelska-Szaniawska (2008, 2009) were confirmed in this broader and more reliable study framework, we also identified a number of new regularities. The particularly important new result was that given more reliable data and a longer time period from the outset of transition under analysis, *de facto* constitutional court independence proved to be particularly significant from the point of view of successful economic reforms in post-socialist countries, while at the same time *de iure* independence turned out irrelevant. In addition to this the results put in question the significance of the factual structure of power in the state for performance in terms of reforms, while

75 We use the word 'external' in quotes as, to be precise, these states are committed internally to fulfilling the requirements for EU accession, which, in itself, acts in this process as an external 'anchor'. This does not mean that we are speaking of a truly external commitment mechanism. For more on internal and external constitutional commitments see Ferejohn and Sager (2003).

76 Except Turkmenistan – see Section 2.3.

at the same time demonstrating even more firmly the country-group specificity in this respect.

Whenever econometric analyses are based on descriptive, qualitative, and not formalized models, several critical remarks can be raised. They may relate to weaknesses and drawbacks connected with the employed quantitative measures, as well as the applied estimation techniques (see Metelska-Szaniawska 2009 for a more detailed discussion). Given what has been said in Section 1.3 on the main caveat of many studies of economic effects of constitutions to date, we are well aware that our study may also suffer from the endogeneity problem, which could not be completely accounted for using the techniques employed so far in this book. The next chapter provides a response to this challenge.

Chapter 4. The synthetic control approach to estimating economic effects of post-socialist constitutions

In response to the problems of endogeneity and causality in comparative studies with relatively small sample sizes, a new statistical approach has recently been developed, called the synthetic control method. In this chapter we apply this method to reassess the effect of constitution-making in post-socialist countries of Europe and Asia on performance of these countries in the field of economic reforms during the post-1989 transition. We verify the existence of such effects and evaluate their statistical significance. Then we search for the explanation of these effects and their magnitude focusing on the characteristics of these constitutions and the solutions that they envisage (structural provisions, bills of rights and enforcement mechanisms). Thanks to employing this approach we are able to avoid several technical caveats that have arisen in earlier studies and verify the validity of their conclusions. In addition, we obtain country-specific results for each individual post-socialist state, as well as formulate detailed insights regarding the actual mechanisms or channels of influence of the constitutional framework on economic reforms. We start by introducing the synthetic control method, its advantages and shortcomings, as well as the design of the study applying this method to re-assess the effects of adopting post-socialist constitutions on economic reforms in transition countries.

4.1 The synthetic control method

In this section we introduce the synthetic control method[77] as a statistical approach allowing to study causal inference in comparative case studies. Comparative cases studies are based on the idea that the effect of an intervention on variables of interest can be inferred from the comparison of the evolution of those

77 In their seminal paper for the development of this approach Abadie et al. (2010) use the plural form i.e. synthetic control methods and discuss the subsequent steps of synthetic control data analysis (constructing the synthetic control group, estimating the synthetic counterfactual, placebo tests etc.). Following the practice of subsequent literature applying this approach, we use the singular form name of this approach (i.e. synthetic control method) understanding it as a series of techniques developed under this heading for comparative case studies.

variables between the unit exposed to the event or intervention and a group of units that are similar to the exposed unit but that were not affected by the event or intervention (Abadie 2015). More specifically, the synthetic control method focuses on the construction of a 'synthetic control group' (also called an "*artificial control group*" – Imbens and Wooldridge 2009, p. 72) by means of searching for a weighted combination of units, which were not exposed to the event or intervention (control countries), selected so as to match, as closely as possible, the country affected by the intervention, before the intervention or event occurs, for a set of predictors of the outcome variable (Campos et al. 2014)[78]. The evolution of the outcome variable for the synthetic control group constructed in this way is the estimate of the counterfactual. The latter shows what the behavior of the outcome variable would have been for the affected country 'had the intervention not happened' in the same way as in the control group. Below we present the formal details of the synthetic control method as applied to comparative case studies, drawing, in particular, on the seminal papers of Abadie et al. (2010, 2015).

Assume a sample of $J + 1$ units (e.g. countries or regions) indexed by j. Among them let unit $j = 1$ be the case of interest ('treated unit', i.e. unit exposed to the event or intervention of interest)[79] and units $j = 2, \ldots, J + 1$ – the potential comparisons (the so-called 'donor pool'). Comparison units are meant to approximate the counterfactual of the case of interest without the intervention, therefore the donor pool should be restricted to units with outcomes that are thought to be driven by the same structural process as for the unit representing the case of interest and that were not subject to structural shocks to the outcome variable during the sample period of the study (Abadie et al. 2015).

Assume further that the sample is a balanced panel, where all units are observed in the same time periods, $t = 1,\ldots, T$. The complete time period can be divided into a positive number of pre-intervention periods, T_0, as well as a positive number of post-intervention periods, T_1, i.e. $T = T_0 + T_1$. Following from this, unit 1 is exposed to the 'treatment' during the periods $T_0 + 1,\ldots, T$, and the intervention has no effect during the pre-treatment period $1,\ldots, T_0$.

78 Such approach brings this method close to (microeconomic) evaluation methods, see more in Imbens and Wooldridge (2009).

79 Without loss of generality we could have multiple units affected by the event or intervention [then the method could be applied to each affected unit separately or to an aggregate of all affected units – Abadie et al. (2015)] but for the sake of clarity and because we further apply the method with a single affected unit, we present this version here.

In order to measure the effect of the 'treatment' on a post-intervention outcome and bearing in mind that pre-intervention characteristics of the treated unit can often be much more accurately approximated by a combination of untreated units than by any single untreated unit, define a synthetic control as a weighted average of the units in the donor pool. Formally, a synthetic control can be represented by a $(J \times 1)$ vector of weights $W = (w_2,\ldots,w_{J+1})$, where $0 \leq w_j \leq 1$ for $j = 2,\ldots, J$ and $w_2 + \ldots + w_{J+1} = 1$. Choosing a particular value for W is equivalent to choosing a synthetic control.

Following John Stuart Mill's method of difference[80], Abadie et al. (2010, 2015) propose selecting the value of W such that the characteristics of the treated unit are best resembled by the characteristics of the synthetic control. In formal terms this comes down to the following. Let X_1 be a $(k \times 1)$ vector containing values of the treated unit's pre-intervention characteristics that we aim to match as well as possible, and let X_0 be the $k \times J$ matrix collecting the values of the same variables for the units in the donor pool. The pre-intervention characteristics in X_1 and X_0 may also include pre-intervention values of the outcome variable. The difference between the pre-intervention characteristics of the treated unit and a synthetic control is given by the vector $X_1 - X_0W$. Now select the synthetic control, W^*, that minimizes the size of this difference. This can be operationalized in the following way. For $m = 1,\ldots, k$, let X_1m be the value of the m-th variable for the treated unit and let X_0m be a $(1 \times J)$ vector containing the values of the m-th variable for the units in the donor pool. Abadie and Gardeazabal (2003), as well as Abadie et al. (2010, 2015) choose W^* minimizing:

$$\sum_{m=1}^{k} v_m \left(X_{1m} - X_{0m}W\right)^2, \qquad (3)$$

80 The so-called 'Mill's methods' are five rules for investigating causes proposed in *A System of Logic* (Mill 1843) – method of agreement, method of difference, joint method of agreement and difference, method of residues, and method of concomitant variation. In his statement of the method of difference Mill writes: "*If an instance in which the phenomenon under investigation occurs, and an instance in which it does not occur, have every circumstance save one in common, that one occurring only in the former; the circumstance in which alone the two instances differ, is the effect, or cause, or a necessary part of the cause, of the phenomenon*" (Mill 1843, p. 455). In other words, according to the method of difference, if you have one situation that leads to an effect and another one which does not and the only difference between them is the presence of a single factor in the first situation, we can infer that this factor is the cause of the observed effect.

where v_m is a weight that reflects the relative importance assigned to the m-th variable, when measuring discrepancy between X_1 and X_0W[81]. It is crucial that the synthetic controls closely reproduce the values that variables with large predictive power on the outcome of interest take for the unit affected by the intervention (Abadie et al. 2015). Accordingly, those variables should be assigned large v_m weights. In the empirical application below, we apply a cross-validation method to choose v_m[82].

Having defined the synthetic control let us move to the post-intervention outcomes. Following further Abadie et al. (2010, 2015), let Y_{jt} be the outcome of unit j at time t. Additionally, let Y_1 be a $(T_1 \times 1)$ vector with the post-intervention values of the outcome for the treated unit [i.e. $Y_1 = (Y_{1\,T_0+1}, \ldots, Y_{1\,T})$] and let Y_0 be a $(T_1 \times J)$ matrix, where column j contains the post-intervention values of the outcome for unit $j + 1$. The synthetic control estimator of the effect of the treatment is then given by the comparison of post-intervention outcomes between the treated unit, which is exposed to the intervention, and the synthetic control, which is not exposed to the intervention, i.e. $Y_1 - Y_0W^*$. That is, for a post-intervention period t (where $t \geq T_0$), the synthetic control estimator of the effect of the treatment is given by the comparison between the outcome for the treated unit and the outcome for the synthetic control at that period:

$$Y_{1t} - \sum_{j=2}^{J+1} W_j^* Y_{jt} \,. \tag{4}$$

The matching variables in X_0 and X_1 are meant to be predictors of post-intervention outcomes and are themselves not affected by the intervention.

To generalize (allowing any unit $i = 1, \ldots, J + 1$ to be exposed to treatment), following the explication in Billmeier and Nannicini (2013), the treatment effect for country i at time T_0 can be defined as:

$$\tau_{it} = Y_{it}(1) - Y_{it}(0) = Y_{it} - Y_{it}(0), \tag{5}$$

where $Y_{it}(1)$ and $Y_{it}(0)$ stand for the potential outcome with and without treatment, respectively. Then the estimand of interest is the vector $(\tau_{i\,T_0+1}, \ldots, \tau_{i\,T})$.

81 For a more formalized statement see Abadie et al. (2015, footnote 5).

82 In particular, in the estimations that we present further we select the fully nested optimization procedure that searches among all positive definite and diagonal V-matrices such that the mean squared prediction error (RMSPE) of the outcome variable is minimized for the pre-intervention periods.

Abadie et al. (2010) show how to identify the above treatment effects under the following general model for the potential outcomes of all units:

$$Y_{jt}(0) = \delta_t + \nu_{jt}, \quad (6)$$
$$Y_{jt}(1) = \tau_{jt} + \delta_t + \nu_{jt}, \quad (7)$$

with $j = 1, \ldots, J + 1$. Given the treatment assignment mechanism described above, τ_{jt} is different from 0 only when $j = i$ and $t > T_0$. Besides the (dynamic) treatment effects τ_{jt}, potential outcomes depend on a common factor δ_t and an error ν_{jt}. Assume that ν_{jt} can be expressed by the following factor model,

$$\nu_{jt} = Z_j\theta_t + \lambda_t\mu_j + \varepsilon_{jt}, \quad (8)$$

where Z_j is a vector of relevant observed covariates that are not affected by the intervention and can be either time-invariant or time-varying, θ_t is a vector of time-specific parameters, μ_j is a country-specific unobservable, λ_t is an unknown common factor, and ε_{jt} are zero-mean transitory shocks. The j subscript to the Z vector does not impose any restriction on the covariates included in the model, which may vary with time or not and may be pre- or post-treatment, as long as they do not depend on the intervention.

4.1.1 Advantages of synthetic control

The synthetic control method, being in a way an extension of the difference-in-difference regression framework, allowing at the same time to make causal inferences in comparative case studies, provides a bridge between quantitative and qualitative studies in comparative politics (Abadie et al. 2015), economics, and in particular at the junction of the two, i.e. in the field of political economy. In doing so the synthetic control method addresses several methodological shortcomings of traditional regression analysis and typical comparative case study research, revealing its various advantages, which we discuss in short in this section.

As Abadie et al. (2010) explain, comparative case study research in the social sciences is obstructed by two problems that affect its empirical implementation. The first concerns ambiguity about how comparison units are chosen, namely researchers often select comparison groups on the basis of subjective measures of affinity between affected and unaffected units. The second problem also relates to the choice of the control group and, in particular, to the uncertainty about the ability of the control group to reproduce the counterfactual outcome trajectory that the affected units would have experienced in the absence of treatment. This type of uncertainty is not reflected by the standard errors constructed using traditional inferential techniques for comparative case studies. The synthetic control method involves a formalization of the selection of the comparison units with the use of a data-driven procedure. Such a procedure reduces discretion in the choice of the comparison control units, requiring that researchers demonstrate the affinities between the affected and unaffected units using observed quantifiable characteristics. As in practice it is usually difficult to find a single unexposed unit that approximates the most relevant characteristics of the units exposed to the event or intervention, the synthetic control method envisages searching for a combination of units providing a more appropriate comparison for the treated unit than any single unit alone. As we will discuss in subsection 4.1.3, the formalization of the control group selection also allows to conduct precise quantitative inference, which is problematic, as mentioned above, in typical comparative case studies.

Comparing with traditional regression methods the synthetic control method has several advantages. The first of them is transparency. Since a synthetic control is constructed as a weighted average of the available control units, this method explicitly specifies the relative contribution of each control unit to the counterfactual of interest, as well as the similarities (or lack thereof) between the affected unit and the synthetic control, in terms of pre-intervention outcomes and other predictors of post-intervention outcomes (Abadie et al. 2010). Secondly, as the set of potential controls can be appropriately restricted to make the underlying unit comparisons more sensible, this method comes also with an advantage of flexibility (Billmeier and Nannicini 2013)[83]. Thirdly, because the weights can be restricted to be positive and sum to one, the synthetic control method provides a safeguard against extrapolation (Abadie et al. 2010). Fourthly, as indicated by Billmeier and Nannicini (2013), the synthetic control method is based on identification assumptions that are weaker than those required by estimators commonly applied in regression panel-data analysis. While panel models control only for confounding factors that are time invariant (fixed effects) or share a common trend (difference-in-difference models), the synthetic control estimation method allows the effect of unobservable confounding factors to vary in time[84]. Thanks to handling the (time-varying) omitted bias, the synthetic

83 At the same time, because the choice of a synthetic control does not require access to post-intervention outcomes, this method allows researchers to decide on their study design without knowing how those decisions will affect the conclusions of their analysis, what allows to promote research honesty in observational studies (Abadie et al. 2010).

84 Campos et al. (2014) indicate that the synthetic control method is in this sense close to the policy-experiment approach as discussed e.g. by Henry (2007).

control method addresses endogeneity and, partially, the omitted variable bias[85]. The latter features make this method particularly attractive and relevant for researchers studying various economic effects of legal and policy interventions[86].

4.1.2 Requirements and potential drawbacks

Several requirements must be fulfilled so as to correctly apply the synthetic control method and obtain results possessing the properties discussed above. They concern the construction of the donor pool, the time period under analysis, the volatility of the outcome variable, and potential problems that may arise due to particular characteristics of the affected unit[87].

Firstly, since constructing the donor pool of comparison units constitutes the crucial step in the implementation of the synthetic control method, it must be given particular care. To this end three aspects are of particular significance (Abadie et al. 2015, Abadie 2015): (1) no interference between units, (2) no idiosyncratic shocks to control units, (3) similar characteristics of control units and the treated unit. By (1) we mean that outcomes of the untreated units must not be affected by the intervention or event, to which the treated unit is exposed. This requires that units affected by the event or intervention of interest, or by interventions/events of a similar nature, should be excluded from the donor pool. This also concerns units, which are indirectly affected by the intervention or event due to spillover effects. Regarding (2), units that may have suffered large idiosyncratic shocks to the outcome of interest during the studied period should also be excluded from the donor pool, if such shocks would have not affected the treated unit in the absence of the treatment. Additionally, (3) requires restricting the donor pool to units with similar characteristics to the treated unit. While the restrictions placed on the weights used for constructing the counterfactual do not allow extrapolation, interpolation biases may arise if the synthetic control matches the characteristics of the affected unit by averaging away large discrepancies between the characteristics of the affected unit and the characteristics of

85 The problem of potentially omitting variables at the time of selecting the pre-treatment characteristics to be used for constructing the counterfactual however remains.

86 One should, however, bear in mind that such studies could nevertheless suffer from reverse causation if the timing of the intervention was decided by expectations regarding future outcomes (see e.g. Billmeier and Nannicini 2013).

87 Most of the requirements listed herein pertain not only to synthetic control methods but also to any other type of comparative case study research design (Abadie 2015).

the units in the synthetic control (Abadie 2015)[88]. Another reason for restricting the size of the donor pool and including only units, which are similar to the treated unit, is to avoid overfitting. The latter arises when the characteristics of the unit affected by the intervention or event are artificially matched by combining idiosyncratic variations in a large sample of unaffected units (Abadie et al. 2015)[89].

Secondly, the synthetic control method also involves requirements concerning the time period under analysis. Since the credibility of a synthetic control depends upon how well it tracks the treated unit's characteristics and outcomes over an extended period of time prior to the treatment, the applicability of this method requires a 'sizable number' of pre-intervention periods (Abadie et al. 2015). At the same time a 'sizable number' of post-intervention periods may be required in studies where the effect of the event or intervention emerges gradually or changes over time. In addition to those two requirements, the synthetic control method is based on the assumption that the intervention has no effect on the outcome before the implementation period. In practice, anticipation effects (impacts of a given intervention prior to its implementation) are not uncommon. Synthetic control estimators may then be biased, if forward looking agents react in advance of the intervention of interest or if certain components of the intervention were put in place in advance of its formal implementation or enactment[90]. Campos et al. (2014) summarize that the choice of the pre-treatment characteristics must include variables that can approximate the path of the

88 As noticed in Abadie et al. (2010), the discrepancies between the characteristics on the unit affected by the intervention and the individual units that compose the synthetic control could, however, be controlled by adding to the objective function in equation (1) presented earlier a set of penalty terms that depend on these discrepancies.

89 Abadie (2015) notices that there is a potential tension between requirements (2) and (3) relating to the construction of the donor pool. On the one hand, one should select for the donor pool units that are affected by the same shocks (if any) as the treated units. However, if spillover effects are substantial and affect units (e.g. countries) in close geographical proximity of the treated unit, those units may provide a biased estimate of the counterfactual outcome for the treated unit. In such cases, whenever units affected by spillover effects are included in the synthetic control, the researcher should be aware of the potential direction of the bias of the resulting estimator (see further Abadie 2015).

90 In such cases, the intervention period (T_0) could usually be redefined (backdated) to be the period before any anticipation effect can be expected, so that the effect of the intervention can be estimated in full extent.

treated unit[91], while at the same time avoiding variables that anticipate the effects of the intervention.

Thirdly, in cases where substantial volatility is present in the outcome of interest effects of events or interventions, which are relatively small when compared with the magnitude of the above volatility, will be indistinguishable. Such situations usually do not preclude the application of the synthetic control method, this volatility in outcome should, however, be removed (by means of time-series filtering techniques) in both the exposed unit, as well as in the units in the donor pool, prior to applying the synthetic control techniques.

Lastly, since synthetic control estimates are based on the idea that a combination of unaffected units can approximate the pre-intervention characteristics of the treated unit, differences in the characteristics of the affected unit and the synthetic control must be small[92]. If the unit affected by the intervention of interest is 'extreme' in the value of a particular variable, such value may not be closely approximated by a synthetic control. A potential solution in such cases may be to transform the outcome level variable to its time differences or growth rates (Abadie 2015).

In addition to the requirements discussed in this section one should also bear in mind a potential methodological shortcoming of the synthetic control method. As Abadie et al. (2015) admit themselves, critics of Mill's method of difference rightfully point out that the applicability of the method may be limited by the presence of unmeasured factors affecting the outcome variable as well as by heterogeneity in the effects of observed and unobserved factors. However, Abadie et al. (2010) argue that if the number of pre-intervention periods is large, then matching on pre-intervention outcomes helps control for these problems. As Abadie et al. (2015) explain, the intuition of this result is straightforward: "*Only units that are alike in both observed and unobserved determinants of the outcome variable as well as in the effect of those determinants on the outcome variable should produce similar trajectories of the outcome variable over extended periods of time. Once it has been established that the unit representing the case of interest and the synthetic control unit have similar behavior over extended periods of time prior to the intervention, a discrepancy in the outcome variable following the intervention is interpreted as produced by the intervention itself*" (Abadie et al. 2015, p. 4).

91 Abadie et al. (2015) also emphasize that it is not recommended to use the synthetic control method when the pre-treatment fit is poor.

92 This requirement is also called the "*convex hull condition*" – for mathematical details see Abadie (2015).

Finally, some authors indicate the shortcoming of the synthetic control method consisting in the inability to assess the significance of the results using standard (large-sample) inferential techniques, due to a relatively small number of observations in the donor pool and periods covered by the sample (Billmeier and Nannicini 2013). As will be discussed below, a solution has recently been proposed to address this drawback by Campos et al. (2014), who use the difference-in-differences estimator for the actual vis-à-vis the synthetic series to produce statements about the statistical significance of the effect of their event of interest on the studies outcome *on average*, before and after treatment. Placebo tests based on permutation techniques can also be implemented to make inferences.

4.1.3 Making inferences with the synthetic control method

The use of statistical inference in comparative case studies raises problems because of the small-sample nature of the data, the absence of randomization, and the fact that probabilistic sampling is not employed to select sample units (Abadie et al. 2015). However, thanks to systematizing the process of estimating the counterfactuals, the synthetic control method allows to conduct falsification exercises, which Abadie et al. (2010) and the literature that draws on their work call 'placebo studies'. Those tests are based on the premise that our confidence that a particular synthetic control estimate reflects the impact of the intervention under scrutiny would be severely undermined if we obtained estimated effects of similar or even greater magnitudes in cases where the intervention did not take place (Abadie et al. 2015).

Two types of such placebo tests can be carried out. The first one, called 'in-time placebos', consists in reassigning the intervention in time and requires data available for a sufficiently large number of time periods when no structural shocks to the outcome variable occurred. The assumption behind these tests is that our confidence about the validity of a result estimating a sizable effect for a certain intervention of interest would dissipate if the synthetic control method also estimated large effects when applied to dates when the intervention did not occur (Heckman and Hotz 1989). The second type of placebo tests involves reassigning the intervention to other units – members of the donor pool. Such tests are referred to as 'in-space placebos' (Abadie et al. 2015). Here the premise is that our confidence that a sizable synthetic control estimate reflects the effect of the intervention would disappear if similar or larger estimates arose when the intervention was artificially reassigned to units not directly exposed to it. Such tests are usually implemented so that placebo effects are estimated for every potential control unit in the donor pool leading to the creation of a distribution of placebo effects, against which the effect estimated for the unit that represents the case of interest can be evaluated. As the latter authors emphasize, our confidence that a large synthetic control estimate reflects the effect of the intervention would be undermined if the magnitude of the estimated effect fell well inside the distribution of placebo effects.

The concept of the presented placebo test is similar to the framework for permutation inference, where the distribution of a test statistic is computed under random permutations of the sample units' assignments to the intervention and nonintervention groups (Abadie et al. 2010). Having applied the synthetic control method to every potential control in the sample this test then aims to assess whether the effect estimated by the synthetic control for the unit affected by the intervention is large relative to the effect estimated for a unit chosen randomly. This 'inferential exercise' is exact in the sense that, regardless of the number of available comparison units, time periods, and whether the data are individual or aggregate, it is always possible to calculate the exact distribution of the estimated effect of the placebo interventions. Examining whether or not the estimated effect of the actual intervention is large relative to the distribution of the effects estimated for the units not exposed to the intervention provides informative inference if under the hypothesis of no intervention effect the estimated effect of the intervention is not expected to be abnormal relative to the distribution of the placebo effects (Abadie et al. 2010).

As in traditional statistical inference, a quantitative comparison between the distribution of placebo effects and the synthetic control estimate can be operationalized with the use of p-values (Abadie et al. 2015). Such a p-value can be constructed by estimating in-space placebo effects for each unit in the sample and then calculating the fraction of such effects greater than or equal to the effect estimated for the treated unit. This 'inferential exercise' reduces to classical randomization inference when the intervention is randomized (Rosenbaum 2005). In the absence of randomization, the p-value still has an interpretation as the probability of obtaining an estimate at least as large as the one obtained for the unit representing the case of interest when the intervention is reassigned at random in the data set (Abadie et al. 2015).

Campos et al. (2014) extend the scope of inference tests available for synthetic control studies by proposing the use of a difference-in-difference estimator for the actual vis-à-vis the synthetic series allowing to draw conclusions on the statistical significance of their differential (i.e. average pre- and post-treatment values). In our study performed in the subsequent sections we employ both the placebo ('in-space') tests proposed by Abadie et al. (2010, 2015), as well as the additional inference tests introduced by Campos et al. (2014). Before developing our own empirical analysis based on the synthetic control method, we devote the next subsection to a short survey of selected studies employing this method, which are aimed to give a meaningful background to the further analysis.

4.1.4 Selected applications of the synthetic control method

Comparative case studies in social sciences have been conducted for long, in particular in order to evaluate large-scale events or aggregate interventions affecting a small number of units (e.g. countries or regions). However, as discussed above, the synthetic control method has a much shorter history[93]. In this section we present, in short, a selection of studies where this method has been applied to study legal-economic and political-economic contexts.

An early study where analysis was based on comparisons between the actual and a synthetic unit in a political-economy context was Abadie and Gardeazabal (2003), who focus on the economic impact of political conflict using as a case the terrorist conflict in the Basque Country during the period 1955–1997. Their approach is based on comparing the economic evolution of the Basque Country during the terrorist era with that of a weighted combination of other Spanish regions selected so as to resemble the characteristics of the Basque Country before terrorist attacks. They conceptualize such a weighted average of other Spanish regions as a 'synthetic' Basque Country without terrorism. The actual Basque Country (with terrorism) is then compared to this 'synthetic' Basque Country. Such analysis reveals a 10-percent average gap which emerges over a period of two decades between Basque per capita GDP and the per capita GDP of a comparable synthetic region without terrorism. Placebo tests supplementing this analysis show that changes in the per capita GDP gap are indeed to be associated with the intensity of terrorist activity.

In their paper published several years later, considered seminal for the synthetic control method, Abadie et al. (2010) develop this approach further and apply it to study the effect of the introduction of a large-scale tobacco control program on cigarette consumption in the American state of California (the so-called Proposition 99, implemented in California in 1991). They demonstrate

93 The Repec IDEAS repositorium lists 113 unique works citing Abadie et al. (2010) (and its earlier working-paper versions) published (at least in form of working papers) during the period 2009–2015 (as of April 4, 2015). In most cases these are studies applying the synthetic control method for comparative case studies to various contexts from within the broad field of Economics.

that following this legal intervention tobacco consumption fell markedly in this state relative to a comparable synthetic control region. In particular, they estimate that by the year 2000 annual per capita cigarette sales in California were about 26 cigarette packs lower than what they would have been in the absence of Proposition 99. In addition to this analysis they also propose new inferential methods to verify the significance of their estimates, i.e. placebo tests discussed in an earlier section of this chapter.

In their subsequent study Abadie et al. (2015) use the synthetic control method to estimate the economic impact of the 1990 German reunification on West Germany. This example also illustrates the potential gains from using synthetic controls in comparative case studies, as compared with other empirical approaches. They begin by demonstrating that no single country is able to closely approximate the values of economic growth predictors for West Germany before the reunification. However, a weighted average of several OECD countries, i.e. Austria, United States, Japan, Switzerland, and the Netherlands, provides a very close approximation of West Germany before 1990. The results of their analysis yield a conclusion that the German reunification did not have much of an effect on West German per capita GDP in the first two years immediately following that event, however from 1992 onward they identify such negative effect on West German income, with GDP per capita being reduced by about 1,600 U.S. dollars per year on average over the 1990–2003 period (approximately 8% of the 1990 baseline level). To evaluate the credibility of these results, Abadie et al. (2015) conduct placebo studies where the treatment of interest is reassigned in the data to a year other than 1990 or to countries different from West Germany. The findings are robust across a series of such placebo studies, as well as to an additional sensitivity check consisting in iterative reestimation of the baseline model to construct a synthetic West Germany omitting in each iteration one of the countries that received a positive weight in the construction of the 'original' synthetic West Germany. In this way they sacrifice some goodness of fit, but are able to check whether their results are driven by any particular control country.

Since 2010 the synthetic control method has been applied in studies of economic consequences of other large-scale events such as natural catastrophes (e.g. Cavallo et al. 2010, Barone and Mocetti 2014) or political conflicts (e.g. Bove et al. 2014 and Costalli et al. 2014 – on civil wars; Bove and Nisticò 2014 – on coups d'état; Acemoglu et al. 2014a – on Egypt's Arab Spring), as well as in studies focusing on effects of different legal and policy interventions (e.g. Bohn et al. 2011, Heim and Lurie 2014, Baum and Ruhn 2013, Doerrenberg and Peichl 2014). Other interesting topics covered by studies using the synthetic control method include effects of granting awards to prominent economists (e.g. Chan et al. 2014), organized crime (Pinotti 2014), and effects of a social media-inspired boycott on firm performance (Richter and Werner 2013).

In this book we are interested, in particular, in studies relating to political and economic reforms, as well as post-socialist transition countries. Below we present a handful of studies concerning related issues.

Billmeier and Nannicini (2013) use the synthetic control method to investigate the impact of economic liberalization, as measured by a widely used indicator that captures the scope of the market in the economy, on real GDP per capita in a worldwide sample of countries. Their study compares the postliberalization GDP trajectory of economies, which have undergone liberalization, with the trajectory of a combination of similar but 'untreated' economies. They find that liberalizing the economy had a positive effect on GDP in most regions, however more recent liberalizations – in the 1990s and in Africa, had no significant effect in this respect.

Campos and Kinoshika (2010) study the effect of various structural reforms on foreign direct investment (FDI) in Latin American and post-socialist transition countries for the period 1989–2004. Their focus is, in particular, on financial liberalization. Applying the synthetic control method they ask how much FDI inflows a given country would have received had it reformed its financial sector in the way as a selected group of other countries. They find, for example, that had Russia implemented financial reform in the same way as Estonia, Latvia, and Lithuania did (that is, had it implemented it like the best combination of these three countries did), then the level of FDI inflows it would have received would have been substantially larger than it actually was (1.6 percent of GDP as compared to 0.5 percent). A similar effect is identified for Argentina (2.2 percent of GDP for 'synthetic Argentina' constructed on the basis of experiences of Mexico, Chile, Brazil, and Venezuela, as compared to 1.2 percent of GDP in reality). The conclusions of this analysis supplement and extend their fixed-effects and GMM panel data analysis.

Pieters at al. (2014) study the effect of a political regime transition (i.e. in their case democratization) on food security and more specifically on child mortality. Using the synthetic control method they find results that contradict typical findings from difference-in-difference studies, namely that a political reform towards democracy does not systematically reduce child mortality. Of the 33 country case studies included in Pieters et al. (2014) they only find a significant and positive relation between food security and political reforms for 4 countries, while for the remaining 29 countries included in their analysis no impact is found.

In one of the most recent applications of the synthetic controls method, which is particularly relevant to the topic of this study, Campos et al. (2014) focus on the economic benefits stemming from economic and political integration within the European Union. Using this method they estimate how GDP per capita and labor productivity would have behaved in countries of the European Union, which joined the latter in subsequent enlargements up to the one in 2004, if those countries had not joined it. This study generally reveals positive effects of EU membership (per capita incomes on average 12 percent lower in absence of EU integration in these countries), with an exception of Greece where the impact is clearly negative. In addition to these conclusions Campos et al. (2014) also make a methodological contribution by addressing one of the main problems of the synthetic control method, i.e. concerning the estimation of confidence intervals for the counterfactual effects and verifying thereby their statistical significance. To this aim they employ the difference-in-difference approach. Finally, they extend the analysis by searching for significant determinants explaining (not in the causal sense, though) the difference between actual levels of GDP per capita (or labor productivity) in the studied countries and those estimated based on the synthetic counterfactuals, which they call the dividends or pay-offs from EU membership. They identify three factors which are closely associated with the magnitude of such average payoff: trade openness, financial integration and the adoption of the Euro. These factors may meaningfully explain the differences between the scope of benefits that countries throughout Europe exert from EU membership.

The studies presented in short above reveal the broad potential of application of the synthetic control method to analyze effects of legal interventions and political events on economic outcomes in cases where comparative case study methods are more suitable than large cross-sectional econometric studies. As mentioned in the previous sections, some of them also bring forward methodological contributions, supplementing and extending the synthetic controls method in a way allowing for more explanative power or addressing additional research questions and hypotheses. We employ some of these extensions in our study of the effect of constitutions on economic reforms in post-socialist countries.

4.2 Study design

In this section we apply the synthetic control method to study the effect of adopting new constitutions in post-socialist countries on their performance in the field of economic reforms, aiming to verify, as well as potentially strengthen and extend, the results of earlier panel-data regression-based studies of this topic. If we obtain similar results, this can be seen as a powerful robustness check.

Moreover, with this method we are able to study the potential significance of the constitutional framework for performance in the field of economic reforms for each post-socialist country separately, what could have earlier been done only in relation to groups of countries.

The outcome variable of interest is, as in Chapter 3, the aggregated transition indicator, also called the index of economic reforms (*econ_reform*), constituting an average of a set of indicators of structural economic reforms, published annually by the European Bank for Reconstruction and Development in subsequent issues of *Transition Report* (EBRD 1994–2013). Recall that the following categories of reforms are included in this indicator: privatization and enterprise restructuring (three indicators: large-scale privatization; small-scale privatization; governance and enterprise restructuring), as well as market liberalization and competition (three indicators: price liberalization; trade and foreign exchange system; competition policy)[94].

The first step of our endeavor consists of the following: In order to study the effect that adopting the constitution by a given post-socialist country (say, Country A) has on its economic reforms process, using the techniques described in Section 4.1, we construct a synthetic Country A that mirrors the values of the independent variables explaining the economic reforms performance in Country A before the adoption of the constitution. All of the remaining post-socialist countries (i.e. save Country A) serve as the donor pool allowing to construct a synthetic Country A. We then estimate the effect of adopting the constitution on Country A's performance in economic reforms as the difference in performance levels between the actual Country A and its synthetic version in the time period following the adoption of the constitution.

Our choice of pre-treatment characteristics is based upon the specification used in the regression studies of the economic effects of constitutions on post-socialist reforms presented in Chapter 3, which are in turn based on earlier studies of the determinants of successful economic reforms in transition (e.g. de Melo et al. 2001; Falcetti et al. 2002; Falcetti et al. 2005; Fish 1998). Recall that they include the initial conditions for undertaking reforms [as measured by the initial conditions index calculated from the first principal component of a factor analysis over 11 indicators, stemming from Falcetti et al. (2002)], the result of the first post-socialist elections [an indicator taken from Fish (1998)], as well as lagged reform variables to account for the fact that past performance significantly

94 Recall also that employing progress in economic reforms, not indicators of economic performance such as GDP growth, as the dependent variable in the study, allows us to focus on the influence of constitutional variables directly on the decision-making by governments in the field of (economic) policy, as suggested by the theory.

influences actual performance in post-socialist economic reforms[95,96]. This model also operates in transition time beginning in 1989 for Poland and Hungary, 1990 – for other Central and Southeastern European countries (except Albania), 1991 – for Albania and the Baltic republics, and 1992 – for remaining former Soviet republics. Such approach allows to account for the fact that transition started at different times in different countries[97].

Several comments and reservations regarding the study design presented above should be made at this point.

Firstly, since the donor pool must be restricted to units with similar characteristics to the unit exposed to the intervention, for each country under examination we construct the donor pool as consisting of all remaining post-socialist countries within the sample. There exists a rather undisputed consensus among transition scholars that the broad-scale institutional change that took place in post-socialist countries of Europe and Asia (involving several dimensions – political, economic, legal, social, etc.) was unprecedented and unique in world history. Therefore, it would not be possible to study the potential significance of constitutions for economic reforms undertaken during post-socialist transition for any other group of countries[98] (or it would render meaningless results).

---

95 Abadie et al. (2010) also use lagged dependent variables in their application of the synthetic control method.

96 Estimations have also been conducted including (lagged) economic growth as an additional independent variable. The inclusion of this variable has however led to a significant decrease in the sample size (down to 13 countries) due to two reasons. Firstly, some countries had to be excluded from the analysis as growth data for their early years of transition is of limited availability and/or reliability. Secondly, with the lag of the growth variable included in the analysis the first year of transition time has to be excluded, what led to an even further decrease in the number of countries encompassed by the analysis (countries, which adopted their constitutions in the first year of their economic transition, could no longer be included). The general conclusions from this analysis do not diverge from those obtained for estimation not including the growth variable, therefore we refrain from presenting them here, putting more emphasis on the results based on the significantly larger sample size.

97 By construction the synthetic control method applied to the model operating in transition time does not allow for the simple inclusion of the stand-alone transition time variable among the independent variables. We have also conducted estimations for the model operating in calendar time. The results are available from the author upon request.

98 A more technical wording of this argument would be that the transition indicators, measuring the performance of countries in the field of various economic reforms, used in the empirical study presented in this chapter, are only available for this group of countries (for the time period under analysis).

Secondly, however, one must bear in mind, that the above approach requires that outcomes of the untreated units (reforms in countries included in the donor pool) are not affected by the intervention (constitution) implemented in the treated unit (i.e. country under examination). In other words, we treat each constitution, understood as a complete and comprehensive constitutional rule-framework for a given country, as a distinct 'intervention'. This implies that a given constitution (potentially) influences the economic reforms process only in the state, where it is enacted (in other words, there are no spillover effects to other post-socialist countries in this respect[99]). Given such approach, in order to study a given country from the sample we are able to construct the donor pool consisting of the remaining post-socialist countries of Europe and Asia.

A third remark concerns the fact that our baseline study, as explained so far, concentrates on constitutions in their entirety, not on specific constitutional rules or their detailed provisions. If one analyzed the effects of specific constitutional rules or regulations, they could be the same or very similar for several countries, what would make applying the synthetic control method inadequate. In order to circumvent this problem, our approach consists of two parts – studying the effect of the constitution as a whole first, and the specific determinants of its magnitude, reflecting inter alia the content of these constitutions, as a second step.

Finally, regarding the time dimension of the study: In order to rule out the potential anticipation effects operating in the period before entrance into force of the given constitutions, we take the treatment period to be the year when a given constitution was adopted[100]. The post-treatment period is in most cases significantly longer than the pre-treatment one (encompassing usually more than 15 years), what makes it justifiable to study the potential gradual, spread over time effects of constitutions on economic reforms. The relatively shorter pre-treatment

99 We emphasize that this concerns spillovers from the constitution of, say, country A to economic reform performance in, say, country B, and not the potential spillover effects between constitutions of countries A and B. As concerns the latter, we would also not expect much effect since, as we have shown in Chapter 2, post-socialist countries in Europe and Asia cannot be said to have adopted the same model constitution or even a set of identical core constitutional solutions. Nevertheless, the validity of our empirical approach here does not even require such assumption to be made.

100 Including the year of adoption of the constitution in the (pre-)treatment period seems also a reasonable choice given the fact that performance in economic reform is not likely to change directly after adoption of the constitution but considerably later (lagged effects).

period is a shortcoming, which is inherent in the presented analysis, as its starting period is the beginning of post-socialist economic reforms.

In the second part of the study we perform a series of placebo tests aiming to find whether the estimated treatment effects for the subsequent post-socialist countries are unusually large comparing to the distribution of the estimates that we obtain when the same treatment is applied to the countries in the donor pool. We then further evaluate the gap in various ways, taking as a starting point the approach developed by Campos et al. (2014) to analyze the growth (in our case: reform) dividends. Finally, we embark on an attempt to explain the magnitude of the reform dividends. We look for explanations in the constitutions themselves (i.e. constitutional rules pertaining to structure of the state power, the constitutional rights and freedoms, constitutional enforcement mechanisms), as well as the environment within which the constitutions operate. We explain the technical details of subsequent steps taken along the discussion of the results in sections 4.3–4.4.

The study covers 20 countries[101] for the time period 1989–2012. Due to the balanced panel requirement, for countries where transition time lasted more than 21 years, the final years of transition are not included[102]. The data sources for the dependent and independent variables are presented in detail in Appendix 3. For the baseline estimations and construction of the placebo tests we use the Stata *synth* software as provided by Abadie et al. (2011, rev. 2014).

---

101 These are countries enumerated in footnote 1, except for: Bosnia and Herzegovina, the Czech Republic, Montenegro, and Serbia (due to unavailable data for some variables); Croatia, Latvia, and Uzbekistan (due to adopting constitutions before or in the year when transition began, rendering the pre-treatment period too short or non-existent); as well as Hungary (due to adopting the constitution very late, outside of the time period of analysis – see next footnote). The design of the study allows, however, for inclusion of the latter four countries within the donor pool.

102 Because of the balanced panel requirement, the entire period under analysis must be the same (in transition years) for each country. Given that 2012 is the last year for which the data are available, the shortest transition period in the sample is for former Soviet republics (excluding the Baltics), where transition time begins in 1992 and the studied period is 1992–2012 (21 years). Therefore, for other countries in the sample the period under analysis must also be limited to 21 years from the outset of transition. For those, where transition time started as early as 1989 (Hungary and Poland) this results in restricting the time period under analysis up to 2009. This is, as a matter of fact, also the reason for the necessity to exclude Hungary from the analysis due to the late adoption of the constitution in this country (2011). Hungary is nevertheless included in the donor pool.

4.3 Baseline results (country studies)

Figure 3 (in Appendix 2) presents the results of baseline estimations using the synthetic control method. Detailed tables reporting the weights attributed to countries from the donor pool for the construction of each synthetic country under examination, as well as the pre-treatment characteristics for each actual and synthetic country, are available in Appendix 4. Two series are plotted in Figure 3 for each post-socialist country under examination. The series represented by the continuous line shows the actual economic reforms performance of a country, while the series represented by the dashed line shows the estimated synthetic counterfactual. The question underlying each of such exercises is, what would have been the performance in economic reforms by the given country had it not adopted the constitution (that it actually did adopt).

Take, for illustration, the case of Azerbaijan. The solid line in Figure 3 shows the evolution of the transition indicator for this country between the 1st and 21st year of transition (in this case in the period 1992–2012). The post-socialist constitution was adopted in this country in 1995, so this year marks the treatment period (vertical line). The dashed line presents synthetic Azerbaijan's performance in economic reforms, i.e. assuming it did not adopt the constitution. The optimal weights for synthetic Azerbaijan constructed on the basis of the donor pool, as explained earlier, are: 0.614 for Tajikistan, 0.368 for Turkmenistan, and 0.018 for Uzbekistan (and 0 for all other countries in the donor pool). A comparison of the evolution of both lines in Figure 3 suggests that performance in economic reforms in Azerbaijan would have been considerably lower in 2012 (and every other year in the period 1996–2012) had it not adopted the constitution in 1995. Before 1995 the series for actual and synthetic Azerbaijan move closely together, while following 1995 they diverge and the gap between actual and synthetic values seems to be nearly constant (with some slight convergence in the most recent years) suggesting permanent, not just temporary, benefits from the constitution for economic reforms.

Positive effects of adopting constitutions for performance in terms of economic reforms are identified in a similar way for most of the other post-socialist countries. Specifically, this is the case for the remaining former Soviet Republics in the Caucasus (Armenia, Georgia), the Baltic republics (Estonia, Lithuania)[103],

103 As explained earlier, Latvia is excluded from the analysis. However, in the additional estimations, which we conducted for the model working in calendar time, Latvia followed a similar pattern (with positive effects).

Southeast Europe (Bulgaria, Macedonia, Romania, Slovenia)[104], as well as Kazakhstan, Slovakia, and Ukraine. The scale of these effects differs between countries, with the largest benefits for Georgia (reaching nearly the value of 1 on the transition indicator) and the smallest ones for Kazakhstan, Macedonia, and Slovakia. In most of these countries the benefits remain relatively stable, with a different pattern in Slovenia (negative effects at the beginning of the post-treatment period and positive later), Macedonia (negative or negligible effects until ca. the 13th year of transition and positive afterwards), Armenia (significant drop in benefits rendering the gap inexistent around the 9th year of transition and positive effects thereafter) and Kazakhstan (decreasing positive effects throughout the transition period).

Negative effects are revealed for a much smaller group of countries, i.e. Albania, Belarus, Moldova, Russia, and Tajikistan[105]. The scale of the effects varies again. While for Albania, Moldova, and Tajikistan they are fairly small, for Belarus they reach nearly 1 point on the transition indicator. The results for Russia should be treated with caution as the pre-treatment fit is questionable (RMSPE = 0.333)[106]. It is notable that for Belarus the negative effects dramatically increase 1–2 years after the constitution was adopted suggesting that the revision of the constitution following the referendum organized on President Lukashenko's initiative in 1996, leading to the reversal of democratization in this country and strengthening of the president's position within the state, could have been a meaningful factor in this respect.

Finally, the effects of adopting constitutions on post-socialist reforms seem negligible in two countries – Kyrgyzstan[107] and Poland. For the latter country this result holds for the entire period of transition, while Kyrgyzstan experienced some positive effects in the first years of transition.

The baseline results presented above suggest considerable variation in the effects of adopting constitutions in post-socialist countries on their performance in economic reforms, while at the same time demonstrating the effectiveness of the synthetic control method in revealing them. In the next section we undertake a further evaluation of these results, assessing the potential significance of the effects and aiming to explain the determinants thereof.

---

104 For Croatia in the model working in calendar time we obtained relatively small but positive effects.

105 We refrain from discussing the case of Turkmenistan, because the pre-treatment fit for this country is poor (RMSPE = 0.439).

106 Given Russia's uniqueness, it seems reasonable that it is difficult to closely 'reproduce' this country by mixing the characteristics of other post-socialist states.

107 No matter which constitution adopted by Kyrgyzstan we consider.

4.4 Evaluating and explaining the reform gaps

In this section we undertake the following tasks. Firstly, we conduct a series of 'conventional' placebo tests, as proposed by Abadie et al. (2010), to draw preliminary conclusions about the significance of the constitutions' effects on economic reforms identified in the previous section. Secondly, we supplement and verify these conclusions using the difference-in-difference approach as proposed by Campos et al. (2014). Thirdly, we study the determinants of the gap between actual and synthetic post-socialist countries in terms of performance in the field of economic reforms, looking at particular characteristics of their constitutions, as well as the broader institutional framework within which the constitutions operate.

To evaluate the significance of the estimates obtained in the previous section, following Abadie et al. (2010), we pose the question, whether our results could be driven entirely by chance, i.e. how often would we obtain results of this magnitude if we had chosen a state at random for the study instead of the given treated unit? To answer this question, we conduct a series of placebo studies by iteratively applying the synthetic control method used to estimate the effect of the constitution adopted in a given state to every other country in the donor pool (moving the treated state to the donor pool). If for a given country the placebo studies show that the gap estimated for the treated unit is unusually large relative to the gaps revealed when subjecting states from the donor pool to the same treatment, then the interpretation is that the analysis presented so far provides significant evidence of the effects of adopting a constitution by a country on its performance in terms of economic reforms.

Figure 4 (in Appendix 2) presents the results of the placebo tests. For each treated country, the thin, colored lines represent the gap associated with subsequent countries in the donor pool subjected to the treatment and their respective synthetic versions. The thicker black line denotes the gap estimated for the treated country. The figure reveals mixed conclusions. While in many cases the effect on economic reforms for the treated country is relatively large (as compared to the other countries), its magnitude is hardly ever largest in the studied group of countries. It should, however, be noted that in some donor countries the pre-treatment mismatch is significant, nevertheless even after removing countries with the pre-treatment RMSPE 20 or 5 times higher than for the given treated country, only for two states – Albania and Belarus, the magnitude of the effect can be considered 'unusually large'[108].

108 The relevant graphs for placebo tests with some countries removed due to high pre-treatment RMSPE (two threshold values have been set, as in Abadie et al. 2010 – 20

We supplement this analysis with inference tests proposed by Campos et al. (2014) consisting in difference-in-difference estimations for the actual and synthetic series for each post-socialist country and check the statistical significance of their differential. Specifically, we assess the significance of the difference in the outcome variable (reform performance) between the average pre-treatment (i.e. prior to the adoption of the constitution) difference (between the actual and synthetic country) and the average post-treatment difference (between the actual and synthetic country). The fact that we are looking at averages may result in producing conservative results as statistical significance may be more difficult to attain for those countries, which experience a gap between the actual and synthetic outcome variable series which is not constant over time in the post-treatment period (Campos et al. 2014).

Table 11 reports the results of these estimations. They reveal that that the differences between the actual and synthetic outcome variable series, associated with the adoption of the post-socialist constitutions, are noticeable for several countries (i.e. statistically significantly different from 0). This is the case for: Central-Asian former Soviet republics, i.e. Armenia (only at the 10% significance level, however), Azerbaijan, and Georgia; the Baltic republics, i.e. Estonia and Lithuania; as well as Bulgaria, Kazakhstan (at the 10% level), Moldova, Romania (at the 10% level), Slovenia (at the 10% level), and Ukraine. For these countries the estimated differential is positive. For Belarus and Russia the differential is significant and negative. These results are to a large extent coherent with the conclusions of the baseline synthetic control study and extend them by allowing to make statements about the statistical significance of the identified effects[109]. The differences concern, in particular, Macedonia and Moldova and can be explained by the fact that averaging the post-treatment effect leads in both of these countries to obtaining a different sign from the effect in the final part of the post-treatment period.

and 5 times higher RMSPE) are available from the author upon request.

109 For a discussion of limitations of the conclusions based on difference-in-difference estimations see Bertrand et al. (2004).

Table 11: Difference-in-difference estimates of the effect of constitutions

Country name	DiD estimate	Standard error	Adjusted R^2	Number of observations
Albania	–0.300	0.336	0.669	42
Armenia	0.196*	0.106	0.784	42
Azerbaijan	0.528***	0.110	0.800	42
Belarus	–0.789***	0.245	0.814	42
Bulgaria	0.310**	0.155	0.461	42
Estonia	0.709***	0.146	0.607	42
Georgia	0.685***	0.125	0.868	42
Kazakhstan	0.390*	0.202	0.880	42
Kyrgystan	0.170	0.104	0.522	42
Lithuania	0.590***	0.144	0.585	42
Macedonia	–0.025	0.118	0.328	42
Moldova	0.559***	0.204	0.879	42
Poland	–0.036	0.363	0.508	42
Romania	0.265*	0.156	0.463	42
Russia	–0.464***	0.109	0.342	42
Slovenia	0.213*	0.120	0.394	42
Slovakia	0.403	0.698	0.677	42
Tajikistan	–0.093	0.126	0.534	42
Turkmenistan	–0.103	0.081	0.636	42
Ukraine	0.731**	0.367	0.778	42
All countries	0.312***	0.116	0.391	840

Note: * Significant at a 10% level, ** Significant at a 5% level, *** Significant at a 1% level.
Source: Author's calculations.

We can now move to the final part of the analysis presented in this chapter aiming to explain the variety in the effects that the adoption of post-socialist constitutions had on economic reforms in different post-socialist countries, as presented in detail above. We first calculate what could be called 'reform dividends' i.e. the benefits in terms of performance in economic reforms associated with the adoption of post-socialist constitutions. They are equivalent to the magnitude of the gap between the actual and synthetic outcome variable series obtained in the previous parts of the analysis. We calculate those gaps not only for the entire post-treatment period for each post-socialist country but also for the first 5 and 10 years after the adoption of the constitution, so as to capture the potential general dynamics.

The reform dividends, calculated in percentage terms, are presented in Table 12. The table reveals considerable variety, both of positive and negative values. The highest positive values are attained by Ukraine (an increasing tendency with a 31.31% reform dividend on average over the complete period after adoption of the constitution, i.e. in 1996–2012) and Georgia (relatively stable benefits throughout the post-treatment period reaching 27.42% reform dividends on average for the 10-year period following the adoption of the constitution, i.e. 1995–2004). Slightly lower but still relatively high dividends are obtained for Estonia (stable throughout the post-treatment period at an average level of 23–24%), Azerbaijan (increasing tendency on average, reaching 23.66% for the complete post-treatment period), Moldova (with an average of 21–22%), Lithuania (18–21%), and Slovakia (decreasing tendency on average, reaching 28.05% in the first 5-years after adoption of the constitution and only 18.79% on average throughout the entire post-treatment period, i.e. 1992–2010[110]). On the other extreme we once again find Belarus (negative reform dividends reaching -21.28% on average in the first 5 years after adopting the 1994 constitution and as much as -28.86% on average throughout the entire post-treatment period, i.e. 1994–2012). Considerable negative benefits are also obtained for Russia (with a noticeable decreasing tendency from only -2.10% on average in the first 5 years after adopting the constitution to as much as -19.86% on average for the entire post-treatment period, i.e. 1993–2012). Relatively stable negative benefits oscillating on average at the level of ca. -8% are found for Albania, while smallest (slightly negative) dividends are experienced for Poland (-1.75% on average throughout the entire post-treatment period, i.e. 1997–2009) and Turkmenistan (-1.97% on average for the period 2008–2012[111]). It is noticeable that for some countries there are considerable dynamics in the average reform dividends following the adoption of their constitutions, e.g.: positive

110 As mentioned earlier, because of the balanced panel requirement, the entire period under analysis amounts to 21 transition years for each country, implicating the period 1990–2010 for Slovakia.

111 As we are only able to study the second post-socialist constitution of Turkmenistan (since the first one was adopted in 1992, i.e. the first year of transition time) and this second constitution was adopted in 2008, the period 2008–2012 is both the 5-year post-treatment period and the complete post-treatment period for this country. See also footnote 105.

and increasing in size in Armenia, Azerbaijan, Bulgaria and Ukraine; positive and decreasing in size in Kazakhstan, Kyrgystan and Slovakia; negative and decreasing in size in Macedonia and Tajikistan; and negative and increasing in size in Belarus and Russia. For Romania and Slovenia the benefits start on average negative and then turn positive with an increasing tendency.

Table 12: Reform dividends (in %)

Country name	5-year post-treatment period	10-year post-treatment period	Complete post-treatment period
Albania	–8.00	–8.31	–8.05
Armenia	3.96	4.06	6.52
Azerbaijan	17.42	22.21	23.66
Belarus	–21.28	–28.47	–28.86
Bulgaria	2.98	4.93	10.48
Estonia	24.20	23.66	23.37
Georgia	26.03	27.42	26.08
Kazakhstan	21.05	18.23	14.73
Kyrgystan	14.29	10.10	6.06
Lithuania	21.26	18.75	20.20
Macedonia	–10.74	–5.86	–1.22
Moldova	21.93	22.22	22.07
Poland	–1.57	–1.72	–1.75
Romania	–11.60	–1.08	8.35
Russia	–2.10	–13.90	–19.86
Slovenia	–2.78	4.24	6.45
Slovakia	28.05	22.37	18.79
Tajikistan	–9.35	–4.27	–3.73
Turkmenistan	–1.97	–	–1.97
Ukraine	23.41	28.84	31.31

Source: Author's calculations.

We now use these values for the final estimations searching for determinants of those dividends. We treat them (or, specifically, the annual dividends, varying year by year, not averaged values) as dependent variables in estimations employing various specifications and techniques of analysis. From the point of view of the focus in this book and bearing in mind that these dividends have been calculated based on the synthetic counterfactuals of countries obtained using a set of pre-treatment characteristics (see equation 8 in section 4.1), including the initial conditions for reform and the result of the initial post-socialist elections, two categories of variables can be identified as potentially explaining the time- and country-variation in these dividends: factors relating to the actual content and characteristics of the adopted constitutions (generally, factors relating to the constitutional framework), as well as factors determining the characteristics of the framework within which these constitutions operate (in particular, the informal institutional framework).

In the study presented here we include both types of determinants, as analyzed earlier using regression techniques in Chapter 3. The first group is the set of constitutional variables including the *de facto* measure of the concentration of power within the state [calculated based on the political constraints index originating from Henisz (2000, 2002, 2013); taking the value of 0 for least concentrated and 1 for most concentrated power], the *de facto* measure of constitutional rights and freedoms [based on the Freedom House (1990–2013) political rights and civil liberties indices; calculated so as to take values between 0 and 1, with 1 for the broadest scope of the functioning bill of rights], as well as two measures of constitutional court independence – *de iure* and *de facto* [based on *de iure* and *de facto* judicial independence indicators proposed by Voigt et al. (2015)]. The second group is represented by the earlier described measure of trust within the society. Expecting considerable inertia in reform dividends (gaps) we also include the lagged gap variable in the regressions.

Table 13 presents the relevant results for various specifications and estimation techniques (OLS with robust standard errors, pooled OLS, FE, RE). They indicate significance of only one constitutional variable throughout all estimations, where is it included, namely *de facto CCI*. At the same time *de iure CCI* is insignificant in all columns of the table, confirming the conclusions from earlier regression studies. The results for concentration of power and rights are not as convincing since the significance of these variables is sensitive to changes in the studied specifications (while *rights* are significant only in the first two columns of Table 13, *concentration* is significant only in the last one; in both cases, however, the signs of the coefficients are as expected based on the theory and results presented in Chapter 3)[112]. The

112 Similar estimations have also been conducted accounting for potential country-group effects of the *concentration* and *rights* variables. No such effects were, however, identified. One possible explanation for this result (incoherent e.g. with the finding of positive effects for concentration in countries which joined the European Union, presented in Chapter 3), could relate to the more limited sample of countries under

presented conclusions confirm the theoretical argumentation based on the credible commitment role attributed to the constitution in the post-socialist transition process, however not its most straightforward aspect, i.e. the extent to which power in the state is *de facto* (de-)concentrated (based on structural provisions or, indirectly, via the limitations on state power imposed by granting broad catalogues of rights and freedoms to the citizens), but rather by ensuring the effectiveness of the last stage in turning promises made by state power into credible commitments, i.e. *de facto* independence of the constitutional judiciary. In addition, the results presented in the last two columns confirm that the role of the informal institutional framework within which constitutions operate in countries should also certainly not be neglected. As expected, evidence is found of inertia in reform dividends (gaps) based on significant positive coefficients for the lagged gap variable in all regressions.

Table 13: Explaining the reform dividends – estimation results
Dependent variable: $reform\_gap_{it}$

Independent variables	Coefficients			
	only *concentration* and *rights*		**including *CCI***	**including *trust***
	I OLS / RE†	**II FE**	**III OLS / RE†**	**IV OLS / RE†**
$concentration_{it}$	-1.610	-2.809	-2.887	-5.702**
$rights_{it}$	0.483*	2.210***	0.487	0.453
CCI_deiure_i	–	–	-0.836	-0.779
$CCI\_defacto_i$	–	–	4.066**	3.378*
$reform\_gap_{i,t-1}$	0.892***	0.642***	0.873***	0.857***
$trust_i$	–	–	–	18.449***
constant	0.481	-3.053	-0.768	-3.418
R^2	0.842	0.791	0.835	0.851
F-stat. / χ^2-stat.	684.65/2115.84	165.63	464.11/1796.14	393.88/1791.42
Number of obs.	400	400	360	320
N. of countries	20	20	18	16

Notes: * Significant at a 10% level, ** Significant at a 5% level, *** Significant at a 1% level.
† Identical coefficients for OLS (robust) and RE estimations, as well as for pooled OLS.
Source: Author's calculations.

examination in the study employing the synthetic control method in comparison with the regression studies presented earlier, due to the reasons explained in footnote 101.

The discussed results constitute a confirmation of the main line of conclusions obtained earlier in Chapter 3 for the panel data regression setting but also their enrichment. Firstly, these results allow to settle that we cannot speak of an overall negative or positive significant effect of concentration of power on economic reforms in the entire sample of post-socialist countries. Secondly, they reveal that constitutional rights and freedoms may also not be the crucial channel either. What comes out of this study as the most vital component of the constitutional framework for economic reforms in post-socialist transition is *de facto* CCI. The latter reflects the essence of the commitment-enhancing role of the constitution for the economic reform process in post-socialist countries since constitutional court independence is obviously an important constraint on power, while at the same time being a vital instrument allowing for effective enforcement of constitutional rights.

4.5 Conclusions

In this chapter we attempted to reassess the relevance of the constitutional framework for performance in the area of economic reforms by post-socialist countries of Europe and Asia after 1989, using the novel synthetic control method. We commenced with a presentation of the method and discussion of its advantages over typical regression analyses proposed to date in studies of the topic, as well as indicated the requirements for the proper application of this method. We then designed a study allowing for verification of the conclusions regarding the role of constitutions for post-socialist economic reforms formulated in Chapter 3, as well as for supplementing them with assessments of the role of constitutions for economic reforms in particular countries on a one-by-one basis. In the latter respect we identified the reform dividends, as well as their determinants related to the enacted constitutional frameworks. From the point of view of the strive to identify the link between constitutions and performance in the field of post-socialist economic reforms the main finding in this chapter confirmed, in particular, the role of *de facto* constitutional court independence constituting the final stage of the constitutional commitment mechanism for reforms.

The study presented in this chapter delivers not only interesting conclusions but also demonstrates the potential of the synthetic control method, as a method allowing to analyze causal inference in comparative case studies, for future investigations in the area of constitutional economics, constitutional law and economics and related fields. This method, being in a way an extension of the difference-in-difference regression framework, provides a bridge between quantitative and qualitative studies in comparative politics (Abadie et al. 2015), economics, and in particular at the junction of the two, i.e. in the field of political economy. While large cross-country studies are often not internally valid because of lacking common support, comparative case studies have the feature of being internally valid, but they often cannot be generalized (Pieters et al. 2014). The synthetic control method succeeds in producing results which are both internally valid (thanks to the specific construction of the counterfactual which allows for good common support) as well as externally valid (thanks to the generalization of results based on tests conducted for large set of units). In this way it allows for "[*p*]*utting qualitative flesh on quantitative bones*" (Tarrow 1995, p. 473).

Having examined the significance of the constitutional framework for decision-making and performance in the field of economic reforms in post-socialist countries after 1989 using both the conventional regression framework and a novel empirical method, we now turn to the final contribution of this book. By incorporating elements of the evolutionary perspective on the functioning of constitutions we attempt not only to a deepen our understanding of the above interrelationship but also to contribute to the further development of the Constitutional Economics research program.

Chapter 5. An evolutionary perspective on the role of post-socialist constitutions

In this chapter we aim to contribute to the research agenda undertaken in this book by incorporating into the analysis of economic effects of constitutions some elements of the view at constitutions from the perspective of Evolutionary Political Economy. As mentioned in Chapter 1, the fact that constitutions are neither everlasting nor exogenous vis-à-vis the political, economic and social spheres, constitutes one of the most important challenges for further development of research on economic effects of constitutions. Systematic studies aimed at explaining constitutional change have recently only began in Constitutional Economics. This field of research could also be of interest to proponents of the evolutionary approach to politics.

Evolutionary Economics and, in particular Evolutionary Political Economy, demonstrated interest in the topic of constitutions as early as in the works of their predecessors, such as Friedrich August von Hayek (e.g. Hayek 1979) or even Joseph Schumpeter (1942/1987)[113]. Also the problem of constitutional change has received attention from scholars evoking some aspects of the evolutionary approach, e.g. Behnke and Benz (2009), as well as Posner (2011). Other studies of interest offer an evolutionary perspective on legal change in general (e.g. Eckhardt 2004, 2011) or focus on evolutionary theory of politics (e.g. Wohlgemuth 2002). None of them however identifies factors influencing constitutional change with the view towards a comprehensive study of economic effects of constitutions. Considering the constitution in this context reveals, for example, a dilemma between its stability (allowing to effectively act as a commitment mechanism) and flexibility (allowing for adaptation to changes in the society).

In this chapter we reach for works and ideas developed within Evolutionary Political Economy which are relevant from the point of view of studying economic effects of constitutions and, in particular, to those that could be related to the constitution's role as a rule framework and commitment device. The chapter is organized as follows. Firstly, we propose several supplementing remarks to the general theoretical approach to economic effects of constitutions based on the perspective of Evolutionary Political Economy. Secondly, in the empirical part, we extend the econometric study of the effects of post-socialist constitutions on

113 See also Oeser (2003) for a more recent interesting account.

economic reforms in transition by incorporating two variables relating to the evolutionary approach proposed in the theoretical section, namely direct democracy mechanisms and popular support for the constitution. The main findings render the study a promising step towards incorporating the evolutionary perspective into economic considerations of the effects of constitutions.

We are aware that evolutionary processes require time, in particular whenever they concern institutions. In the case of post-socialist countries of Europe and Asia the institutional or, in particular, constitutional framework is rather recent, if one compares it with e.g. many consolidated democracies. We nevertheless believe that the 25-year period that has already passed since the outset of transition warrants a preliminary study including elements of the evolutionary perspective that can be treated as a first step on an avenue of very promising future research. The examination presented in this chapter should therefore be regarded as an additional reflection on the implications of the remaining evidence collected in this book referring to economic effects of post-socialist constitutions.

5.1 The role of the constitution from an evolutionary perspective

As explained in Chapter 1 the principal role of constitutions from the point of view of an economist consists in the fact that they determine the 'rules of the game' for ordinary politics and economic activity. In Buchanan and Tullock's seminal contribution to the development of the Constitutional Economics research program (Buchanan and Tullock 1962) the political process can be divided into two stages – the constitutional and post-constitutional one. The rules laid down at the constitutional stage (the constitutional contract) constitute a binding framework, or constraints, within which choices of political and economic actors are made in the course of their every-day activity.

From the point of view of Evolutionary Institutional Economics constitutional rules are constitutive (0th order) rules which form the opportunity space for 1st order generic rules (institutions). As Potts (2007) argues, constitutive rules are in essence not economic but political. They may concern the economic system (e.g. fundamental rules regarding property rights protection or economic freedom) but the environment in which they are selected, where they evolve and are replicated, is political in nature and not (or at least not necessarily) subject to economic forces. However, since the 0th and 1st order rules co-evolve both at the micro and macro levels, the study of constitutive rules is also of interest to economists. Research on how institutions affect economic evolution cannot abstract from how 0th order rules affect the dynamics of 1st order rules.

Evolutionary Political Economy is in particular interested in conceptualizing constitutive rules as "*the evolved outcome of a political meso trajectory in which political rules (cf. economic rules) are subject to an origination, adoption and retention trajectory*" (Potts 2007, p. 348). This point of view on constitutional rules is well in line with the general understanding of these rules as determining the framework for political and economic action. Proponents of the Constitutional Economics approach also point to the fact that constitutional rules, while forming this framework, are themselves the outcome of the political process. At a first glance both approaches to the economic role of the constitution seem highly consistent with each other and mutually reinforcing (i.e. the arguments raised by evolutionists could be seen as strengthening the conclusions of Constitutional Economics). In this section we reconsider this in more detail with the focus on how the evolutionary approach contributes to the consideration of economic effects of constitutions.

5.1.1 Crucial rules

Research in the field of Constitutional Economics, both theoretical and empirical, revealed that from the point of view of economic performance one aspect of the constitutional framework is of particular importance – the (potential) commitment-enhancing feature of constitutional rules. The focus on the commitment feature of constitutional rules turns the attention of economists from those provisions of constitutions which directly concern the economic system to the study of rules determining the functioning of the political system – the government and its relations with voters and economic agents.

Evolutionary Political Economy offers an evolutionary approach to the functioning of the political sphere based on two building blocks: (1) the assumption of bounded rationality of individuals acting in various contexts in politics (these individuals differ in skills, knowledge, expectations, practices and learning heuristics); (2) process analysis of systems characterized by endogenous change, permanent creation of novelty, competitive selection, path-dependent imitation (instead of static equilibrium) (Wohlgemuth 2002). This approach focuses inter alia on the process of creating and changing political opinions and solutions to political problems, changing knowledge constraints of political actors, as well as dissemination of information within the political process. Much inspiration is drawn from Schumpeter's writings on political leadership and irrationality of voters in politics (e.g. Schumpeter 1942/1987), as well as from Hayek's theory of the evolutionary political opinion formation process with particular focus on learning (e.g. Hayek 1960, 1976). Wohlgemuth (2002) presents this approach in more detail and applies the evolutionary perspective to political competition and democracy.

In the evolutionary view constitutions provide a rule framework for the functioning of the political sphere perceived as given above. They should therefore allow for competition, which enables the discovery of individual preferences, abilities, information, as well as learning[114]. Competition within the political sphere implies pluralism of views and enables an open process of opinion formation. Dynamic concepts, such as innovation, creativity, and accumulation of knowledge, play a particularly important role. In explaining the evolutionary approach to politics Wohlgemuth (2002) mentions Popper's (1945) argument, according to which the quality of a system of government cannot be assessed on the basis of the effects (in terms of welfare or happiness) that it produces, but depends on institutions and processes which allow (or not) for open criticism and potential replacement of the politicians in power. Similarly, Hayek (e.g. 1960) views democracy as a procedure for the formation, discovery and verification of opinions and solutions to political problems. The rules governing such process should be tailored to the complexity of the everyday world of politics. They also ought to allow for constant evolution of – and within – the political sphere.

Three out of the constitutional rules mentioned in the preceding chapters of this book are of particular significance for the commitment-enhancing role of the constitution. Firstly, credibility of government commitment increases together with an increase in the number of veto players that can influence policy decisions in a state. The more players engaged, the less likely are changes or reversals of these decisions. Obviously, this aspect relates to the structure of government laid down in the constitution, as well as to the actual political fragmentation. However, credibility of commitment also depends on the scope and enforcement of constitutional systems of rights and freedoms of individuals and their groups. These rights and freedoms constitute constraints on discrete activity of government. The last aspect of the commitment-enhancing role of the constitution concerns the effectiveness of its enforcement mechanism. As in

114 In his discussion of the evolutionary approach to politics with particular emphasis on political competition Wohlgemuth (2002) stresses the differences between market competition and political competition, e.g. relating to the fact that individuals and their groups acting in the political sphere are not able to receive only those goods which they prefer and are willing to pay for, but receive a complete bundle of goods and services regardless of their preferences and willingness to pay (since election results are the same for all voters). This results in much weaker incentives for knowledge creation than in the market setting.

most systems this role is fulfilled by the constitutional judiciary, the degree of the latter's independence is examined.

A more detailed view at constitutions as frameworks for political action based on Evolutionary Political Economy, presented above, reveals that the same three constitutional rules, which are considered by constitutional economists as primary sources of the commitment-enhancing constitutional mechanism, are also of central importance for the evolutionary approach to the role of constitutions. Firstly, in a political system with numerous actors holding the power to decisively influence policy decisions (veto-players) one expects more competition of ideas, pluralism, accumulation of knowledge etc. This means that the number of veto-players in the system of government can also be regarded as a particularly important aspect of the role of constitutions from an evolutionary perspective. Secondly, pluralism, creation and evolution of ideas, accumulation of knowledge, as well as competition would not flourish without a broad and effective system of constitutional rights and freedoms granted to individuals and their groups. As Wohlgemuth (2002) argues, what is required are "*extended spheres of private autonomy and freedom to act, which allow groups to pursue different aims and test different practices at the same time, as long as they do not violate the freedom of others to do so as well*" (Wohlgemuth 2002, p. 232)[115]. Thirdly, the mechanism allowing for implicit change (evolution) of constitutional systems within states is in the hands of the constitutional judiciary, which interprets and supplements the formal constitutional framework allowing for its constant evolution and adjustment to the development of societies in various spheres of their members' activity. One could expect that an independent constitutional judiciary will serve this function in a more neutral (and therefore from the society's point of view more effective) way than a politically-biased one.

Viewing the functioning of the political sphere through the lens of Evolutionary Political Economy reveals however that one other aspect of the constitutional framework is of particular importance as it determines whether, and to what extent, individuals are capable of voicing their views and opinions in the political sphere. This relates to mechanisms of direct democracy allowing for popular participation in politics through referenda or initiatives. As mentioned in Chapter 1, these issues have already been the focus of study of Constitutional Economics, also with relevance to economic effects of constitutional rules. Proponents of this approach view direct democracy primarily from the perspective

115 This relates to Hayek's arguments about the role of minority opinions for the growth of civilization (see Hayek 1960).

of the principal-agent problem, as a mechanism allowing for issue unbundling and greater transparency of the political process (see e.g. Blume et al. 2009a, Blume and Voigt 2010). However, these studies have often taken only a partial view at the problem, considering the role of direct democracy mechanisms to a large extent in isolation from the remaining aspects of the constitutional framework. Based on a more complex view of the functioning of the political sphere offered by the evolutionary approach we argue that rules governing the structure of power, constitutional rights and freedoms, independence of the constitutional judiciary, as well as direct democracy mechanisms complement each other in forming the fundamental constitutional framework for the functioning of states and economies. This hypothesis remains to be tested empirically.

5.1.2 Stability vs. flexibility of the constitution

As a starting point for the considerations on stability of constitutions recall Williamson's (2000) classification of institutions on four levels (L1-L4) starting from informal institutions, customs, traditions, norms, religions, and embeddedness (constituting level L1 with a frequency of change of 100 to 1000 years) and finishing with resource allocation and employment on level L4 (changing continuously). In this classification constitutions would in principle fall on level L2 (institutional environment: formal rules of the game) with the frequency of change oscillating between 10 and 100 years. Constitutions can serve effectively as commitment mechanisms if they are stable in time. If they are often changed or replaced, they will not succeed in acting as a binding constraint on political behavior and will fail to play a significant role in counteracting the time-inconsistency problem in policy-making. Recent empirical studies demonstrate that changes of constitutions of various countries happen every year, either by amendment of the existing document or replacement[116]. While the exact meaning of the term 'constitutional stability' is not unambiguous (see e.g. Negretto 2008), the second case mentioned above (replacement of a constitution) is of particular concern for the study of the commitment feature of the constitution by economists[117]. In some countries constitutions persist much longer without

116 Other possibilities are the suspension or reinstatement of a constitution.

117 Changing selected provisions of the constitution in accordance with the amendment procedure provided in the constitution (i.e. a form of renegotiation of the constitution) can be regarded as a response to adjust the constitution text to the changes in the political, economic or social environment and may not influence the perception of its stability by political and economic actors.

replacement (e.g. the Constitution of United States in force since 1789), while in others they are replaced every few years (e.g. Venezuela has seen 26 different constitutions since its independence in 1811, out of which 16 were adopted since 1900). As mentioned briefly in Chapter 1, according to a recent study of endurance of national constitutions conducted by Elkins et al. (2009) the life expectancy of a constitution is 19 years[118].

Since constitutional changes are indisputable facts, several scholars have recently also undertaken the challenge to provide explanations of this phenomenon. Theoretical political science literature suggests an important role of time in sustaining constitutions, arguing that constitutional stability is a self-enforcing equilibrium (e.g. Hardin 1989). In this view the longer a constitution is in force, the more likely it is to last further (positive time dependence). Changes of long-lasting constitutions are unlikely due to internal costs of collective action required to conduct them successfully. A similar approach is taken by Hadfield and Weingast (2011), who view the law in general, and the constitution in particular, as a coordination device, and explain its stability by reference to the coordination focal solution, which becomes an equilibrium in a game between the sovereign and citizens of a state. Voigt (1999) also presents the constitution as an outcome of a bargaining game, where the players involved are the most powerful interest groups in the society. Changes in the constitution may occur in such setting when the relative bargaining power of various groups changes over time (e.g. due to technological innovation) and those, whose relative bargaining power has increased, will demand constitutional renegotiation.

Recent empirical studies of constitutional stability and endurance reveal an important role of environmental factors (in particular stability of the political and social environment), as well as constitutional design (or institutions connected with the content and drafting process of the constitution) for the lifespan of constitutions. Several studies, drawing on general theories of institutional change, emphasize that constitutional change occurs at the wake of social or economic crises or other exceptional circumstances such as revolutions, political regime collapses, wars etc. (e.g. Elster 1995). Negretto (2008) confirms that stability of the political and social environment, which the constitution regulates, has been one of the crucial factors determining the 'durability' of Latin American constitutions over the period 1946–2000. In particular, such aspects as regime transitions, transformations of party systems, irregular interruptions

118 Calculated based on the survival model for data from Elkins et al. (2014) as the age before which 50% of constitutions will have died.

of governments and antigovernment demonstrations significantly increased the risk of constitutional replacement in this part of the world (which has been experiencing most frequent constitutional change). Negretto (2008) however also identifies factors connected with constitutional design that influenced constitutional durability, e.g. bicameralism of the legislature and the existence of constitutional adjudication mechanisms (these two factors contributed to lowering the risk of constitutional replacement). Elkins et al. (2009) argue, more generally, that up to a certain point constitutions which are more flexible (i.e. they are easier to amend, formally and informally, allowing them to adjust to changing circumstances), more inclusive (i.e. include a wide range of social and political actors at the time of drafting and further functioning of constitutions), and more specific (i.e. those with more detailed provisions) are more enduring than others. They also confirm the significance of several environmental factors.

Some studies have recently also been conducted regarding the determinants of change of particular constitutional rules, e.g. Ticchi and Vindigni (2010) seeking to identify the factors determining the choice between 'majoritarian' and 'consensual' constitutions as classified by Lijphart (1999). In their important contributions Hayo and Voigt (2010a, 2013) study changes in the form of government worldwide since ca. 1950 and find, in particular, that such changes in the constitutions can be explained by characteristics of the political system, internal and external political conflicts, as well as political leadership, whereas economic and socio-demographic variables are not significant factors in this respect. In a different study (Hayo and Voigt, 2010b) these authors also seek to explain the degree of formal constitutional court independence laid down in constitutions of various countries and find that legal origins, religious factors and distribution of resources are significant factors in this respect.

An evolutionary approach to constitutions suggests caution when embarking on the challenge to establish the conditions for durability of national constitutions and particular constitutional rules. This view at the problem emphasizes that in order to serve the changing needs of the society and the economy in a state, the constitution must be well suited to these dynamically evolving spheres. This suggests a potential conflict between the understanding of constitutions as maximally stable rule systems and their essential flexibility to remain in coherence with the society's evolving needs. Since, according to this approach, the rationale behind enacting and enforcing the constitution are primarily the needs and interests of various groups within the society, changes within these spheres may render the solutions proposed by the constitution dysfunctional and necessitate its adaptation. Depending on the extent to which the constitution is flexible and capable of accommodating such change, this may require introducing either implicit or explicit amendments, or may demand replacement of the constitution[119]. This aspect of the constitutional stability problem is of particular significance in federal systems where destabilizing effects might be caused by various social, economic and cultural factors affecting the balance of tasks and resources between governments at different levels, as well as continuous struggle for power of actors from the various federal units and pressure towards secession. Behnke and Benz (2009) study the dynamics of constitutional policy in federal states distinguishing between explicit change (reform) and implicit change (evolution). They argue, inter alia, that those two modes of constitutional change complement each other in allowing federal systems to achieve a stable balance of constitutional rigidity and flexibility. The choice of a particular mode depends on formal rules of amending constitutions, the actual constellation of actors participating in negotiation of changes and the existing federal power structure[120].

The problem of adjusting constitutions to the changing needs of societies is, however, not solely the problem of federal states. Studies confirming the importance of environmental factors for constitutional change, mentioned above, illustrate this problem in its extreme variant, when the political, social (or in some cases economic) changes in a country take the form of crises, revolutions, regime collapses, etc. But even in less extreme situations, when popular support for the operating constitution is weak (a sign of low coherence of the constitution with the society's needs), the society (and, in particular, its well-organized groups) may lower compliance with the operating constitution and seek constitutional change. This has important consequences for the commitment-enhancing feature of constitutions, which will be significantly weaker in constitutionally unstable environments. The role of popular (social) support for the constitution, so far largely neglected by Constitutional Economics studies of economic effects of

---

119 The latter case, when evolving social needs lead to dysfunctionality and replacement of the constitution, could be perceived as a peculiar 'lifecycle' of the constitution. While institutional lifecycle theories have been proposed and discussed alongside analyses of evolution and dynamics of institutional orders (e.g. Brousseau and Raynaud 2011), the particular lifecycle theory of the constitution is yet to be developed.

120 For an interesting early account of the stability-flexibility trade-off see Hamburger (1989) on how this dilemma was perceived by drafters of the United States Constitution.

constitutions, is therefore another aspect that a more detailed analysis inspired by evolutionary considerations suggests to include[121].

5.1.3 Imperfect incentives

According to the Constitutional Economics approach to analyzing economic consequences of constitutions the latter act as commitment mechanisms by means of providing incentives to politicians in power (which make their promises credible in the eyes of other non-state actors within the state), as well as to individuals and their groups (to develop their individual and group activity in various fields, within the framework determined by constitution rules). An important contribution to this understanding can be made by relaxing the assumption that the addressees of these incentive mechanisms respond to them in a perfectly rational way. Such view of the incentive structure that the constitution produces, both for the actors within the political sphere (especially politicians in power), as well as individuals and other non-state entities, can draw inspiration from behavioral and evolutionary theory.

Since constitutions are meant to establish 'rules of the game' within the political sphere, they should exert particular influence on political actors. Strengthening credibility of these actors' (policy decision-makers') commitment will often contradict their particular interests. Expecting that these actors will credibly commit to long run goals, even if that is in conflict with satisfying their short-run preferences, constitutes in fact the essence of the counteracting time-inconsistency mechanism provided by the constitution. However, with such approach it seems crucial to ask why politicians in power would at all commit to such mechanism and not defer for the sake of their own benefit. Levinson (2011) provides a broad account of this problem, discussing in detail several relevant mechanisms. He argues, in particular, that "*the success of constitutional law, in both its constitutive and constraining roles, depends on the willingness and the*

121 Another important issue which the evolutionary approach suggests to take into account when constitutional change is considered is constitution-makers' bounded rationality. Although actors involved in drafting constitutions may want to structure constitutional rules tailored to the society's needs, for reasons of bounded rationality (limited knowledge and cognition of constitution-makers facing the complexity of the real world of politics and economics, in particular its dynamics) the choices that they make may prove erroneous and may need to be corrected by means of consecutive explicit (and to some extent possibly also implicit) constitutional change. This is one reason for assuring broad popular participation in the constitution-making process (see Voigt 2003).

ability of powerful social and political actors to make sustainable commitments to abiding by and upholding constitutional rules and institutions. The positive puzzle of constitutional commitment lies in explaining the sources of this willingness and ability" (Levinson 2011, p. 4). Most of the explanations that Levinson (2011) proposes fall within the rationality-based approach (e.g. relating to benefits from coordination, connected with reputation, repeat-play and reciprocity in politics, etc.). Some, however, reach beyond the rationality-based way of thinking and relate e.g. to the status quo bias (psychologically and sociologically embedded political arrangements and the role of inertia), as well as explanations pertaining to sunk costs in politics (political asset-specific investment). Chafetz (2011) supplements Levinson's account by bringing in the issues of legitimacy, Aristotelian virtue and Republican virtue, which although seldom included directly in economic analyses of constitutions, should not be completely set aside when one attempts to view the problem with focus on complexity and irregularity.

An interesting account of why constitutional commitment works (at least to a certain extent) has also been provided by Posner (2011). He makes use of evolutionary game theory to show that constitutions act as focal points for political behavior and when behavior is organized around such points this allows for avoiding conflict. The argument is based on the view at constitutions as sets of conventions that have evolved together with changes of tastes and technologies (a view that can be attributed particularly to Strauss 1996). Individuals obey conventions, just as they obey the rules of the road – so as not to fall in conflict with others who obey the conventions. While individuals could possibly improve their situation by deviating from a convention (constitution) collectively (to better suit their tastes and the environment), they will not achieve this by deviating individually[122]. The constitution, perceived as a convention, will then prevail because it is self-enforcing. The argument is further extended by Posner (2011) to separation of powers. An important role is attributed in this setting to the judiciary (in particular, the Supreme Court in the American system) which prevents politicians (legislatures) from violating constitutions-conventions that are "*desired by the public*" and assists them in overcoming the "*undesirable*" ones.

The problem of constitutions as 'parchment barriers' has recently been brought up with increasing frequency in research falling within the broadly-construed field of Constitutional Economics. This has, however, been done primarily as a starting point for attempts at explaining the relationship between *de iure* and *de*

122 This setting resembles Axelrod's (2006) prisoner's dilemma; see also Bendor and Swistak (1997).

facto constitutional rules (e.g. Melton 2013, Law and Versteeg 2013) and not as motivation for closer studies on imperfect incentives that the constitutional commitment mechanism may produce. While research on the latter topic has so far been scarce, with the recent emergence of the field of Behavioral Political Economy (see DellaVigna 2009, Beggren 2012, and a recent survey by Schnellenbach and Schubert 2015) one can expect more focus in this area in the upcoming future.

5.2 Empirical tests

On the basis of the considerations presented in Section 5.1 one may suggest several hypotheses that could be incorporated into the framework of studies of economic effects of constitutions conducted to date in order to allow for broadening and deepening of the analysis. Firstly, a more detailed look at the political sphere of countries suggests that mechanisms of direct democracy allowing for popular participation in politics should be taken into account alongside the three crucial constitutional rules identified earlier as turning promises of politicians in power into credible commitments. Secondly, the stability vs. flexibility debate suggests that it is important to take into account whether, and if so – to what extent, individuals and their groups support the existing constitution (generally, they will support it if they perceive that it serves their interests well). If this support is present, they can be expected to comply with the constitution. If not, they may seek constitutional change. Thirdly, relaxing the rationality in politics assumption leads to the conclusion that one should not expect perfectly rational responses of individuals and their groups to incentives which the constitution generates, both within the political sphere (for politicians and voters), as well as in the economic sphere. Some examples are Schumpeter's irrational voters and the failure to take advantage of rights granted to individuals and their groups.

The operationalization of the latter problem remains beyond the scope of this study[123]. Here we propose a preliminary empirical test regarding the first two hypotheses formulated above. In particular, we extend the model linking post-socialist constitutions with performance in economic reforms, developed in chapters 3 and 4, to include two new potentially relevant variables. In subsection 5.2.1 we study the role of direct democracy mechanisms, while in subsection 5.2.2 we focus on support for the constitution within the society.

123 As the focus here is essentially on behavioral questions, this could be studied with the use of experimental methods.

5.2.1 Introducing direct democracy mechanisms

In this section we undertake a more detailed examination of direct democracy mechanisms implemented and applied in post-socialist countries of Europe and Asia with a view on the potential role that they play in linking the rule framework for political decisions on economic reforms and the progress in the implementation of the latter during the time period as long as nearly 25 years of post-socialist transition. As explained earlier in this chapter, such mechanisms, allowing for popular participation in politics through referenda or initiatives, determine whether, and to what extent, individuals are capable of voicing their views and opinions in the political sphere. This activity could also be an additional check on government power, strengthening the commitment mechanism envisaged by the remaining constitutional rule-framework.

Mechanisms of direct democracy in post-socialist countries of Europe and Asia have not received much attention of constitutional economists to date. However, as Table 14 demonstrates, the legal solutions adopted by post-socialist states in this respect differ significantly. There is one single country providing (*de iure*) for all types of direct democracy mechanisms used in contemporary political systems at the national level, i.e. mandatory referenda, optional referenda, citizens' initiative, agenda initiatives, and recall (Belarus[124]). Eight countries provide for four out of these five possibilities (except for recall), while another nine establish three of them (different sets, with recall being least common). No type of mechanism is applied in all post-socialist countries of Europe and Asia. These countries differ also in respect to whether referenda are binding, or not, and what issues can be brought before them. In addition to direct democracy at the national level most countries also evoke such mechanisms at the regional or local levels. The factual use of these mechanisms by the post-socialist societies during the last nearly 25 years has also been far from uniform. In order to examine the potential influence of direct democracy mechanisms on the economic reform process of post-socialist countries we first estimate the model developed in Chapter 3 supplemented with an additional variable relating to direct democracy (*DD*) and, subsequently, turn to discuss the results pertaining to this issue obtained using the synthetic control method.

124 This observation also immediately raises doubts whether analysis of *de iure* direct democracy would be sufficient for identifying its effects. We return to this issue shortly.

Table 14: De iure mechanisms of direct democracy in post-socialist countries

Country	Legal provisions for mandatory referendums (national level)	Legal provisions for optional referendums (national level)	Legal provisions for citizens' initiatives (national level)	Legal provisions for agenda initiatives (national level)	Legal provisions for recall (national level)	Are referendum results binding?	What can be brought to a referendum?	Legal provisions at the regional level	Legal provisions at the local level
Albania		+	+	+		A	B	+	+
Armenia	+	+				A	B		+
Azerbaijan	+	+				A	B		+
Belarus	+	+	+	+	+	A	B	+	+
Bosnia and Hercegovina								+	+
Bulgaria		+				S	B	+	+
Croatia	+	+	+			A	B	+	+
Czech Republic	+					A	O		+
Estonia	+	+				A	B		+
Georgia		+	+	+		A	B		
Hungary	+	+	+	+		S	B		+
Kazakhstan		+				S	B		
Kyrgyzstan		+		+	+	A	B		+
Latvia	+	+	+	+		A	B		

Country	Legal provisions for mandatory referendums (national level)	Legal provisions for optional referendums (national level)	Legal provisions for citizens' initiatives (national level)	Legal provisions for agenda initiatives (national level)	Legal provisions for recall (national level)	Are referendum results binding?	What can be brought to a referendum?	Legal provisions at the regional level	Legal provisions at the local level
Lithuania	+	+	+	+		S	B		
Macedonia	+	+	+	+		A	O		+
Moldova	+	+	+	+			B	+	+
Montenegro	+			+					+
Poland	+	+		+		A	B	+	+
Romania	+	+		+		A	B	+	+
Russia	+	+	+			A	B	+	+
Serbia	+	+	+	+		A	B	+	+
Slovakia	+	+	+	+		S	B	+	+
Slovenia	+	+	+	+		A	B		+
Tajikistan	+	+				A	B		
Turkmenistan		+	+	+			B		+
Ukraine	+	+	+			A	B	+	+
Uzbekistan	+	+					B		

Notes: A – always, S – sometimes, B – both constitutional and other issues, O – other issues only.

Source: Own elaboration of the basis of IDEA (2008, Annex A).

Several measures of the extent to which a country uses direct democracy mechanisms and allows for popular participation in policy decisions have been proposed (e.g. Fiorino and Ricciuti 2007, see also Blume et al. 2009a). Most of these measures are time-invariant for a given period. For our panel-data study we find it most adequate to employ a cumulative measure of the number of popular (direct democracy) votes conducted in post-socialist countries during the period under investigation. This includes mandatory and optional referenda, as well as initiatives and plebiscites[125]. The data for our *DD* variable have been assembled based on the information provided by the Centre for Research on Direct Democracy related to the University of Zurich Law School (C2D 1989–2012). In our sample we find countries which did not make any use of direct democracy mechanisms during the period 1989–2012 (e.g. Bulgaria), as well as countries which applied them quite intensively (e.g. Lithuania and Slovenia – 19 votes each, Azerbaijan – 41 votes). As mentioned above, we believe that the use of direct democracy mechanisms may act as an additional factor contributing to the reform- and credibility-enhancing feature of the constitution and therefore expect a positive coefficient on the *DD* variable[126].

Table 15 presents the estimation results for specification (1) from Chapter 3 supplemented by the *DD* variable: for the larger sample of countries without *trust* in Columns 1–2 and for the smaller sample with *trust* in Columns 3–4 (in both cases the *CCI* variables are included). We refrain from presenting the detailed results of the system estimations including *DD* as they do not offer any new insights beyond the conclusions based on the single equation framework. The coefficients for other constitutional and control variables in Columns 1–4 of Table 15 are consistent with the results obtained earlier. The *DD* variable is found significant in estimations for the larger sample. The coefficient value indicates weak positive influence of the use of direct democracy mechanisms on performance

125 This approach is consistent with the conclusions of a more general study of the economic effects of direct democracy by Blume et al. (2009a), according to which it is the factual use of referenda that matters, not the sole inclusion of such institution in the constitution.

126 Including the direct democracy measure in the model together with the rights indicator (in particular, its 'political rights' component) does not raise concerns since the latter does not relate to direct democracy (see Freedom House 2005). The simple correlation between the *DD* variable and the *rights* index (as well as its political rights component separately) is 0.1 (-0.07). Additional estimations including the *DD* variable conducted for separated 'political rights' and 'civil liberties' components of the *rights* index, as well as without the 'political rights' component, did not alter the presented conclusions regarding direct democracy.

in economic reforms. Such results confirm that this influence is complementary to the effects of concentration of power and rights. Together these constitutional rules contribute to turning promises made by governments in transition countries regarding economic reforms into (more) credible commitments.

Table 15: Estimation results for specification (1) including direct democracy, 1989–2012 Dependent variable: $econ\_reform_{it}$

Independent variables	Coefficients			
	I OLS, without *trust*	II RE, without *trust*	III OLS, with *trust*	IV RE, with *trust*
$concentration_{it}$	−0.38*** (−3.25)	−0.51*** (−5.80)	−0.54*** (−5.24)	−0.56*** (−6.31)
$rights_{it}$	0.11*** (7.98)	0.12*** (6.43)	0.11*** (9.29)	0.13*** (6.61)
CCI_deiure_i	−0.25*** (−2.29)	−0.45* (−1.93)	−0.22*** (−2.24)	−0.24 (−1.03)
$CCI\_defacto_i$	0.29*** (2.56)	0.40*** (2.05)	0.33*** (3.31)	0.32* (1.69)
DD_{it}	5.1×10^{-3}*** (2.27)	5.2×10^{-3}* (1.68)	1.9×10^{-3} (0.95)	2.7×10^{-3} (0.82)
$trtime_{it}$	0.20*** (6.31)	0.20*** (24.90)	0.20*** (6.62)	0.20*** (24.07)
$trtime^2_{it}$	-6.1×10^{-3}*** (−5.00)	-5.9×10^{-3}*** (−18.16)	-6.1×10^{-3}*** (−5.20)	6×10^{-3}*** (−17.00)
$(IC\times trtime)_{it}$	-4.8×10^{-3}* (−1.94)	3.5×10^{-4} (0.12)	6.9×10^{-4} (−0.28)	-1.7×10^{-3} (−0.52)
$(IC\times trtime^2)_{it}$	3.1×10^{-4}*** (2.34)	1.1×10^{-4} (0.89)	1.1×10^{-4} (0.78)	1.3×10^{-4} (0.92)
$elections_i$	0.13*** (8.46)	0.09*** (3.41)	0.13*** (13.85)	0.12*** (4.44)
$trust_i$	–	–	1.12*** (3.43)	1.04* (1.77)
constant	1.19*** (10.28)	1.47*** (6.54)	0.90*** (5.50)	0.93*** (3.08)
R^2	0.857	0.853	0.878	0.877
F-stat. / χ^2-stat.	3363.06	2428.89	8467.25	2482.40
Number of obs.	502	502	439	439
N. of countries	23	23	20	20

Note: Values of the *t*-statistic in brackets.
* Significant at a 10% level, *** Significant at a 5% level.

Source: Author's calculations.

This general conclusion, however, fails to hold for the slightly smaller sample, as presented in Columns 3–4, where the *DD* variable is found insignificant. While one could search for reasons why accounting for trust within the society weakens the role of direct democracy, we propose instead a more detailed look at the influence of direct democracy mechanisms in different groups of countries (recall that all Central Asian countries are eliminated from the smaller sample). This is possible, similarly to the approach adopted in Chapter 3, when one includes interactions of the *DD* variable and dummy variables representing particular groups of countries. Table 16 presents the most interesting results of such estimations. It only reports the coefficients on the *DD* variable and its interactions with country-group dummies since the remaining variables in these regressions behave as discussed in the previous sections[127]. The first conclusion that stems from these results is a negative coefficient on the interaction variable for those countries of the region, which applied for EU membership during the transition period, and an altogether negative effect of direct democracy mechanisms for these countries (as revealed by the comparison of coefficients for the *DD* and the *EU* interaction variable in all three columns of Table 16). This finding is in line with the result of country-group-specific estimations conducted for post-socialist EU Member States in Chapter 3 highlighting the role of the constraints relating to the preparation for EU accession as an 'external' commitment mechanism ('anchor') for reforms. In such setting direct democracy becomes more of a cost than a positive determinant of a successful economic reforms. While we find no particular regularity as regards the effect of direct democracy in the former Soviet republics (excluding the Baltics and Central Asia), the use of direct democracy mechanisms may have played a significant positive role for reforming the economies of those republics located in Central Asia (this conclusion follows from the result of the extended system estimation reported in the last column of Table 16).

The differences in the role that direct democracy has to play in different groups of countries for economic reforms in transition, which we found above, may be partly responsible for the differences in the results obtained for the *DD* variable in estimations including the *trust* variable (due to unavailability of data, excluding Central Asia from the analysis) and those not including the *trust* variable (but encompassing Central Asia). However, to check the robustness of these results we now shift to the synthetic control method framework (allowing to circumvent the potential endogeneity problem that could have flawed the results

127 As earlier, next to the interaction we include all constitutive terms in the regressions (see footnote 72).

of the discussed regressions[128]) and, in particular, verify whether the use of direct democracy mechanisms explains any part of the reform dividends (positive or negative) accrued by post-socialist countries from adopting constitutions and identified in Section 4.4.

Table 16: Estimation results for direct democracy in country groups, 1989–2012 Dependent variable: econ_reform$_{it}$

	OLS	RE	3SLS (extended)
$(DD{\times}EU)_{it}$	−0.023*** [0.013***]	−0.014*** [0.008***]	−0.010*** [0.003]
$(DD{\times}FSU)_{it}$	0.003 [−0.0002]	0.015* [−0.009]	−0.001 [−0.002]
$(DD{\times}CA)_{it}$	0.016 [0.005*]	−0.030* [0.005*]	0.023*** [0.0004]
Number of observations	439 / 502†		334 / 388†
Number of countries	20 / 23†		20 / 23†

Notes: Values of the coefficient on the *DD* variable in brackets.
* Significant at a 10% level, *** Significant at a 5% level.
† See Table 10.
Source: Author's calculations.

Table 17 presents the relevant results, once again limited to the coefficients for direct democracy and, based on the insights from earlier parts of this section, its interactions with country-group dummies[129]. While we obtain a confirmation of the conclusion of an overall negative effect for post-socialist countries which applied for EU membership, the effect of direct democracy is positive (or, to be more precise, overall less negative) when one focuses on the former Soviet republics (excluding the Baltics and Central Asia). For Central Asia we find no particular statistically significant result.

128 For a very recent attempt at identifying the determinants of direct democracy see e.g. Blume et al. (2015)

129 The remaining explanatory variables behave as expected and conclusions presented in Section 4.4 based on Table 13 retain their validity. The *CCI* variables are included in all specifications (just as all the relevant constitutive terms of the interactions). In some specifications including the interaction terms the *de facto CCI* variable marginally looses significance.

Table 17: Direct democracy and reform dividends – estimation results
Dependent variable: $reform\_gap_{it}$

Independent variables	Coefficients		
	I OLS, robust	II pooled OLS	IV RE
DD_{it}	−0.040	−0.040	−0.040
$(DD \times EU)_{it}$	−0.231*** [0.085*]	−0.231* [0.085]	−0.231* [0.085]
$(DD \times FSU)_{it}$	0.314*** [−0.323***]	0.314* [−0.323***]	0.314* [−0.323***]
$(DD \times CA)_{it}$	−0.041 [−0.039]	−0.041 [−0.039]	−0.041 [−0.039]
Number of observations	360	360	360
Number of countries	18	18	18

Notes: When country groups are studies, values of the coefficient on the *DD* variable in brackets.
* Significant at a 10% level, *** Significant at a 5% level.
† See Table 10.
Source: Author's calculations.

To sum up, the results that we obtained in this section may be treated as preliminary evidence that use of direct democracy mechanisms is of potential importance as part of the framework for decision-making in the field of economic policy (here, specifically, in the area of post-socialist economic reforms). This could be explained by the role that these mechanisms may play for the functioning of competition within the political sphere, as well as enhancing credible commitment of governments to pursuing policy. These effects are, however, clearly not uniform throughout the region, but rather country-group specific. This specificity may be related to the fact that in exercising their functions in the state these mechanisms complement other elements of the framework for counteracting the time-inconsistency problem in policy making rooted in other constitutional rules or, as in the case of countries which applied for EU membership, based on external 'anchor' mechanisms.

5.2.2 Support for the constitution

The process of constitution making in post-socialist countries after 1989 represents in itself a compelling research area for authors interested in explaining constitutional change, also with regard for the evolutionary perspective and the stability vs. flexibility debate evoked earlier in this chapter. The determinants of post-socialist constitutional design have been analyzed e.g. by Elster (1993, 1996), Elster et al. (1998), Ordeshook (1997, 2002), as well as Voigt and Wagener (2002). These studies indicate the relevance of an array of factors for this process and focus, in particular, on the complex interaction at three levels of analysis – legacies, institutions, and decisions (Elster et al. 1998). Legacies refer to path dependence associated with the past, including the communist past and the 'deep' past of the pre-communist era; institutions refer to the configuration of actors and rules that emerged in the short period after the breakdown of the old regime, as well as the mode of the breakdown itself; while decisions refer to the strategic actions of key political and economic actors. The issue of 'importing' constitutional principles from the United States and Western Europe to the newly-created constitutional systems in the transition countries has also not gone unnoticed (e.g. Ordeshook 2002). From the point of view of the approach to explaining constitutional endurance proposed by Elkins et al. (2009) one can see constitutional change in post-socialist countries as primarily driven by environmental factors, in particular by the collapse of the pre-1989 regime.

As discussed in Chapter 2, constitutions of post-socialist countries have been adopted primarily during the period 1990–1996. This means that in some of these states the complex transition process began already under a new set of meta rules laid down in the post-socialist constitution, resembling to a certain extent, in Hayekian terms, the constructivist case (with socio-political order that coordinates individual actions constructed through top-down planning). In other countries, where post-socialist constitutions were adopted later in the transition process, one could in principle speak of a period with more opportunity for spontaneous action within the society and economy, however under the more or less strictly enforced constitutional rules from the pre-transition period (with consecutive amendments). Finally, some countries deliberately opted for the so-called stop-gap constitutionalism, adopting provisional (interim) constitutions early in the transition process and the 'ultimate' post-socialist constitutions in a few years' time (e.g. Albania in 1991 and 1998, Poland in 1992 and 1997 – see more in Table 2 in Chapter 2). Whether the moment of adopting the post-socialist constitution mattered for its role as a commitment mechanism from the point of view of performance in the field of economic reforms was studied already by Hellman (1997). As mentioned briefly in Section 1.4, Hellman's (1997) econometric tests suggest that postponing the adoption of new post-socialist constitutions did not advance the process of economic reforms.

This result holds both for the entire set of post-socialist countries of Central and Eastern Europe and former Soviet Union, as well as for the narrower set of post-socialist countries, where constitutions have been ratified through a democratic process. This study also finds no evidence to suggest that adopting post-socialist constitutions hindered economic reforms and, instead, indicates some positive effects of their adoption for these reforms. Bearing in mind the approach to the constitution's role in fostering the post-socialist economic reforms process presented in previous chapters of this book, one may treat Hellman's (1997) conclusions as a supplementary confirmation of the arguments presented by negative constitutionalists in their debate with advocates of positive constitutionalism.

As already mentioned, post-socialist constitutions have nearly all undergone amendments, as illustrated by Table 2 in Chapter 2. Roberts (2009) presents an interesting study of determinants of these changes arguing, in particular, that the causes of these amendments rest less in formal institutions (constitutional obstacles in the way, e.g. supermajorities) but rather in the political and social context, meaning that countries alter their constitutions as circumstances change. However, most importantly from the perspective of constitutional stability, only seldom have the post-socialist constitutions been replaced. Leaving interim constitutions (i.e. deliberate stop-gap constitutionalism) aside, replacement as such took place only in Kyrgyzstan, Turkmenistan, Serbia and Montenegro. With regard to the latter two countries this was connected with their turbulent history at the turn of the 21st century, resulting in separation of these states in 2006 and the need for new constitutions (adopted, respectively, in 2006 and 2007). A simple calculation for 28 post-socialist countries yields 18.96 years as the average age of a post-socialist constitution (calculated as of 2015 on the basis of constitutions then in force), which is nearly equal to the world average life expectancy of a constitution mentioned earlier (19 years). If one excludes the four cases of constitutional replacement mentioned above, this number increases to 20.92. Bearing in mind the limited time period since the outset of post-socialist transition in these countries, the small number of constitutional replacement cases, as well as considerably high average lifespans calculated above could be regarded as evidence of relative stability of the constitutional framework in the region during the post-socialist times.

In this book we are interested primarily in the working of the constitutional commitment mechanism. While, as argued in Section 5.1.2, constitutional stability is a crucial precondition for effective functioning of this mechanism, the role of popular support for the constitution in this respect, as a way of reflecting the adjustment of a constitution to the changing needs of a society, should also not be neglected. As the data evoked later in this section show, post-socialist societies are far from uniform as regards this support. Therefore, a second hypothesis that we aim to consider in the empirical study presented in this chapter concerns the role of popular support for the constitution in the latter's functioning as a commitment mechanism for policy-making by the government, based again on the evidence for post-socialist countries of Europe and Asia in transition. If this support is high we can expect that members of the society, both political and economic actors, will comply with the constitution increasing thereby its stability and commitment-enhancing potential. If not, they may seek constitutional change making the constitutional framework for the political and economic sphere less stable and the commitment mechanism significantly weaker.

Since we argue that support for the constitution from the society is necessary for the commitment mechanism that the constitution establishes to function properly, we propose to introduce an additional interaction variable into the empirical framework analyzed in previous parts of this book. This variable, being an interaction of the *concentration of power index* used earlier and the popular support measure, will allow to capture the effect that concentration of state power has on establishing credible commitment for policy-making by the government adjusted by, or conditional upon, the higher or lower level of support for this arrangement within the society.

We are not aware of the existence of detailed data regarding the level of support for the constitution as such in different countries, which would allow for cross-country comparisons in this respect. Having the choice between employing a measure of support for the law in general or for the political system established in a country, we opt for the second possibility since we are in particular interested in government-structure related provisions of the constitution. The popular support variable included in the study (*polsystemrate*) represents therefore the way the society rates the political system operating within the country. The data for this variable have been extracted from World Value Survey studies (4th wave for the years 1999–2002[130]). The scores for post-socialist countries in this database, i.e. the mean ratings of the political system within these societies classified on a

130 We do not include earlier waves due to very limited availability of data for post-socialist countries for the first years of transition. Armenia, Azerbaijan and Georgia were however not included in the 4th wave of WVS, therefore data for the 3rd wave (1996/1997) have been used for these countries.

10-point scale, range from 2.6 to 6.7[131]. The model specification takes the following form[132]:

$$econ\_reform_{it} = \alpha_1 concentration_{it} + \alpha_2 rights_{it} + \alpha_3 CCI\_deiure_i + \alpha_4 CCI\_defacto_i + \\ +\alpha_5 (concentration \times polsystemrate)_{it} + \alpha_6 trtime_{it} + \alpha_7 trtime_{it}^2 + \\ +\alpha_8 (IC \times trtime)_{it} + \alpha_9 (IC \times trtime^2)_{it} + \alpha_{10} elections_i + \alpha_{11} polsystemrate_i + \varepsilon_{it}. \quad (9)$$

Table 18 presents the results of estimations including the interaction variable *concentration×polsystemrate*. In the first column we present the outcomes of the panel regression based on specification (9)[133], while in the second column – their verification obtained using the synthetic control method. In both columns the interaction variable is significant and its coefficient takes a positive value. These results indicate that when support within the society for the political system determined by the constitution is higher, power need not be as deconcentrated to allow for a successful economic reforms process as in the lack of this support. In other words, support for the political system is an important aspect that should be taken into account when the constitution is studied as a commitment mechanism. This result passes the robustness check performed on the basis of the synthetic control method. The control variables employed in the

131 We are aware that such time-invariant measure of support for the constitution is highly simplified and, in particular, that a more dynamic view of the changes in support in time for each country would certainly enrich the analysis conducted here and its conclusions. At this moment such extensions were, however, not feasible, due to highly limited availability of data that would be required for such analysis.

132 As previously, testing for interaction effects we include all constitutive terms, i.e. also *polsystemrate* as a proxy for the level of support within the society for the political system, allowing to capture its potential direct influence on the reform process. We refrain from including the *trust* variable in these specifications as correlation between this variable and *polsystemrate* is considerably high. In this version of the study we do not include the direct democracy variable. The analyzed sample is slightly smaller than in previous regression studies presented in this book, as studying support for the constitution required excluding the early years of transition, as in most countries they preceded the adoption of constitutions, or even if constitutions were adopted, one could not yet discuss the popular support relating to them.

133 As the result of the Hausman test suggests inconsistency of the random effects estimator, while the fixed effects model does not allow to include time-invariant variables (such as e.g. *polsystemrate* and the *CCI* variables), in this first empirical approach to the topic we report results based on pooled OLS with Driscoll-Kraay standard errors. We refrain from presenting the results of system estimations as they do not alter the general conclusions.

studied specifications, including the constitutional variables, generally behave as expected based on our earlier findings, with concentration of power in the state confirming it significance in this setting (importantly, from the point of view of the key conclusion of this section). The same holds for *de facto* constitutional court independence, while for *rights*, as in Chapter 4, the results are more ambiguous (this factor turns out insignificant in the synthetic control setting).

Table 18: Estimation results for specification (9), 1989–2012
Dependent variable: $econ\_reform_{it}$ (I) / $reform\_gap_{it}$ (II)

Independent variables	**Coefficients**	
	I **panel regression**	**II** **SCM**
$concentration_{it}$	−0.641*** (−4.46)	-14.895*** (-2.18)
$rights_{it}$	0.107*** (8.20)	0.187 (0.78)
CCI_deiure_{i}	−0.324*** (−3.73)	-1.127 (−0.60)
$CCI\_defacto_{i}$	0.223*** (2.34)	0.774* (1.73)
$(concentration{\times}polsystemrate)_{it}$	0.080*** (2.64)	2.722* (1.82)
$trtime_{it}$	0.775*** (10.84)	–
$trtime^2_{it}$	−0.002*** (−6.43)	–
$(IC{\times}trtime)_{it}$	$-1.7{\times}10^{-3}$ (−0.15)	–
$(IC{\times}trtime^2)_{it}$	$-2.5{\times}10^{-6}$ (−0.04)	–
$elections_{i}$	0.179*** (9.66)	–
$polsystemrate_{i}$	0.060*** (2.80)	-1.398 (-1.27)
$reform\_gap_{i,t-1}$	–	0.927*** (43.63)
constant	1.594*** (22.27)	8.213* (1.88)

Independent variables	Coefficients	
	I panel regression	II SCM
R^2	0.904	0.937
F-stat. / χ^2-stat.	28337.26	617.58
Number of observations	338	272
Number of countries	20	16

Note: Values of the t-statistic in brackets.
* Significant at a 10% level, *** Significant at a 5% level.
Source: Author's calculations.

While we are well aware of the very preliminary nature of the results presented in this section, we believe that they are indicative of the likely existence of a significant but so far largely neglected factor, which relates the constitutional framework, as a commitment mechanism, to economic policy – the (popular) support for the constitution. While theoretical considerations pronounced within the debate on 'constitutions as parchment barriers' provide ground for questioning the strength and effectiveness of the constraints that the constitution places on political decision makers, further empirical studies confirming the role of this factor remain on the future agenda for constitutional economics researchers and may take the results of this section as the starting point[134].

5.3 Conclusions

In this chapter we made a first attempt at incorporating some evolutionary aspects of analysis into the study of economic effects of constitutions. We discussed potential channels of influence and provided a preliminary empirical study for the post-socialist countries. Based on this extended approach we were able to demonstrate that two additional aspects connected with the constitutional frameworks in these countries are relevant from the point of view of the economic reform process: direct democracy mechanisms (for some groups of countries) and popular support for the constitution as a reflection of the conformity of the constitution with the society's needs and expectations. We must emphasize that we limited our discussion to aspects connected with the evolutionary

134 Future studies should also consider constructing a more fine-tuned (and best if time-varying) measure of popular support for the constitution, which could allow for much more meaningful analysis.

approach which could have revealed themselves in the setting of post-socialist countries where the constitutional framework is relatively young and constitutions have only seldom been replaced. Nevertheless, even in such circumstances we succeeded in showing that the constitutional economics approach to economic effects of constitutions developed so far omits several significant aspects and should be broadened to include more insights from the evolutionary perspective.

The evolutionary approach to politics offers a much more comprehensive and sophisticated view at the political sphere and, in particular, on its dynamics. Since constitutional rules influence the economy *via* the developments within the political sphere (political outcomes), such view at politics contributes in a significant way to a deeper understanding of the problem of economic effects of constitutions. With respect to some constitutional rules, in particular the ones which have been identified as crucial from the point of view of providing credibility to promises made by political actors in power (or enhancing their credibility), the evolutionary approach provides additional convincing arguments why these aspects of the constitutional framework are significant. But an even more important contribution of the evolutionary approach could be in identifying mutual relationships and interactions between different constitutional rules, as well as their critical re-assessment taking into account the imperfect reaction of individuals and other non-state actors (due to bounded rationality or limited access to information) to incentive structures generated by constitutional rules. These issues would require studying constitutional frameworks over a much longer time perspective and remain on the future outlook for the promising field of research at the intersection of Constitutional Economics and Evolutionary Political Economy.

Conclusions

With this book we intended primarily to contribute to Constitutional Economics and, in particular, to its empirical dimension, in order to open the doors for shifting the respective theory to a higher generalization level. The central claim was that constitutional solutions, adopted by post-socialist countries after 1989, which enhanced the credibility and commitment of decision makers in the field of economic reforms conducted by these countries during the transition period, constituted a framework conducive to such reforms. The theoretical model, suggested in Chapter 1 on the basis of the existing Constitutional Economics and Political Economics literature, laying down the fundament for what could be called constitutional political economy of transition, or constitutional political economy of reform, indicated the role of constitutional constraints on discretionary power of political decision makers, as well as building the latter's capacity to push through difficult reforms, for the constitutional commitment-enhancing mechanism to effectively support the reform process in post-socialist economies. We also suggested to concentrate the focus in this respect on the significance of structural provisions, bills of rights, as well as constitutional enforcement mechanisms. The overview of post-socialist constitutions presented in Chapter 2 revealed considerable variation in the solutions adopted in these areas by post-socialist countries, both in the *de iure* and *de facto* dimensions, rendering the studies of potential links between these constitutional rules and performance in the field of post-socialist economic reforms a particularly compelling research problem.

The results obtained from three empirical studies presented in Chapters 3–5 of this book generally confirmed the significance of the constitutional framework for post-socialist countries' performance in economic reforms including privatization, liberalization, enterprise restructuring, competition policy and so forth. As expected, the link was found to be based on the role of the constitution in building credible commitment of political actors vis-à-vis economic actors and the entire society. The crucial element of the credibility-enhancing constitutional framework that emerged from the results obtained in all variants of the empirical study and for all of the included countries[135] was *de facto* independence of their constitutional courts, while at the same time *de iure* independence of these courts turned out irrelevant. As the last stage in turning promises made

135 Except Turkmenistan – see Section 2.3.

by political decision makers into credible commitments *de facto* constitutional court independence is obviously an important constraint on discretionary power, while at the same time being a vital instrument allowing for effective enforcement of constitutional rights. For the remaining constitutional rules under examination the results revealed more variation and country- or country-group specificity. With regard to concentration of state power we cannot speak of an overall negative or positive significant effect on economic reforms in the entire sample of post-socialist countries. In particular, countries committed to European integration, i.e. those which experienced a strong 'external' commitment-enhancing mechanism, seem to have benefited from more concentration of power, while for other groups of studied countries this conclusion is not valid, in fact they rather demonstrate the opposite. With regard to constitutional rights and freedoms, the results of our studies reveal that they may not be the crucial channel either. An interesting exception in this respect is the significantly positive link between rights and economic reforms in Central Asian countries, where, in fact, there is much room for broadening the scope of the currently functioning catalogues of rights and freedoms and improving the effectiveness of their protection[136]. Finally, two additional aspects connected with the constitutional frameworks in post-socialist countries are relevant from the point of view of the economic reform process: direct democracy mechanisms (for some groups of countries) and popular support for the constitution (as potentially weakening or strengthening the constitutional commitment mechanism). To sum up, while our broader and more reliable study framework confirmed several results of earlier analyses by Metelska-Szaniawska (2008, 2009), we also came up with a number of new and refined findings. While these results in themselves deliver valuable conclusions, we treated them as a starting point for two further contributions brought by this book to the development of Constitutional Political Economy.

In Chapter 4 we succeeded in demonstrating the results of a carefully designed empirical study, conducted using the novel synthetic control method, showing that with account for potential endogeneity of constitutional rules, many of them reaffirm their vital importance for the way policy decisions are made in the state, while for other rules such claims are repudiated by the evidence or at least questionable. The presented study also revealed the usability and effectiveness of the synthetic control method for further research within Constitutional Economics and related fields, the development of which has been seriously obstructed

136 However, recall that we were not able to confirm this result in the synthetic control framework due to data limitations.

by problems relating to endogeneity and causality in empirical studies. While, as mentioned in Section 1.3, studies aimed at identifying the determinants of constitutional change have been on the agenda of Constitutional Economics scholars for a few years already and will certainly broaden our understanding of mechanisms linking constitutions and the economic sphere, such research faces various methodological and technical challenges and therefore one cannot expect advancement in this field to take place in a short period of time. A fortiori, the possibility that the application of synthetic control method to studies of economic effects of constitutions offers, i.e. to circumvent problems of endogeneity and causality and deliver more reliable results, is particularly valuable to researchers in this field.

A second input that we attempted to make in this book was bringing in to the theoretical approach to economic effects of constitutions new elements inspired by the evolutionary approach to politics. In a preliminary empirical examination that we conducted in Chapter 5 we succeeded in showing that the constitutional economics approach to economic effects of constitutions developed so far omits several significant aspects and should be broadened to include more insights from the evolutionary perspective.

While we believe that the book has brought valuable contributions as concerns new results, new methods, reconciling Constitutional Economics with the evolutionary perspective and new implications stemming from it, we are aware that much remains to be developed in future research within this promising field.

In the studies presented here we worked with empirical evidence from post-socialist countries of Europe and Asia. This comes with its advantages but also limitations in the context of generalization of the obtained results. The limitations are particularly connected with the problem that characterizes much of research within Political Economy, Institutional Economics and related fields – cross-country comparability. Proponents of the approach treating systemic changes in post-socialist countries after 1989 as a "*gigantic natural experiment*" (e.g. Elster 1991, Weimer 1997, Elster et al. 1998) argue that because of a common legacy from the past and similar characteristics at the outset of transition, cross-country studies for this group of states are relatively well grounded. However, extrapolation of results obtained from these studies to other regions that differ in terms of historical legacies, culture, age and maturity of their democracies, or their informal institutional framework, bears a significant risk of overinterpretation. Therefore, we do not aim to generalize the recommendations stemming from our studies to other groups of countries, even those which seem to be undergoing partially similar large-scale constitutional changes over the recent years (e.g. the Arab Spring countries[137]).

The fact that we are able to draw implications from the studies conducted in this book for post-socialist countries of Europe and Asia is, however, in itself a noteworthy accomplishment. These conclusions can have both a practical dimension, as well as be of value for development of the relevant theory. As far as the first are concerned, the constitutional framework can be of significance for further economic reforms, as required by a given post-socialist country, as well as for extending the time horizon for policy-making activity in more general settings. Taking as an illustration the case of Poland which is approaching the 19th year of its 1997 Constitution (i.e. the average survival age of a constitution in the world, as mentioned earlier), our results suggest that while increasing concentration of state power in this country (either due to constitutional amendment or a change in factual distribution of power between political parties in consequence of elections) does not threaten the reforms process (in fact, the effect may be reform-enhancing), this country should not underestimate the role of the constitutional judiciary and, in particular, its independence. Therefore actions that may undermine this independence, such as the recent hasty process of adopting the new Constitutional Tribunal Act by the Polish Sejm (i.e. lower chamber of Parliament), just two days after the results of the presidential elections have revealed in May 2015 the defeat of the incumbent candidate connected with the then majority in Parliament, as well as the events that followed[138], should be

137 Recent constitutional change in the Arab countries did not go unnoticed among Constitutional Economics scholars – see e.g. Gutmann and Voigt 2015. Many research projects are ongoing while this book is being published.

138 The new draft of the Act adopted initially by the Sejm on May 27, 2015 established, e.g., a new rule relaxing the requirements for candidates for Constitutional Tribunal judges and allowing entry for those with 10 years of experience in public institutions connected to law-making or implementation of law. This obviously opened the door for nominating judges with a political background and was likely to undermine the court's independence. While this doubt-raising provision was later removed from the draft, another problematic aspect resulted in much more serious consequences. The draft, adopted finally by the Parliament on June 25 and signed by the outgoing President on July 21, 2015, also envisaged the modification of dates pertaining to the judges' election process in such way that several judges would be nominated earlier than under the previous Act, allowing the majority in Parliament at that time to take the decision on their election ('avoiding' the risk of having this decision taken by the next Parliament after the October 2015 parliamentary elections, which were likely to witness, and did witness indeed, another defeat of that majority). This, however, turned out to be only

avoided. It is also important to bear in mind that a sole *de iure* change need not be advantageous or detrimental in this respect, as it is *de facto* constitutional court independence that matters.

Implications for post-socialist countries from our studies can also enrich the theories explaining the process of economic reforms and, in particular, the influence of political and institutional determinants in this respect. As argued in Chapter 1 and mentioned earlier in this section, the model explaining the role of constitutions for the post-socialist economic reforms process, developed in this book, may be considered the theoretical fundament for what could be named constitutional political economy of reform or constitutional political economy of transition. The book certainly contributes to a vast literature that attempts to explain variation in post-socialist economic reforms by reference to such determinants. Frye (2007) suggests to distinguish between deep and middle-range causal mechanisms in this respect. Deep mechanisms relate to initial conditions for the economic reforms process, such as bureaucratic legacy and the relative distortions of central planning (see e.g. de Melo et al. 2001; Kitschelt 2001b). Middle-range theories emphasize the role of political and economic institutions that emerged in the early years of transition (e.g. Fish 1998, Frye and Mansfield 2003). As institutions are themselves shaped by initial conditions, some authors indicate the significance of tactics chosen by policy makers during the transition period to overcome historical constraints (Shleifer and Treisman 2000). According to, inter alia, Mishler and Rose (2007), these institutional aspects gain importance over time as societies learn how to operate within them. Treisman (2014), who recently reviewed the experience of post-socialist countries of Europe and Asia from the broad political-economy perspective, emphasizes three crucial factors determining successful post-socialist transformation. Firstly, historical traditions influenced political reforms, i.e. democracy broke through quicker in countries where socialism (or communism) had been installed more recently, while predominantly Muslim countries of Central Asia and Azerbaijan became

the beginning of a "political battle for the Tribunal" as in November 2015, with support of the new majority, the Parliament amended the Constitutional Tribunal Act overnight (the new President signed the document immediately on the next day). Based on this amendment the Sejm deemed the election of five judges on the basis of the Constitutional Tribunal Act adopted in June ineffective and initiated the election process anew. While this book is being published the struggle continues (both the new Act adopted in June and its amendment adopted in November, have been subjected to constitutional review). Whatever its outcome is, the factual independence of the Polish Constitutional Tribunal has already been seriously undermined by these events.

consolidated autocracies[139]. Secondly, individual leaders made a difference. "*At times, what was needed was the type of leadership required to devise a competent and sufficiently ambitious plan and then plunge ahead against a typhoon of criticism. At other moments, successful leadership meant having the flexibility and strategic sense to switch coalitions at crucial moments, disappointing former allies, compromising with former opponents, doing whatever was necessary to move things forward*" (Treisman 2014, p. 294). Thirdly, what mattered most for successful transformation was the nature of political institutions that handled the wide range of conflicts between different economic groups in these countries. He argues, in particular, that democratic institutions pushed decision-making in the direction of more economic freedom, while reforms leading to more responsive, accountable, and transparent governance, allowed for more successful market reforms. In this book we focused on the role of constitutions, which establish the political institutions in place in a country and shape the functioning of political actors by providing a stronger or weaker commitment mechanism that can be crucial from the point of view of policy making, also in the field of post-socialist economic reforms. By identifying 'which constitutional rules matter', as well as the various inter-connected channels of influence of these rules on successful economic transformation, we enriched the grand picture of the political-economic account of post-socialist transition 25 years from the outset of this process.

139 This argument pertaining to the importance of varying historical legacies is often raised by authors criticizing the approach treating post-socialist transition as a (gigantic) natural experiment – see more in Gehlbach and Malesky (2014).

References

Abadie A. (2015), *Using Synthetic Controls to Evaluate an International Strategic Positioning Program in Uruguay: Feasibility, Data Requirements, and Methodological Aspects*, Inter-American Development Bank Document No. 37312864, Inter-American Development Bank.

Abadie A., Diamond A., Hainmueller J. (2015), "Comparative Politics and the Synthetic Control Method", *American Journal of Political Science*, 59(2), pp. 495–510.

Abadie A., Diamond A., Hainmueller J. (2011, rev. 2014), http://EconPapers.repec.org/RePEc:boc:bocode:s457334

Abadie A., Diamond A., Hainmueller J. (2010), "Synthetic Control Methods for Comparative Case Studies: Estimating the Effect of California's Tobacco Control Program", *Journal of the American Statistical Association*, 105(490), pp. 493–505.

Abadie A., Gardeazabal J. (2003), "The Economic Costs of Conflict: A Case Study of the Basque Country", *American Economic Review* 93(1), pp. 112–32.

Acemoglu D. (2005), "Constitutions, Politics, and Economics: A Review Essay on Persson and Tabellini's *The Economic Effects of Constitutions*", *Journal of Economic Literature*, 43, pp. 1025–1048.

Acemoglu D., Hassan T.A., Tahoun A. (2014a), *The Power of the Street: Evidence from Egypt's Arab Spring*, NBER Working Papers No. 20665, National Bureau of Economic Research.

Acemoglu D., Naidu S., Restrepo P., Robinson J.A. (2014b), *Democracy Does Cause Growth*, NBER Working Paper No. 20004, National Bureau of Economic Research.

Acemoglu D., Johnson S., Querubin P., Robinson J.A. (2008), "When Does Policy Reform Work? The Case of Central Bank Independence", *Brookings Papers on Economic Activity*, 39(1), pp. 351–429.

Acemoglu D., Robinson J. (2006), *Economic Origins of Dictatorship and Democracy*, New York: Cambridge University Press.

Acemoglu D., Johnson S. (2005), "Unbundling Institutions", *Journal of Political Economy*, 113(5), pp. 949–995.

Ahrens J. (2007), "Governance in the process of economic transformation", in: Jovanovic M., Dalgon L., Seliger B. (eds.), *System Transformation in Comparative Perspective. Affinity and Diversity in Institutional, Structural and Cultural Patterns*, Münster: LITVerlag.

Ahrens J., Meurers M. (2001). *Institutions, Governance, and Economic Performance in Post-Socialist Countries: A Conceptual and Empirical Approach*, unpublished manuscript.

Alesina A., Persson T., Tabellini G. (2006), "Reply to Blankart and Koester's *Political Economics versus Public Choice Two Views of Political Economy in Competition*", *Kyklos*, 59, pp. 201–208.

Alt J., Lassen D. (2003), "The Political Economy of Institutions and Corruption in American States", *Journal of Theoretical Politics*, 5(3), pp. 341–65.

Amsden A.H., Kochanowicz J., Taylor L. (1998), *The Market Meets Its Match. Restructuring the Economies of Eastern Europe*, Cambridge, Mass. and London: Harvard University Press.

Antoszewski A., Herbut R. (1998), *Demokracje Europy Środkowo-Wschodniej w perspektywie porównawczej* (Democracies of Central and Eastern Europe in a Comparative Perspective), Wrocław: Wydawnictwo Uniwersytetu Wrocławskiego.

Arrow K.J. (1951), *Social Choice and Individual Values*, New York: Wiley.

Aslund A. (2002), *Building Capitalism: The Transformation of the Former Soviet Bloc*, Cambridge: Cambridge University Press.

Aslund A., Djankov S. (eds.) (2014), *The Great Rebirth: Lessons from the Victory of Capitalism over Communism*, Washington D.C.: Peterson Institute for International Economics.

Axelrod R. (2006), *The Evolution of Cooperation*, revised edition, New York: Basic Books.

Babetskii I., Campos N.F. (2007). *Does Reform Work? An Econometric Examination of the Reform-Growth Puzzle*, IZA Discussion Paper No. 2638, Institute for the Study of Labor (IZA).

Balcerowicz L. (1996), *Socialism, Capitalism, Transformation*, Budapest: Central European University Press.

Barone G., Mocetti S. (2014), "Natural disasters, growth and institutions: A tale of two earthquakes", *Journal of Urban Economics*, 84(C), pp. 52–66.

Barro R. (2000), *Rule of Law, Democracy, and Economic Performance*, in: *2000 Index of Economic Freedom*, Washington D.C.: Heritage Foundation, pp. 31–49.

Bates R.H. (1981), *Markets and States in Tropical Africa: The Political Basis of Agricultural Policies*, Berkeley: University of California Press.

Baum Ch.L., Ruhm Ch.J. (2013). *The Effects of Paid Family Leave in California on Labor Market Outcomes*, NBER Working Papers No. 19741, National Bureau of Economic Research.

Beard Ch. (1913/1986), *An Economic Interpretation of the Constitution of the United States; with a New Introduction by Forrest Mc Donald*, New York: Free Press.

Beck T., Clarke G., Groff A., Keefer P., Walsh P. (2001), "New Tools in Comparative Political Economy: The Database of Political Institutions", *World Bank Economic Review*, 15(1), pp. 165–176.

Becker Th.L. (1970), *Comparative Judicial Studies*, Chicago: Rand McNally & Co.

Behnke N., Benz A. (2009), "The Politics of Constitutional Change between Reform and Evolution", *Publius*, 39(2), pp. 213–240.

Bendor J., Swistak P. (1997), "The evolutionary stability of cooperation", *American Political Science Review*, 91, pp. 290–307.

Berggren N. (2012), "Time for behavioral political economy? An analysis of articles in behavioral economics", *Review of Austrian Economics*, 25, pp. 199–221.

Bertrand M., Duflo E., Mullainathan S. (2004), "How Much Should We Trust Differences-in-Differences Estimates?", *Quarterly Journal of Economics*, 119 (1), pp. 249–275.

Billmeier A., Nannicini T. (2013), "Assessing Economic Liberalization Episodes: A Synthetic Control Approach", *The Review of Economics and Statistics*, 95(3), pp. 983–1001.

Bjoernskov Ch. (2015), "Constitutional property rights protection and economic growth: evidence from the post-communist transition", *Constitutional Political Economy*, 26(3), pp. 247–280.

Black D. (1948), "On the Rationale of Group Decision-Making", *Journal of Political Economy*, 56(1), pp. 23–34.

Blankart Ch.B., Koester G.B. (2007), "The Economic Analysis of Constitutions: Fatalism Versus Vitalism", *Econ Journal Watch*, 4(2), pp. 169–183.

Blankart Ch.B., Koester G.B. (2006). "Political Economics versus Public Choice", *Kyklos*, 59(2), pp. 171–200.

Blume L., Hayo B., Voigt S. (2015), *Correlates and Determinants of Direct Democracy*, MAGKS Joint Discussion Paper Series in Economics No. 1–2015, Universities of Aachen, Gießen, Göttingen, Kassel, Marburg, Siegen.

Blume L., Müller J., Voigt S. (2009a), "The Economic Effects of Direct Democracy – A First Global Assessment", *Public Choice*, 140, pp. 431–61.

Blume L., Müller J., Voigt S., Wolf C. (2009b), "The Economic Effects of Constitutions: Replicating – and Extending – Persson and Tabellini", *Public Choice*, 139, pp. 197–225.

Blume L., Voigt S. (2013), "The Economic Effects of Constitutional Budget Institutions", *European Journal of Political Economy*, 29, pp. 236–251.

Blume L., Voigt S. (2011), "Does Organizational Design of Supreme Audit Institutions Matter? A Cross-country Assessment", *European Journal of Political Economy*, 27(2), pp. 215–229.

Blume L., Voigt S. (2010), *Institutional Details Matter – More Economic Effects of Direct Democracy*, working paper, http://ssrn.com/abstract=1639487.

Blume L., Voigt S. (2007). "The Economic Effects of Human Rights", *Kyklos*, 60(4), pp. 509–538.

Bohn S., Lofstrom M., Raphael S. (2014), "Did the 2007 Legal Arizona Workers Act Reduce the State's Unauthorized Immigrant Population?", *The Review of Economics and Statistics*, 96(2), pp. 258–269.

Bove V., Eliay L., Smith R.P. (2014). *The relationship between panel and synthetic control estimators of the effect of civil war*, BCAM Working Paper No. 1406, Birkbeck Centre for Applied Macroeconomics.

Bove V., Nisticò R. (2014). "Coups d'état and defense spending: a counterfactual analysis", *Public Choice*, 161(3), pp. 321–344.

Bradbury J.C. and Crain W.M. (2001), "Legislative organization and government spending: crosscountry evidence", *Journal of Public Economics*, 82, pp. 309–325.

Brambor Th., Clark W.R., Golder M. (2006), "Understanding Interaction Models: Improving Empirical Analyses", *Political Analysis*, 14, pp. 63–82.

Brennan G., Hamlin A. (1994), "A Revisionist's View of the Separation of Powers", *Journal of Theoretical Politics*, 6(3), pp. 345–368.

Brennan G., Kliemt H. (1990), "Logo Logic", *Constitutional Political Economy*, 1(1), pp. 125–127.

Brousseau E., Raynaud E. (2011), "'Climbing the hierarchical ladders of rules': A life-cycle theory of institutional evolution", *Journal of Economic Behavior & Organization*, 79, pp. 65–79.

Buchanan J.M. (1990), "The Domain of Constitutional Economics", *Constitutional Political Economy*, 1(1), pp. 1–18.

Buchanan J.M. (1987), "Constitutional Economics", in: Eatwell J., Milgate M., Newman P. (eds.), *The New Palgrave – A Dictionary of Economics*, London/Basingstoke: MacMillian.

Buchanan J.M. (1977), *Freedom in Constitutional Contract – Perspectives of a Constitutional Economist*, College Station and London: Texas A&M University Press.

Buchanan J.M., Tullock G. (1962), *The Calculus of Consent. Logical Foundations of Constitutional Democracy*, Ann Arbor: The University of Michigan Press.

C2D (1989–2012), *Direct Democracy database*, Centre for Research on Direct Democracy (c2d), http://www.c2d.ch/.

Campos N.F., Coricelli F., Moretti L. (2014), *Economic Growth and Political Integration: Estimating the Benefits from Membership in the European Union Using the Synthetic Counterfactuals Method*, CEPR Discussion Papers No. 9968, Center for Economic and Policy Research.

Campos N.F., Coricelli F. (2002), "Growth in Transition: What We Know, What We Don't, and What We Should", *Journal of Economic Literature*, 40(3), pp. 793–836.

Campos N.F., Kinoshita Y. (2008), *Foreign Direct Investment and Structural Reforms; Evidence From Eastern Europe and Latin America*, IMF Working Papers No. 08/26, International Monetary Fund.

Carey J.M. (2000), "Parchment, Equilibria, and Institutions", *Comparative Political Studies*, 33(6–7), pp. 735–761.

Cavallo E., Galiani S., Noy I., Pantano J. (2013), "Catastrophic Natural Disasters and Economic Growth", *The Review of Economics and Statistics*, 95(5), pp. 1549–1561.

Chafetz J. (2011), *The Political Animal and the Ethics of Constitutional Commitment*, Cornell Law Faculty Publications Paper 182, Cornell University.

Chan H.F., Frey B.S., Gallus J., Torgler B. (2014). "Academic honors and performance", *Labour Economics*, 31, pp. 188–204.

Cheibub J.A. (2007). *Presidentialism, Parliamentarism, and Democracy*, Cambridge: Cambridge University Press.

Cheibub J.A., Elkins Z., Ginsburg T. (2013), "Beyond Presidentialism and Parliamentarism", *British Journal of Political Science*, 44(03), pp. 515–544.

Cingranelli D.L., Richards D.L., Clay K.Ch. (2014), *The CIRI Human Rights Dataset*, version 2014.04.14, http://www.humanrightsdata.com.

Cooter R.D. (2000), *The Strategic Constitution*, Princeton: Princeton University Press.

Costalli S., Moretti L., Pischedda C. (2014), *The Economic Costs of War: Synthetic Counterfactual Evidence and the Effects of Ethnic Fractionalization*, HiCN Working Papers 184, Households in Conflict Network.

Cox G.W., McCubbins M.D. (2001), "The Institutional Determinants of Economic Policy Outcomes", in: Haggard S., McCubbins M.D. (eds.), *Presidents, Parliaments, and Policy*, Cambridge: Cambridge University Press, pp. 21–63.

Crain W.M., Tollison R.D. (1979), "Constitutional Change in an Interest-Group Perspective", *Journal of Legal Studies*, 8(1), pp. 165–175.

Dąbrowski M., Gortat R. (2002a), *Political and Economic Institutions, Growth and Poverty – Experience of Transition Countries*, Human Development Report 2002, New York: UNDP.

Dąbrowski M., Gortat R. (2002b), *Political Determinants of Economic Reforms in Former Communist Countries*, CASE Studies and Analyses 242, Center for Social and Economic Research.

de Haan J., Klomp J. (2010), "Inflation and Central Bank Independence: A Meta-Regression Analysis", *Journal of Economic Surveys*, 24(4), pp. 593–621.

DellaVigna S. (2009), "Psychology and economics: evidence from the field", *Journal of Economic Literature*, 47, pp. 315–372.

de Melo J., Denizer C., Gelb A., Tenev S. (2001), "Circumstance and Choice: The Role of Initial Conditions and Policies in Transition Economies", *The World Bank Economic Review*, 15(1), pp. 1–31.

Dewatripont M., Roland G. (1997), "Transition as a Process of Large Scale Institutional Change", in: Kreps D., Wallis K. (eds.), *Advances in Economics and Econometrics: Theory and Applications*, Vol. II, Cambridge: Cambridge University Press, pp. 240–278.

Dincer N.N., Eichengreen B. (2014), "Central Bank Transparency and Independence: Updates and New Measures", *International Journal of Central Banking*, 10(1), pp. 189–253.

Doerrenberg Ph., Peichl A. (2014), "The impact of redistributive policies on inequality in OECD countries", *Applied Economics*, 46(17), pp. 2066–2086.

Doucouliagos H., Ulubasoglu M.A. (2008), "Democracy and Economic Growth: A Meta-Analysis", *American Journal of Political* Science, 52(1), pp. 61–83.

Downs A. (1957), *An Economic Theory of Democracy*, New York: Harper and Row.

Dupre C., *Importing the Law in Post-Communist Transitions: The Hungarian Constitutional Court and the Right to Human Dignity,* Oxford: Hart Publishing.

EBRD (1994–2013), *Transition Report*, London: European Bank for Reconstruction and Development, subsequent issues.

Eckhardt M. (2011), "Legal Evolution Between Stability and Change", in: Zumbansen P., Calliess G.-P. (eds.), *Law, Economics, and Evolutionary Theory*, Cheltenham: Edward Elgar, pp. 202–225.

Eckhardt M. (2004), *Evolutionary Approaches to Legal Change*, Thünen-Series of Applied Economic Theory Working Paper No. 47, Thünen-Reihe Angewandter Volkswirtschaftstheorie.

Elkins Z., Ginsburg T., Melton J. (2014), *The Comparative Constitutions Project*, data available at http://www.comparativeconstitutionsproject.org/.

Elkins Z., Ginsburg T., Melton J. (2009), *The Endurance of National Constitutions*. New York: Cambridge University Press.

Elster J. (2000), "Arguing and Bargaining in Two Constituent Assemblies", *University of Pennsylvania Journal of Constitutional Law*, 2, pp. 345–421.

Elster J. (1996), "The Role of Institutional Interest in East European Constitution-Making – Explaining Legislative Dominance", *East European Constitutional Review*, 5(6), pp. 63–65.

Elster J. (1995), "Forces and mechanisms in constitution-making", *Duke Law Review*, 45, pp. 364–396.

Elster J. (1991), "Constitutionalism in Eastern Europe: An Introduction", *The University of Chicago Law Review*, 58(2), pp. 447–482.

Elster J., Offe C., Preuss U.K. (1998), *Institutional Design in Post-communist Societies: Rebuilding the Ship at Sea*, New York: Cambridge University Press.

Enikolopov and Zhuravskaya (2007), "Decentralization and Political Institutions", *Journal of public economics*, 91(11), pp. 2261–2290.

Falcetti E., Lysenko T., Sanfey P. (2005), *Reforms and Growth in Transition: Re-Examining the Evidence*, EBRD Working Paper No. 90, European Bank for Reconstruction and Development.

Falcetti E., Raiser M., Sanfey P. (2002), "Defying the Odds: Initial Conditions, Reforms, and Growth in the First Decade of Transition", *Journal of Comparative Economics*, 30, pp. 229–250.

Fałkowski J., Metelska-Szaniawska K. (2015), "Przyczyny ustanawiania i stabilność konstytucji państwa – perspektywa ekonomiczna" (Establishing State Constitutions and Their Stability – An Economic Perspective), *Gospodarka Narodowa*, 3, pp. 79–105.

Farber D. (2002), "Rights as Signals", *Journal of Legal Studies*, 31, pp. 83–98.

Feld L.P., Kirchgässner G. (2001), "The Political Economy of Direct Legislation: Direct Democracy and Local Decision-Making", *Economic Policy*, 33, pp. 329–363.

Feld L.P., Savioz M. (1997), "Direct Democracy Matters for Economic Performance: An Empirical Investigation", *Kyklos*, 50(4), pp. 507–538.

Feld L.P., Voigt S. (2003), "Economic Growth and Judicial Independence: Cross-Country Evidence Using a New Set of Indicators", *European Journal of Political Economy*, 19(3), pp. 497–527.

Feld L.P., Zimmermann H., Döring Th. (2004), *Federalism, Decentralization and Economic Growth*, Discussion Paper Series "Fiscal Federalism and National Growth" No.1, University of Marburg.

Fidrmuc J. (2003), "Economic Reform, Democracy and Growth during Post-Socialist Transition", *European Journal of Political Economy*, 19, pp. 583–604.

Fiorino N., Ricciuti R. (2007), *Determinants of Direct Democracy*, CESifo Working Paper No. 2033, Ifo Institute, Center for Economic Studies.

Fischer S., Sahay R. (2004), *Transition Economies: The Role of Institutions and Initial Conditions*, paper presented at the IMF conference "Festschrift in Honor of Guillermo A. Calvo", International Monetary Fund, April 15–16.

Fish M.S. (1998), "The Determinants of Economic Reform in the Post-Communist World", *East European Politics and Societies*, 12(1), 31–78.

Freedom House (1990–2013), *Freedom in the World*, Washington, D.C.: Freedom House, subsequent issues.

Frey B., Stutzer A. (2006), "Direct Democray: Designing a Living Constitution", in: Congleton R. (ed.), *Democratic Constitutional Design and Public Policy – Analysis and Evidence*, Cambridge: The MIT Press, pp. 39–80.

Frye T. (2007), "Economic Transformation and Comparative Politics", in: Boix C., Stokes S. (eds.), *The Handbook of Comparative Politics*, Oxford: Oxford University Press, pp. 940–968.

Frye T., Mansfield E.D. (2003), "Fragmenting Protection: The Political Economy of Trade Policy in the Post-Communist World", *British Journal of Political Science*, 33, pp. 635–57.

Geddes B. (1994), "Challenging the Conventional Wisdom", *Journal of Democracy*, 5(4), pp. 104–118.

Gehlbach S., Malesky E.J. (2014), "The Grand Experiment That Wasn't? New Institutional Economics and the Postcommunist Experience", in: Galiani S., Sened I. (eds.), *Institutions, Property Rights, and Economic Growth: The Legacy of Douglass North*, New York: Cambridge University Press, pp. 223–247.

Gehlbach S., Malesky E.J. (2010), "The Contribution of Veto Players to Economic Reform", *The Journal of Politics*, 72(4), pp. 957–975.

Gerring J., Thacker S. (2004), "Political Institutions and Corruption: the Role of Unitarism and Parliamentarism", *British Journal of Political Science*, 34, pp. 295–330.

Giavazzi F., Tabellini G. (2005), "Economic and political liberalizations", *Journal of Monetary Economics*, 52, pp. 1297–1330.

Gifford A. (1991), "A Constitutional Interpretation of the Firm", *Public Choice*, 68, pp. 91–106.

Ginsburg T., Melton J. (2015), *Innovation in Constitutional Rights*, paper presented at the NYU Workshop on Law, Economics and Politics, http://www.law.nyu.edu/sites/default/files/upload_documents/November%2019%20Ginsburg%20Melton%20Innovation%20in%20Constitutional%20Rights%20.pdf.

Godoy S., Stiglitz J. (2006). *Growth, Initial Conditions, Law and Speed of Privatization in Transition Countries: 11 Years Later*, NBER Working Papers No. 11992, National Bureau of Economic Research.

Greif A. (2008), "The Impact of Administrative Power on Political and Economic Developments, Toward a Political Economy of Implementation", in: Helpman E. (ed), *Institutions and Economic Performance*, Cambridge: Harvard University Press, pp. 17–63.

Grossman G.M., Helpman E. (1994), "Protection for Sale", *American Economic Review*, 84(4), pp. 833–850.

Gutmann J., Voigt S. (2015), "The Rule of Law and Constitutionalism in Muslim Countries", *Public Choice*, 162(3–4), pp. 351–380.

Hadfield G.K., Weingast B.R. (2011), *Endogenous Institutions: Law as a Coordinating Device*, University of Southern California Law School Law and Economics Working Paper Series Paper No. 141, University of Southern California.

Hainmueller J. (2015), *Synth Package*, http://web.stanford.edu/~jhain/synthpage.html.

Hamburger P.A. (1989), "The Constitution's Accommodation of Social Change", *Michigan Law Review*, 88, pp. 239–327.

Hardin R. (1989), "Why a Constitution?", in: Grofman B., Wittman D. (eds.), *The Federalist Papers and the New Institutionalism*, New York: Agathon Press, pp. 100–120.

Hare P.G. (2001), "Institutional Change and Economic Performance in the Transition Economies", in: *Economic Survey of Europe*, Geneva: United Nations, UNECE, pp. 77–94.

Hare P., Turley G. (eds.) (2013), *Handbook of the Economics and Political Economy of Transition*, London: Routledge.

Hartwell Ch.A. (2013), *Institutional Barriers in the Transition to Market: Examining Performance and Divergence in Transition Economies*, London: Palgrave Macmillan.

Havrylyshyn O., van Rooden R. (2003), "Institutions Matter in Transition but So Do Policies", *Comparative Economic Studies*, 45, pp. 2–24.

Hayek F.A. (1979), *Law, Legislation and Liberty: Vol. 3. The Political Order of a Free People*, Chicago: University of Chicago Press.

Hayek F.A. (1976), *Law, Legislation and Liberty: Vol. 2. The Mirage of Social Justice*, Chicago University Press, Chicago.

Hayek F.A. (1960), *The Constitution of Liberty*, Chicago: University of Chicago Press.

Hayo B., Voigt S. (2013), "Endogenous constitutions: Politics and politicians matter, economic outcomes don't", *Journal of Economic Behavior & Organization*, 88(C), pp. 47–61.

Hayo B., Voigt S. (2010a), "Determinants of Constitutional Change: Why Do Countries Change Their Form of Government?", *Journal of Comparative Economics*, 38, pp. 283–305.

Hayo B., Voigt S. (2010b), *Mapping Constitutionally Safeguarded Judicial Independence – A Global Survey*, MAGKS Joint Discussion Paper Series in Economics Paper No. 34–2010, Universities of Aachen, Gießen, Göttingen, Kassel, Marburg, Siegen.

Hayo B., Voigt S. (2007), "Explaining de facto judicial independence", *International Review of Law and Economics*, 27(3), pp. 269–290.

Heckman J., Hotz V.J. (1989), "Choosing among Alternative Nonexperimental Methods for Estimating the Impact of Social Programs: The Case of Manpower Training", *Journal of the American Statistical Association*, 84(408), pp. 862–74.

Heim B., Lurie I. (2014), "Does health reform affect self-employment? Evidence from Massachusetts", *Small Business Economics*, 43(4), pp. 917–930.

Hellman J.S. (1997), "Constitutions and Economic Reform in Post-Communist Countries", in: Pistor K., Sachs J.D. (eds.), *The Rule of Law and Economic Reform in Russia*, Boulder: Westview Press, pp. 55–78.

Henisz W.J. (2013), *POLCON Database*, 2013 release.

Henisz W.J. (2002), "The Institutional Environment for Infrastructure Investment", *Industrial and Corporate Change*, 11(2), pp. 355–389.

Henisz W.J. (2000), "The Institutional Environment for Economic Growth", *Economics and Politics*, 12(1), pp. 1–31.

Henry P.B. (2007), "Capital Account Liberalization: Theory, Evidence, and Speculation", *Journal of Economic Literature*, XLV, pp. 887–935.

Herron E.S., Randazzo K.A. (2003), "The Relationship Between Independence and Judicial Review in Post-Communist Courts", *The Journal of Politics*, 65(2), pp. 422–438.

Holmes S. (1995), "Conceptions of Democracy in the Draft Constitutions of Post-Communist Countries", in: Crawford B. (ed.), *Markets, States and Democracy. The Political Economy of Post-Communist Transformation*, Boulder: Westview Press, pp. 71–81.

IDEA (2008), *Direct Democracy. The International IDEA Handbook*, Stockholm: International Institute for Democracy and Electoral Assistance.

Imbens G.W., Wooldridge J.M. (2009), "Recent Developments in the Econometrics of Program Evaluation", *Journal of Economic Literature*, 47(1), pp. 5–86.

IMF (2000), *World Economic Outlook 2000*, Washington, D.C.: International Monetary Fund.

Kager J.H., Roth A.E. (1995), *The Handbook of Experimental Economics*, Princeton: Princeton University Press.

Keefer P., Stasavage D. (2003), "The Limits of Delegation: Veto Players, Central Bank Independence, and the Credibility of Monetary Policy", *American Political Science Review*, 97(3), pp. 407–423.

Kitschelt H. (2001a), "Constitutional Design and Postcommunist Economic Reform", in: Beyer J., Wielgohs J., Wiesenthal H. (eds.), *Successful Transitions: Political Factors of Socio-Economic Progress in Post-socialist Countries*, Baden Baden: Nomos.

Kitschelt H. (2001b), *Post-Communist Economic Reforms: Causal Mechanisms and Concomitant Properties*, paper presented at the 2001 Annual Meeting of the American Political Science Association in San Francisco, August 29 – September 2.

Klomp J., de Haan J. (2009), "Central Bank Independence and Financial Instability", *Journal of Financial Stability*, 5(4), pp. 321–338.

Knack S., Keefer P. (1995), "Institutions and Economic Performance: Cross-Country Tests Using Alternative Institutional Measures", *Economics and Politics*, 7(3), pp. 207–227.

Kocher M., Strauß S., Sutter M. (2006), "Individual or Team Decision-Making – Causes and Consequences of Self-Selection", *Games and Economic Behavior*, 56, pp. 259–270.

Kołodko G. (2001), "Postcommunist Transition and Post-Washington Consensus: The Lessons for Policy Reforms", in: Blejer M.I., Škreb M. (eds.), *Transition. The First Decade*, Cambridge, Mass. and London: MIT Press, pp. 45–83.

Kołodko G. (2000), *From Shock to Therapy: The Political Economy of Post-Socialist Transformation*, Oxford: Oxford University Press.

Law D.S., Versteeg M. (2013), "Sham Constitutions", *California Law Review*, 101, pp. 863–952.

Lederman D., Loayza N., Soares R. (2005), "Accountability and Corruption", *Economics and Politics*, 17(1), pp. 1–35.

Levinson D. (2011), "Parchment and Politics: The Positive Puzzle of Constitutional Commitment", *Harvard Law Review*, 124, pp. 657–746.

Lijphart A. (1999), *Patterns of Democracy – Government Forms and Performance in Thirty-Six Countries*. New Haven: Yale University Press.

Linzer D., Staton J. (2012), *A Measurement Model for Synthesizing Multiple Comparative Indicators: The Case of Judicial Independence*, paper presented at the 2011 Annual Meeting of the American Political Science Association, Seattle, September 1–4.

Lissowska M. (2006), "New Research Problems for Institutional Economics Arising from the Experience of Transition to a Market Economy: The Evolution of Institutions", *Journal of Economics and Business*, IX(2), pp. 53–80.

Ludwikowski R.R. (2000), "Constitutional Culture of the New East-Central European Democracies", *Georgia Journal of International and Comparative Law*, 29(1), pp. 1–29.

Ludwikowski R.R. (1998), "'Mixed' Constitutions – Product of an East-Central European Constitutional Melting Pot", *Boston University International Law Journal*, 16(1), pp. 1–70.

Macey J.R. (1987), "Competing Economic Views of the Constitution", *The George Washington Law Review*, 56(1), pp. 50–80.

Matsusaka J. (1995), "Fiscal Effects of the Voter Initiative: Evidence from the Last 30 Years", *Journal of Political Economy*, 102(2), pp. 587–623.

McGregor J. (1994), "The presidency in East Central Europe", *RFE/RL Research Report*, 3(2), pp. 23–31.

Melton J. (2013), *Do Constitutional Rights Matter? The Relationship between De Jure and De Facto Human Rights Protection*, working paper, http://citeseerx.ist.psu.edu/viewdoc/download?doi=10.1.1.375.9784&rep=rep1&type=pdf.

Melton J., Ginsburg T. (2014), "Does De Jure Judicial Independence Really Matter?: A Reevaluation of Explanations for Judicial Independence", *Journal of Law and Courts*, 2(2), 187–217.

Metelska-Szaniawska K. (2012), „Ekonomia konstytucyjna – ekonomia polityczna ładu gospodarczego" (Constitutional Economics – Political Economy of the Economic Order), in: Wilkin J. (ed.), *Teoria wyboru publicznego. Główne nurty i zastosowania* (Public Choice. Main Strands and Interests), Warszawa: Wydawnictwo Naukowe Scholar, pp. 109–135.

Metelska-Szaniawska K. (2009), "Constitutions and economic reforms in transition: an empirical study", *Constitutional Political Economy*, 20(1), 1–41.

Metelska-Szaniawska K. (2008), *Konstytucyjne czynniki reform gospodarczych w krajach postsocjalistycznych* (Constitutional determinants of economic reforms in post-socialist countries), Warszawa: Wydawnictwa Uniwersytetu Warszawskiego.

Milczarek D. (2002), *Privatisation as a Process of Institutional Change. The Case of State Farms in Poland*, Aachen: Shaker Verlag.

Mill J.S. (1843), *A System of Logic*, London: John W. Parker, West Strand.

Mishler W., Rose R. (2007), "Generation, Age, and Time: The Dynamics of Political Learning during Russia's Transformation", *American Journal of Political Science*, 51(4), pp. 822–34.

Mueller D.C. (ed.) (1997), *Perspectives on Public Choice: A Handbook*, Cambridge: Cambridge University Press.

Negretto G.L. (2008), *The Durability of Constitutions in Changing Environments: A Study on Constitutional Stability in Latin America*, The Helen Kellogg Institute for International Studies Working Paper No. 350, Kellogg Institute for International Studies.

Norris P (2009), *Democracy Time-Series Data,* release 3.0, http://www.pippanorris.com.

North D.C. (1997), *The Contribution of the New Institutional Economics to an Understanding of the Transition Problem*, Helsinki: United Nations University, World Institute for Development Economics Research.

North D.C. (1990), *Institutions, Institutional Change and Economic Performance*, New York: Cambridge University Press.

North D.C., Wallis J.J., Weingast B.R. (2009), *Violence and Social Orders: a Conceptual Framework for Interpreting Recorded Human History*, New York: Cambridge University Press.

North D.C., Weingast B.R. (1989), "Constitutions and Commitment: The Evolution of Institutions Governing Public Choice in 17th Century England", *Journal of Economic History*, vol. 49, pp. 803–832.

Oeser E. (2003), *Evolution and Constitution. The Evolutionary Selfconstruction of Law*, Dordrecht: Springer Verlag.

Olson M. (1965), *The Logic of Collective Action: Public Goods and the Theory of Groups*, Cambridge, MA: Harvard University Press.

Opper S. (2008), "New Institutional Economics and Its Application on Transition and Developing Economies" in: Brousseau E., Glachant J.-M. (eds.), *New Institutional Economics. A Guidebook*, Cambridge: Cambridge University Press, pp. 389–406.

Ordeshook P.C. (2002), "Are 'Western' Constitutions Relevant to Anything Other than They Serve?", *Constitutional Political Economy*, 13(1), pp. 3–24.

Ordeshook P.C. (1997), "Constitutions for New Democracies: Reflections of Turmoil or Agents of Stability?", *Public Choice*, 90, pp. 53–72.

Ordeshook P.C. (1992), "Constitutional Stability", *Constitutional Political Economy*, 3, pp. 137–75.

Osiatynski W. (2003), "Paradoxes of constitutional borrowing", *International Journal of Constitutional Law*, 1(2), pp. 244–268.

Persson T., Roland G., Tabellini G. (2000), "Comparative Politics and Public Finance", *Journal of Political Economy,* 108(6), pp. 1121–1161.

Persson T., Roland G., Tabellini G. (1997), "Separation of Powers and Political Accountability", *Quarterly Journal of Economics,* 112(4), pp. 1163–1202.

Persson T., Tabellini G. (2006), "Democracy and Development: The Devil in the Details", *American Economic Review,* 96(2), pp. 319–324.

Persson T., Tabellini G. (2003), *The Economic Effects of Constitutions,* Cambridge: The MIT Press.

Persson T., Tabellini G. (2000), *Political Economics – Explaining Economic Policy,* Cambridge: The MIT Press.

Pieters H., Curzi D., Olper A., Swinnen J. (2014), *Political Reforms and Food Security,* paper presented at the 2014 International Congress of the European Association of Agricultural Economists in Ljubljana, August 26–29.

Plümper Th., Martin, Ch. (2003), "Democracy, government spending, and economic growth: A political-economic explanation of the Barro-effect", *Public Choice,* 117, pp. 27–50.

Popper K.R. (1945), *The Open Society and its Enemies,* Princeton: Princeton University Press.

Posner E. (2011), "Constitutional Possibility and Constitutional Evolution", in: Zumbansen P., Calliess G.-P. (eds.), *Law, Economics, and Evolutionary Theory,* Cheltenham: Edward Elgar, pp. 131–155.

Posner R. (1986), *Economic Analysis of Law,* 3rd ed., New York: Little, Brown and Company.

Potts J. (2007), "Evolutionary Institutional Economics", *Journal of Economic Issues,* 41(2), pp. 341–350.

Przeworski A. (1991), *Democracy and the Market: Political and Economic Reforms in Eastern Europe and Latin America,* New York: Cambridge University Press.

Radulescu R., Barlow D. (2002), "The Relationship between Policies and Growth in Transition Countries", *Economics of Transition,* 10(3), pp. 719–745.

Raiser M., Haerpfer Ch., Nowotny T., Wallace C. (2001), *Social Capital in Transition: A First Look at the Evidence,* EBRD Working Paper No. 61, European Bank for Reconstruction and Development.

Rasch B.E., Congleton R. (2006), "Constitutional Amendment Procedures", in: Congleton R. (ed.), *Democratic Constitutional Design and Public Policy – Analysis and Evidence,* Cambridge: MIT Press, pp. 319–342.

Raudla R. (2010), *Constitution, Public Finance, and Transition Theoretical Developments in Constitutional Public Finance and the Case of Estonia,* Frankfurt am Mein: Peter Lang Internationaler Verlag der Wissenschaften.

Rios-Figueroa J., Staton J.K. (2014), "An Evaluation of Cross-National Measures of Judicial Independence", *Journal of Law, Economics, and Organization*, 30(1), pp. 104–137.

Roberts A. (2009), "The politics of constitutional amendment in postcommunist Europe", *Constitutional Political Economy*, 20, pp. 99–117.

Roland G. (2002), "The Political Economy of Transition", *Journal of Economic Perspectives*, 16(1), pp. 29–50.

Roland G. (2000), *Transition and Economics. Politics, Markets, and Firm*, Cambridge, MA and London: MIT Press.

Roland G. (1994), "The Role of Political Constraints in Transition Strategies", *Economics of Transition*, 2(1), pp. 27–41.

Rosenbaum P.R. (2005), "Heterogeneity and Causality: Unit Heterogeneity and Design Sensitivity in Observational Studies", *The American Statistician*, 59(2), pp. 147–152.

Sadurski W. (2014), *Rights Before Courts – A Study of Constitutional Courts in Postcommunist States of Central and Eastern Europe*, 2nd edition, Dordrecht: Springer.

Sadurski W. (2002), "Postcommunist Charters of Rights in Europe and the US Bill of Rights", *Journal of Law and Contemporary Problems*, 65, pp. 101–127.

Sadurski W. (2001), *Postcommunist Constitutional Courts in Search of Political Legitimacy*, European University Institute Working Papers No. 2001/11, European University Institute.

Schnellenbach J., Schubert C. (2015), "Behavioral political economy: a survey", *European Journal of Political Economy*, http://dx.doi.org/10.1016/j.ejpoleco.2015.05.002.

Shleifer A., Treisman D. (2000), *Without a Map: Political Tactics and Economic Reform in Russia*, Cambridge, MA: MIT Press.

Schumpeter J.A. (1942/1987), *Capitalism, Socialism, and Democracy*, 6th edition, London: Unwin.

Sen A. (1999), *Development as Freedom*, Oxford: Oxford University Press.

Shugart M.S., Carey J.M. (1992), *Presidents and Assemblies: Constitutional Design and Electoral Dynamics*, New York: Cambridge University Press.

Smithey S., Ishiyama J. (2000), "Judicious Choices: Designing Courts in Post-Communist Politics", *Communist and Post-Communist Studies*, 33, pp. 163–182.

Stigler G.J. (1972), "Economic Competition and Political Competition", *Public Choice*, 13, pp. 91–106.

Stigler G.J. (1970), "Director's Law of Public Income Redistribution", *Journal of Law and Economics*, 13(1), pp. 1–10.

Strauss D. (1996), "Common Law Constitutional Interpretation", *University of Chicago Law Review*, 63, pp. 877–935.

Sutter M., Haigner S., Kocher M. (2010), "Choosing the Carrot or the Stick? Endogenous Institutional Choice in Social Dilemma Situations", *The Review of Economic Studies*, 77(4), pp. 1540–1566.

Tarrow S. (1995), "Bridging the Quantitative-Qualitative Divide in Political Science", *American Political Science Review*, 89(2), pp. 471–474.

Testa C. (2010), "Bicameralism and Corruption", *European Economic Review*, 54(2), pp. 181–198.

Thießen U. (2000), *Fiscal Federalism in Western European and Selected Other Countries: Centralization or Decentralization? What is Better for Economic Growth*, DIW Discussion Papers No. 224, German Institute for Economic Research (DIW Berlin).

Thießen U. (2003), "Fiscal Decentralization and Economic Growth in High Income OECD Countries", *Fiscal Studies*, 24(3), pp. 237–274.

Ticchi D., Vindigni A. (2010), "Endogenous Constitutions", *Economic Journal*, 120, pp. 1–39.

Tollison R.D. (1988), "Public Choice and Legislation", *Virginia Law Review*, 74, pp. 339–371.

Treisman D. (2014), "The political economy of change after communism", in: Aslund A., Djankov S. (eds.), *The Great Rebirth: Lessons from the Victory of Capitalism over Communism*, Washington D.C.: Peterson Institute for International Economics, pp. 273–296.

Treisman D. (2007), "What Have We Learned About the Causes of Corruption from Ten Years of Cross-National Empirical Research?", *Annual Review of Political Science*, 10, pp. 211–244.

Tsebelis G. (2002), *Veto Players: How Political Institutions Work*, Princeton: Princeton University Press.

Tsebelis G. (1995), "Decision-Making in Political Systems: Veto Players in Presidentialism, Parliamentarism, Multicameralism and Multipartyism", *British Journal of Political Science*, 25(3), pp. 289–325.

Tushnet M. (2009), "Constitutional Workarounds", *Texas Law Review*, 87, pp. 1499–1516.

Vanberg V.J. (1992), "Organizations as Constitutional Systems", *Constitutional Political Economy*, 3(2), pp. 223–253.

Van den Hauwe L. (2000), "Public Choice, Constitutional Political Economy and Law and Economics", in: Bouckaert B., De Geest G. (eds.), *Encyclopedia of Law and Economics*, Cheltenham: Edward Elgar, pp. 603–659.

Voigt S. (2011a), "Empirical Constitutional Economics: Onward and Upward?", *Journal of Economic Behavior & Organization*, 80(2), pp. 310–330.

Voigt S. (2011b), "Positive Constitutional Economics II – A Survey of Recent Developments", *Public Choice*, 146(1–2), pp. 205–256.

Voigt S. (2003), "The Consequences of Popular Participation in Constitutional Choice – Towards a Comparative Analysis", in: van Aaken A., List Ch., Lutge Ch. (eds.), *Deliberation and Decision: Economics, Constitutional Theory, and Deliberative Democracy*, Aldershot: Ashgate, pp. 199–229.

Voigt S. (1999), *Explaining Constitutional Change – A Positive Economics Approach*, Cheltenham: Edward Elgar.

Voigt S., Gutmann J., Feld L. (2015), "The Effects of Judicial Independence 10 Years on: Cross-Country Evidence Using an Updated Set of Indicators", *European Journal of Political Economy*, 38, pp. 197–211.

Voigt S., Wagener H.-J. (eds.) (2002), *Constitutions, Markets and Law: Recent Experiences in Transition Economies*, Cheltenham: Edward Elgar.

Wacziarg R., Welch K. (2008), "The Liberalization and Growth: New Evidence", *World Bank Economic Review*, 22(2), pp. 187–231.

Wagner R.E. (1987), "James M. Buchanan – Constitutional Political Economist", *Regulation: AEI Journal on Government and Society*, 1, pp. 13–17.

Weimer D.L. (ed.) (1997), *The Political Economy of Property Rights: Institutional Change and Credibility in the Reform of Centrally Planned Economies*, New York: Cambridge University Press.

Weingast B. (1997), "The Political Foundations of Democracy and the Rule of Law", *American Political Science Review*, 91, pp. 245–263.

Weingast B. (1993), "Constitutions as Governance Structures: The Political Foundations of Secure Markets", *Journal of Institutional and Theoretical Economics*, 149, pp. 286–311.

Wicksell K. (1896/1958), *Finanztheoretische Untersuchungen*, Jena: Gustav Fischer (English translation: *A new principle of just taxation*), in: Musgrave R., Peacock A.T. (eds.), *Classics in the Theory of Public Finance*, New York: St. Martin's Press, pp. 72–118.

Winiecki J. (ed.) (2001), *Institutional Barriers to Economic Development: Poland's Incomplete Transition*, London: Routledge.

Wohlgemuth M. (2002), "Evolutionary Approaches to Politics", *Kyklos*, 55(2), pp. 223–246.

World Bank (2013). *World Development Indicators 2013.* Washington, D.C.: The World Bank.

World Values Survey (1995–1998, 1999–2004), World Values Survey Association, 3rd and 4th wave, http://www.worldvaluessurvey.org.

Appendices

Appendix 1. Additional tables

Table 1: Selected empirical studies of economic effects of constitutional rules and their results

Constitutional rule/ component[a]	Dependent variable	Source	Primary result	Estimation method
Electoral rules				
Proportional representation	Labor productivity	Persson and Tabellini (2003)	+(*)	OLS (n = 74)
	Total factor productivity	Persson and Tabellini (2003)	+	OLS (n = 73)
	Government revenue	Persson and Tabellini (2003)	+	OLS (n = 76)
		Blume et al. (2009b)	+(*)	OLS (n = 78)
	Government expenditure (central)	Persson and Tabellini (2003)	+*	OLS (n = 80)
	Government expenditure (total)	Blume et al. (2009b)	+	OLS (n = 77)
	Budget deficit	Persson and Tabellini (2003)	+*	OLS (n = 60)
Size of electoral district	Labor productivity	Persson and Tabellini (2003)	-*	OLS (n = 73)
	Total factor productivity	Persson and Tabellini (2003)	-*	OLS (n = 72)
	Corruption	Persson and Tabellini (2003)	+(*)	OLS (n = 68)
Structure of power				
Form of government (results reported for the presidential variant)	Labor productivity	Persson and Tabellini (2003)	-(*)	OLS (n = 74)
		Blume et al. (2009b)	-	OLS (n = 79)
	Total factor productivity	Persson and Tabellini (2003)	-	OLS (n = 73)
		Blume et al. (2009b)	-*	OLS (n = 79)
	Government revenue	Persson and Tabellini (2003)	-*	OLS (n = 76)
		Blume et al. (2009b)	-	OLS (n = 79)

Constitutional rule/ component[a]	Dependent variable	Source	Primary result	Estimation method
Form of government (results reported for the presidential variant)	Government expenditure (central)	Persson and Tabellini (2003)	-*	OLS (n = 80)
	Government expenditure (total)	Blume et al. (2009b)	-	OLS (n = 77)
	Corruption	Persson and Tabellini (2003)	-	OLS (n = 68)
		Gerring and Thacker (2004)	+*	WLS (n = 125)
		Lederman et al. (2005)	+*	probit/OLS (n = 87–97)
Bicameralism	Government expenditure (central)	Bradbury and Crain (2001)	-*	WLS (n = 37, 1971–89)
		Plümper and Martin (2003)	-*	OLS, (n = 83, 1975–97)
	Corruption	Testa (2010)	*	panel, (n = 34, 1996–2000)
Number of veto players	Economics growth	Henisz (2000)	+*	OLS (n = 82, 1965–90) , GLS (n = 64–88, 1960–90), GMM (n = 64–71, 1965–90)
Decentralization	Goverment revenue	Feld et al. (2004)	-,*	panel, TSLS (n = 26, 80–98, Switzerland)
Decentralization (of revenues)	Economic growth	Enikolopov and Zhuravskaya (2007)	-	OLS (n = 73)
		Thießen (2000)	-*	GLS (n = 26)
			∩	panel (n = 26, 1975–95)
Decentralization (of spending)	Economic growth	Thießen (2003)	+*	GLS (n = 25)
Constitutional rights and freedoms				
Basic human rights	Accumulation of physical capital (investment)	Blume and Voigt (2007b)	+*	OLS (n = 135)

Constitutional rule/ component[a]	Dependent variable	Source	Primary result	Estimation method
Political rights	Investigated primarily under the heading 'economic effects of democracy' – see Doucouliagos and Ulubasoglu (2008) for results of a meta-analysis covering 81 earlier studies with 470 published estimates of the democracy-growth relationship, more recently e.g. Acemoglu et al. (2014b)			
Property rights	Economic growth	Blume and Voigt (2007)	+*	OLS (n = 126)
	Accumulation of physical capital (investment)	Blume and Voigt (2007)	+*	OLS (n = 135)
	Total factor productivity	Blume and Voigt (2007)	+*	OLS (n = 135)
Civil rights	Accumulation of physical capital (investment)	Blume and Voigt (2007)	+*	OLS (n = 135)
	Total factor productivity	Blume and Voigt (2007)	+*	OLS (n = 135)
Emancipatory rights	Total factor productivity	Blume and Voigt (2007)	+*	OLS (n = 135)
Judicial independence				
De facto judicial independence	Economic growth	Feld and Voigt (2003)	+*	OLS (n = 73)
De facto judicial independence	Economic growth	Voigt et al. (2015)	+*	OLS (n = 104)
Direct democracy				
Direct democracy	Budget deficit	Blume et al. (2009a)	-*	OLS (n = 45)
	Life satisfaction (happiness)	Frey and Stutzer (2006)	+*	WLS (n = 6134, Switzerland)
Mandatory referenda	State and local tax revenues	Feld and Kirchgässner (2001)	-*	panel, OLS (N = 26, 1986–97, Switzerland, fiscal)
	Government expenditure (total)	Blume et al. (2009a)	-*	OLS (n = 62)
	State and local government expenditure	Matsusaka (1995)	-*	panel, OLS (n = 49, 1960–90, US)

Constitutional rule/ component[a]	Dependent variable	Source	Primary result	Estimation method
Initiatives	State and local tax revenues	Matsusaka (1995)	-*	panel, OLS (n = 49, 1960–90, US)
	State and local government expenditure	Matsusaka (1995)	-*	panel, OLS (n = 49, 1960–90, US)
		Blume et al. (2009a)	+*	OLS (n = 62)
	Corruption	Alt and Lassen (2003)	-*	OLS (n = 45, US)
Fiscal referenda	Total factor productivity	Feld and Savioz (1997)	+*	GLS (n = 26, Switzerland)
Other rules (examples)				
Constitutional deficit rule	Government expenditures (total)	Blume and Voigt (2013)	-*	OLS (n = 47)
Supreme audit institutions (court model of auditing)	(Perceived) corruption	Blume and Voigt (2011)	+*	OLS (n = 35)
Central bank independence	Investigated primarily for effects on inflation – see de Haan and Klomp (2010) for results of a meta-analysis covering 59 earlier studies (confirming a significant genuine effect on inflation), more recently (with account for transparency) e.g. Dincer and Eichengreen (2014); on a negative effect on financial instability Klomp and de Haan (2009)			

Notes: [a] Constitutional rules as defined broadly in Section 1.1, in some (infrequent) cases specified by a country within ordinary legislation. +/- reports the sign of the estimated coefficient in the regression, * denotes significance, (*) – low significance.

Source: Own elaboration on the basis of Voigt (2011b; Tab. 2) and sources mentioned in the table.

Table 3: Systems of government in post-socialist countries

Country	Constitution adoption year	Cheibub (2007)	Metelska-Szaniawska (2009)	Norris (2009)	DPI (2013)	Cheibub et al. (2013)
Albania	1998	parliamentary	parliamentary	mixed executive	parliamentary	parliamentary
Armenia	1995	mixed (semi–presidential)	presidential	mixed executive	presidential	semi–presidential
Azerbaijan	1991	–	presidential	mixed executive	presidential	presidential
Belarus	1994	–	authoritarian presidential; (semi–) presidential; presidential–parliamentary	mixed executive	presidential	semi–presidential
Bosnia and Hercegovina	1995	–	–	mixed executive	parliamentary	semi–presidential
Bulgaria	1991	mixed (semi–presidential)	parliamentary	mixed executive	assembly–elected president[a]	semi–presidential
Croatia	1991	mixed (semi–presidential)	semi–presidential; parliamentary with a strong presidential component	mixed executive	presidential[b]	semi–presidential
Czech Rep.	1993	parliamentary	(pure) parliamentary	mixed executive	parliamentary	parliamentary
Estonia	1992	parliamentary	parliamentary	mixed executive	assembly–elected president	parliamentary
Georgia	1995	–	presidential	presidential republic	presidential	presidential
Hungary	1949	–	pure parliamentary	–	parliamentary	parliamentary
Kazakhstan	1995	–	close to presidential	mixed executive	presidential	semi–presidential

Country	Constitution adoption year	Cheibub (2007)	Metelska-Szaniawska (2009)	Norris (2009)	DPI (2013)	Cheibub et al. (2013)
Kyrgyzstan	1993	–	presidential–parliamentary	mixed executive	presidential	semi–presidential
Latvia	1922	–	parliamentary (rationalized)	–	parliamentary	parliamentary
Lithuania	1992	mixed (semi–presidential)	parliamentary–presidential; parliamentary with elements of presidentialism; parliamentary	mixed executive	presidential	semi–presidential
Macedonia	1991	mixed (semi–presidential)	parliamentary	mixed executive	parliamentary	semi–presidential
Moldova	1994	–	parliamentary	mixed executive	presidential[c]	semi–presidential
Montenegro	1992	–	–	–	–	semi–presidential
Poland	1992	mixed (semi–presidential)	–	mixed executive	presidential	semi–presidential
	1997	mixed (semi–presidential)	parliamentary (rationalized)	mixed executive	presidential	semi–presidential
Romania	1991	mixed (semi–presidential)	semi–presidential; close to semi–presidential; parliamentary with elements of semi–presidentialism; parliamentary	mixed executive	parliamentary	semi–presidential
Russia	1993	mixed (semi–presidential)	presidential–parliamentary; close to semi–presidential	–	presidential	semi–presidential

Country	Constitution adoption year	Cheibub (2007)	Metelska-Szaniawska (2009)	Norris (2009)	DPI (2013)	Cheibub et al. (2013)
Serbia	1992	–	–	–	–	semi–presidential
	2003	–	–	mixed executive	–	parliamentary
	2006	–	–	–	–	semi–presidential
Slovakia	1992	parliamentary	(pure) parliamentary	–	parliamentary	semi–presidential
Slovenia	1991	mixed (semi–presidential)	parliamentary (rationalized)	mixed executive	parliamentary	semi–presidential
Tajikistan	1994	–	–	mixed executive	presidential	presidential
Turkmeni-stan	1992	–	authoritarian presidential	mixed executive	presidential	presidential
Ukraine	1996	mixed (semi–presidential)	presidential–parliamentary; parliamen-tary–presidential	mixed executive	presidential	semi–presidential
Uzbekistan	1992	–	authoritarian presidential	mixed executive	presidential	presidential

Notes: [a] from 2002 parliamentary; [b] from 2001 parliamentary; [c] from 2001 assembly-elected president.
Source: Own elaboration on the basis of the sources mentioned in the table.

Table 6: De facto protection of rights and freedoms in post-socialist constitutions

Country	GP	NP	Constitutional underperformance						Constitutional overperformance						Constitution type
			FU	PU	Personal integrity rights	Civil and political freedoms	Socioeconomic and group rights	Overall score	FU	PU	Personal integrity rights	Civil and political freedoms	Socioeconomic and group rights	Overall score	
Albania	12	12	6	6	0.750	0.800	0.667	0.750	1	0	1.000	–	0.000	0.333	strong
Armenia	14	13	6	2	0.600	0.400	0.667	0.538	0	0	–	–	0.000	0.000	strong
Azerbaijan	13	13	4	4	0.500	0.300	0.625	0.462	1	0	1.000	–	0.000	0.500	sham
Belarus	14	14	3	5	0.375	0.200	0.600	0.393	0	0	0.000	–	–	0.000	sham
Bosnia and Herzegovina	7	6	3	2	0.500	0.750	–	0.667	5	1	0.833	–	0.750	0.786	modest
Bulgaria	12	12	6	6	0.625	0.800	0.833	0.750	3	0	1.000	–	1.000	1.000	strong
Croatia	13	13	7	5	0.800	0.700	0.667	0.731	0	1	–	–	0.250	0.250	strong
Czech Rep.	13	13	12	1	1.000	0.900	1.000	0.962	0	1	–	–	0.250	0.250	strong
Estonia	13	13	11	2	0.875	1.000	0.875	0.923	1	1	1.000	–	0.500	0.750	strong
Georgia	12	12	4	6	0.375	0.700	0.667	0.583	2	0	1.000	–	0.500	0.667	strong
Hungary	12	12	9	2	0.750	0.900	0.833	0.833	1	0	1.000	–	0.000	0.333	strong
Kazakhstan	6	6	3	0	1.000	0.250	1.000	0.500	0	4	0.375	0.000	0.125	0.222	weak
Kyrgyzstan	12	12	4	5	0.600	0.400	0.750	0.542	1	0	–	–	0.333	0.333	strong
Latvia	10	10	6	4	0.833	0.700	1.000	0.800	1	3	0.750	–	0.333	0.500	strong
Lithuania	13	13	8	5	0.875	0.700	0.875	0.808	1	1	1.000	–	0.500	0.750	strong
Macedonia	13	13	8	5	0.900	0.800	0.667	0.808	0	1	–	–	0.250	0.250	strong
Moldova	13	12	6	4	0.700	0.600	0.750	0.667	1	1	–	–	0.750	0.750	strong
Poland	13	12	9	2	0.875	0.900	0.667	0.833	1	1	1.000	–	0.500	0.750	strong
Romania	15	15	6	6	0.700	0.500	0.600	0.600	–	–	–	–	–	–	strong

Country	GP	NP	Constitutional underperformance						Constitutional overperformance						Constitution type
			FU	PU	Personal integrity rights	Civil and political freedoms	Socioeconomic and group rights	Overall score	FU	PU	Personal integrity rights	Civil and political freedoms	Socioeconomic and group rights	Overall score	
Russia	12	12	2	2	0.125	0.000	0.833	0.250	1	0	1.000	–	0.000	0.333	sham
Slovakia	13	13	10	3	0.900	0.800	1.000	0.885	0	1	–	–	0.250	0.250	strong
Slovenia	14	13	12	1	0.900	1.000	1.000	0.962	0	1	–	–	0.500	0.500	strong
Tajikistan	12	12	3	3	0.500	0.200	0.500	0.375	1	0	1.000	–	0.000	0.333	sham
Turkmenistan	13	13	4	2	0.700	0.000	0.500	0.385	0	0	–	–	0.000	0.000	sham
Ukraine	14	14	5	6	0.500	0.700	0.500	0.571	1	0	1.000	–	–	1.000	strong
Uzbekistan	13	13	3	2	0.625	0.000	0.325	0.308	1	0	1.000	–	0.000	0.500	sham

Notes: GP – gross number of rights promised in the constitution; NP – net number of rights promised for which *de facto* performance data is available; FU – number of rights in the constitution (or in case of overperformance – omitted from the constitution) that were fully upheld; PU – number of rights in the constitution (or in case of overperformance – omitted from the constitution) that were partially upheld.

Source: Own elaboration on the basis of Law and Versteeg (2013, appendices II and III).

Appendix 2. Additional figures

Figure 3: Baseline synthetic control estimates for subsequent post-socialist countries

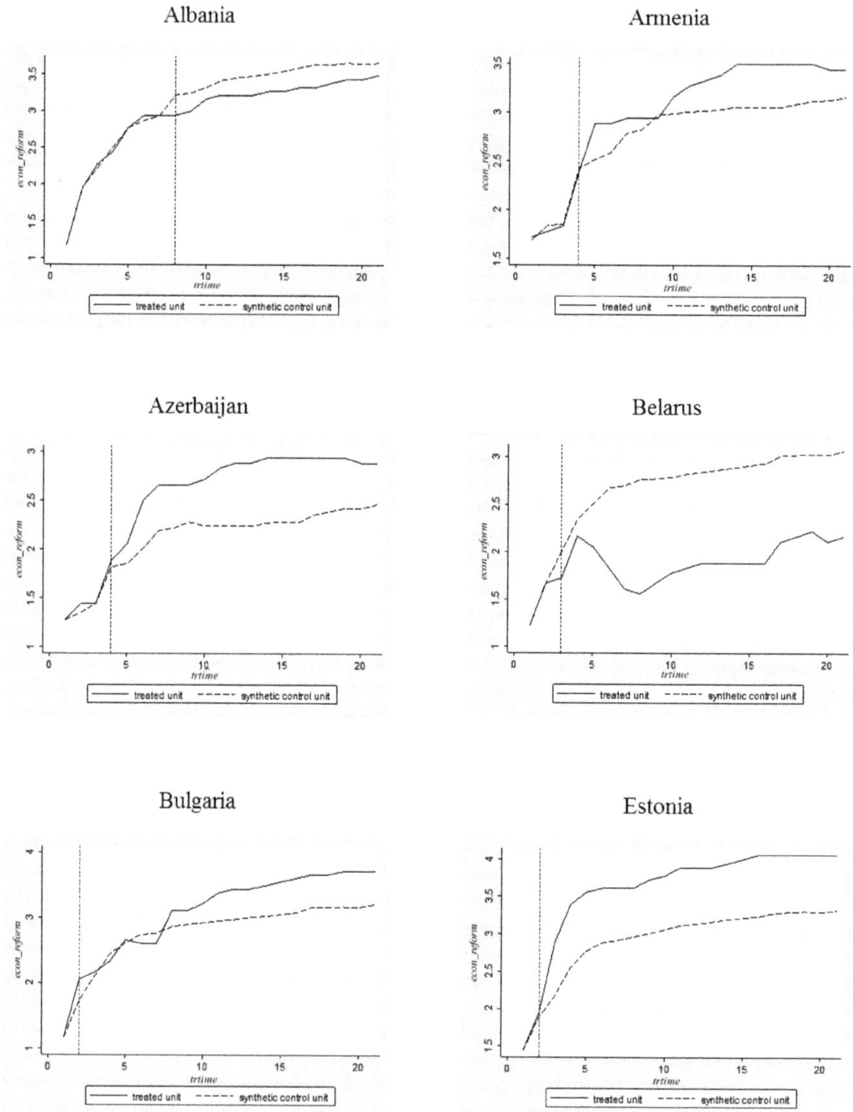

Source: Author's calculations and graphs.

Figure 3: Baseline synthetic control estimates for subsequent post-socialist countries (contd.)

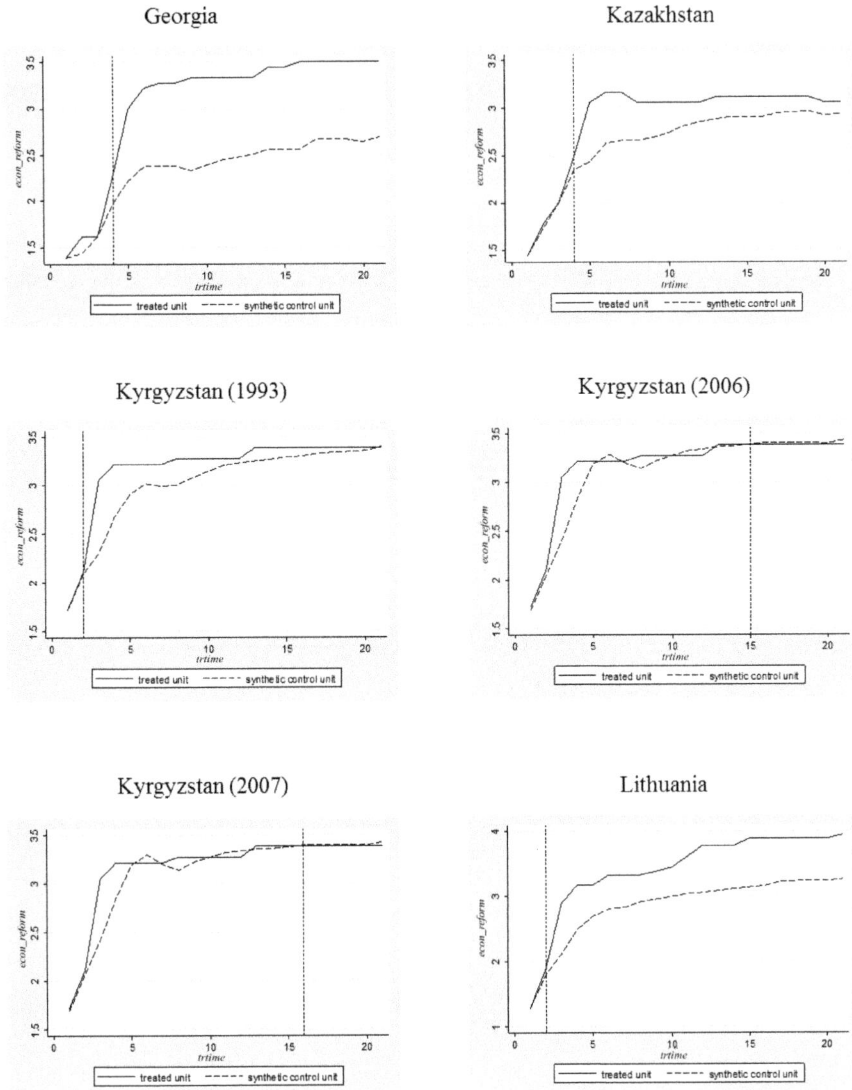

Source: Author's calculations and graphs.

Figure 3: Baseline synthetic control estimates for subsequent post-socialist countries (contd.)

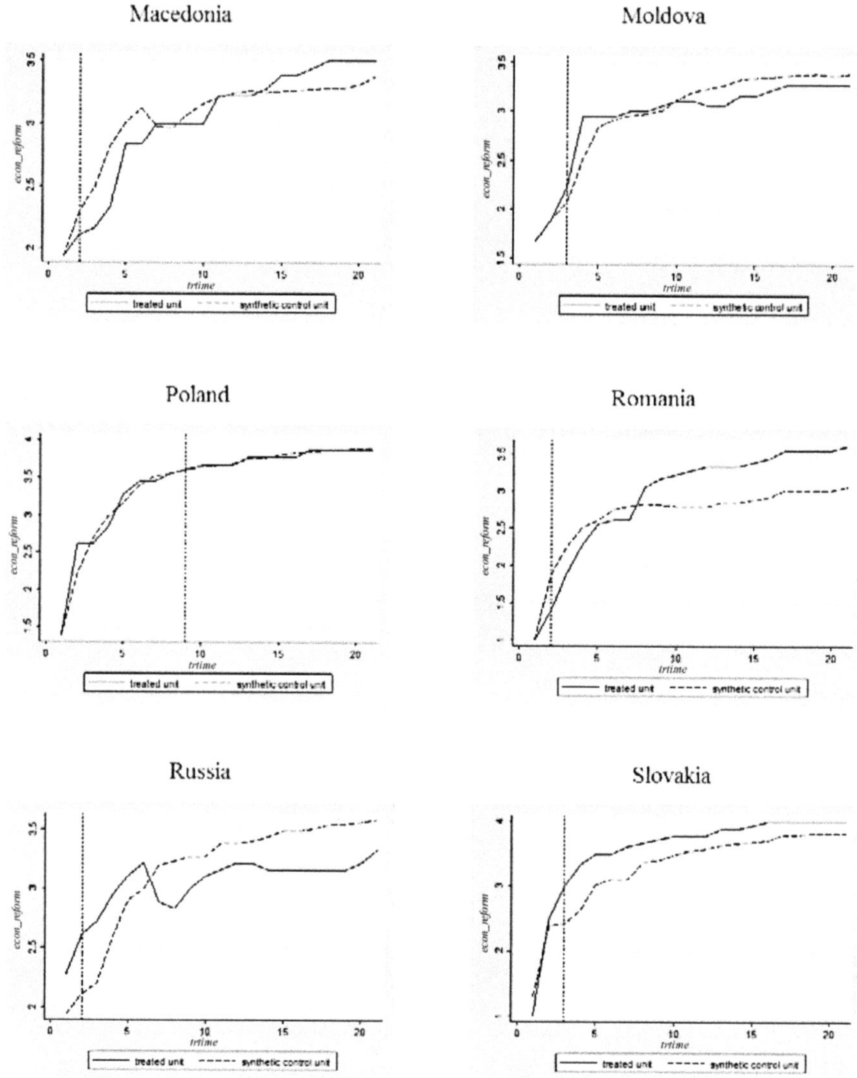

Figure 3: Baseline synthetic control estimates for subsequent post-socialist countries (contd.)

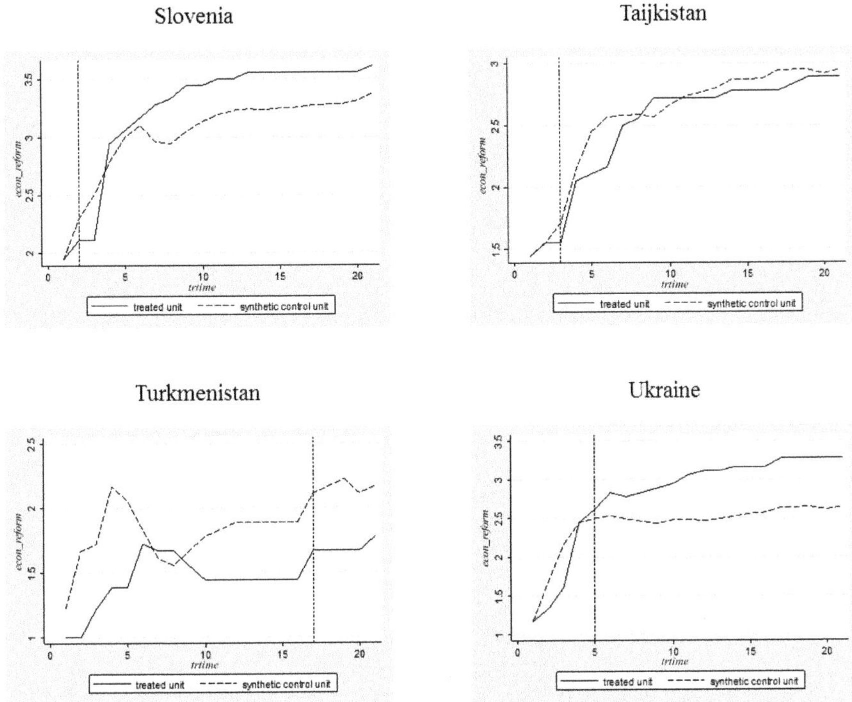

Source: Author's calculations and graphs.

Figure 4: Placebo tests results for subsequent post-socialist countries

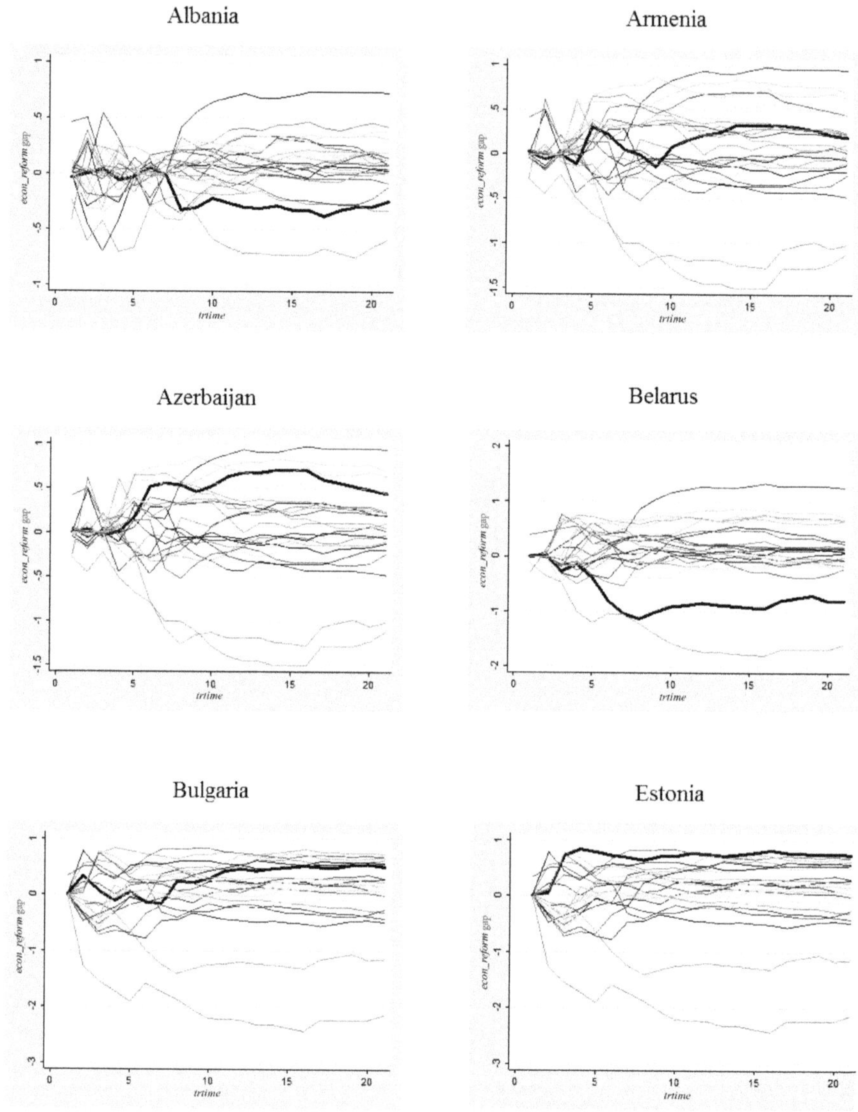

Source: Author's calculations and graphs.

Figure 4: Placebo tests results for subsequent post-socialist countries (contd.)

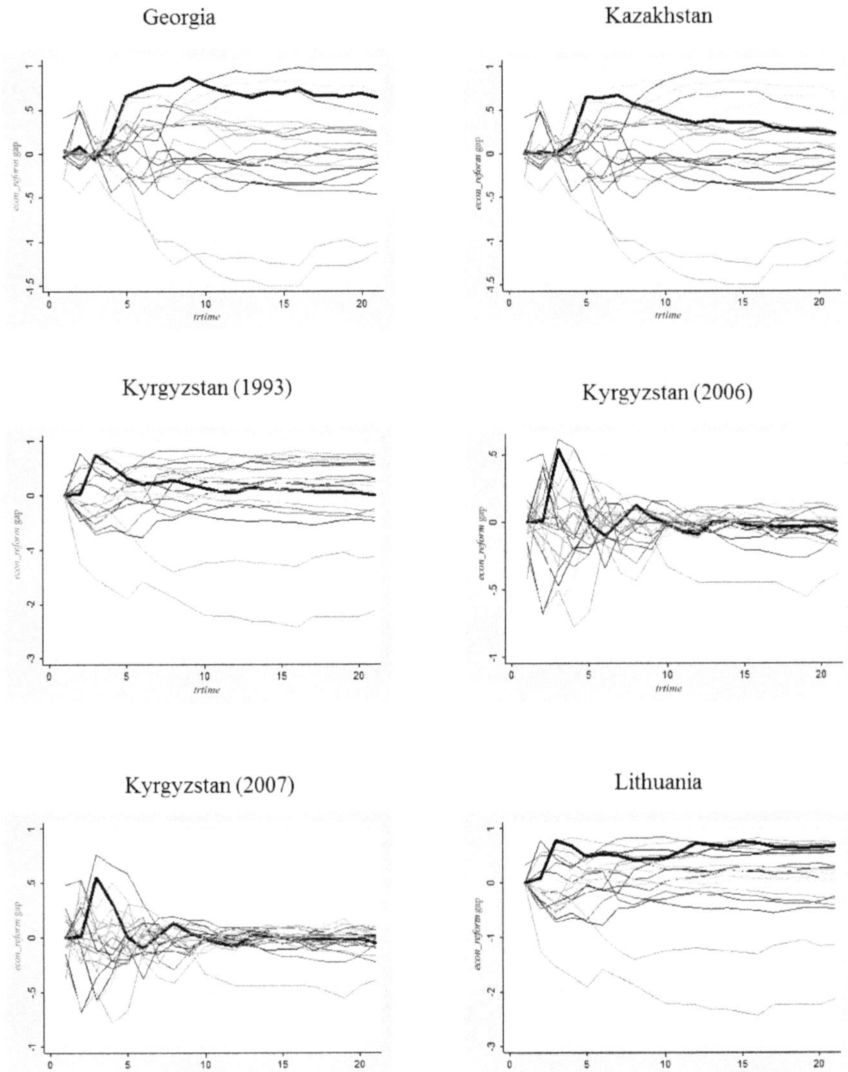

Source: Author's calculations and graphs.

Figure 4: Placebo tests results for subsequent post-socialist countries (contd.)

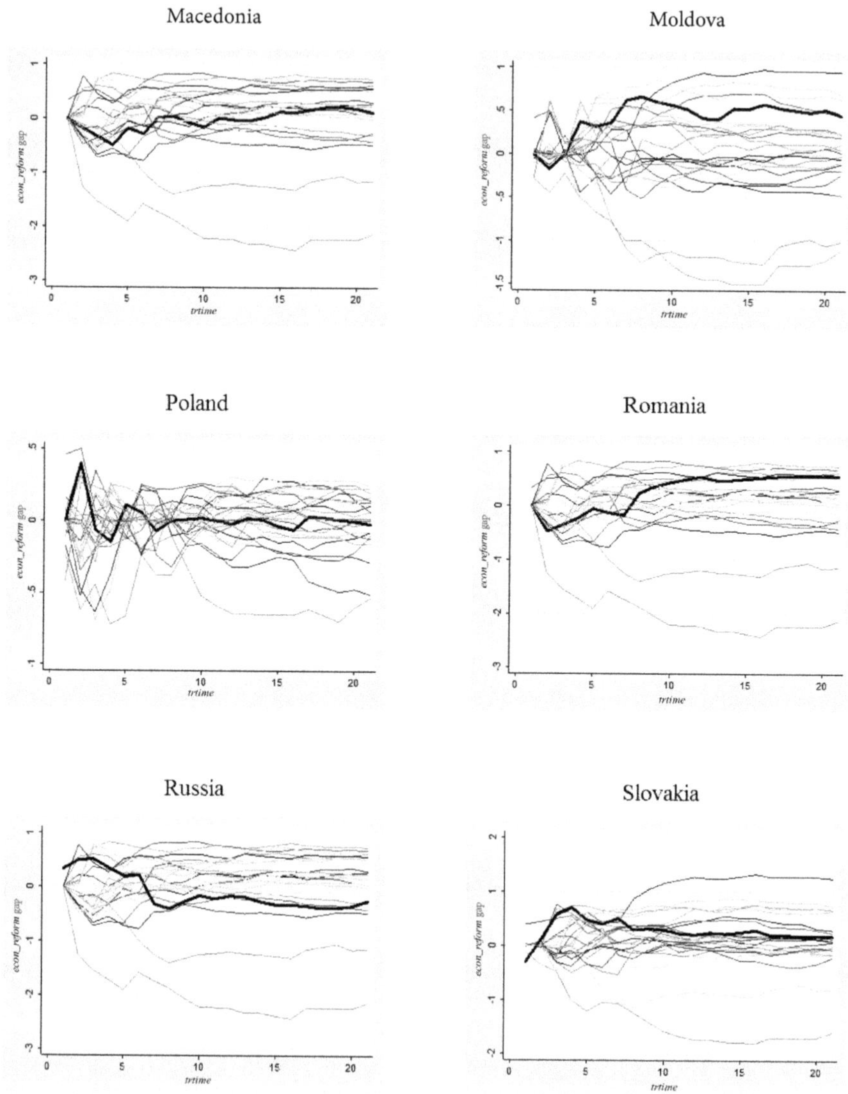

Source: Author's calculations and graphs.

Figure 4: Placebo tests results for subsequent post-socialist countries (contd.)

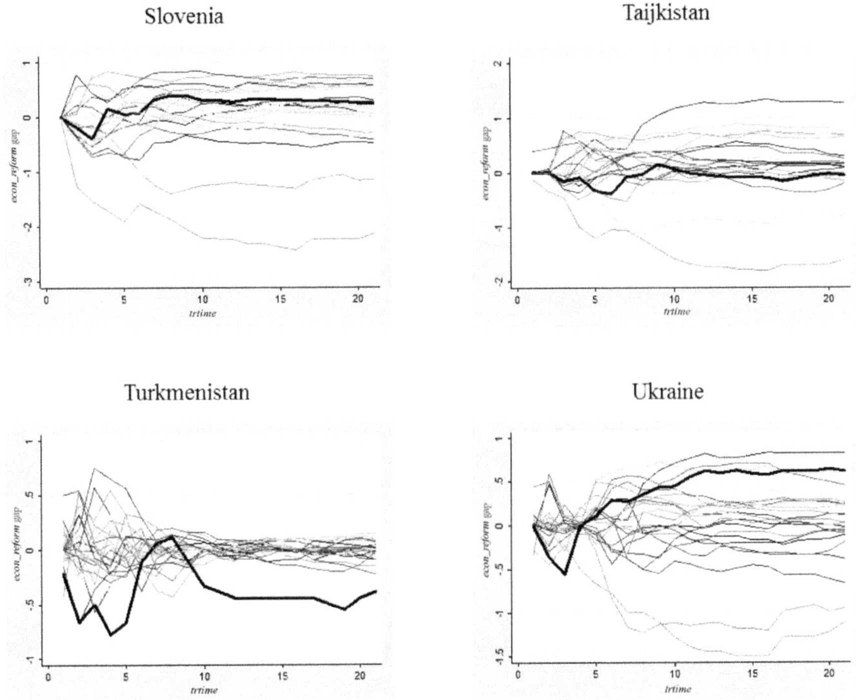

Source: Author's calculations and graphs.

Appendix 3. Description of variables and data sources

Variable name	Description	Data source
CA	Dummy variable for Central Asian countries	-
CCI_defacto	*De facto* constitutional court independence indicator	Voigt et al. (2015)
CCI_deiure	Formal constitutional court independence indicator	Voigt et al. (2015)
concentration	Concentration of state power index reflecting the extent to which a single political actor is capable of decisively influencing state policy	Author's calculations based on Henisz (2013)
DD	A cumulative measure of the number of conducted popular votes (direct democracy)	Author's calculations based on C2D (1989–2012)
econ_reform	Aggregate transition indicator (index of economic reforms) constituting an average of a set of six indicators of structural economic reforms	Author's calculations based on EBRD (1994–2013)
elections	An indicator reflecting the result of the initial post-socialist elections in a country (including some aspects of their organization)	Fish (1998)
EU	Dummy variable for EU membership / EU applicant (depending on specification)	-
fiscal	Share of the general government fiscal balance in GDP (in %)	EBRD (1994–2013)
FSU	Dummy variable for former Soviet Union countries (excluding the Baltic republics)	-
growth	Annual GDP growth rate (in %)	World Bank (2013)
IC	Initial conditions index calculated from the first principal component of a factor analysis over 11 indicators	Author's calculations based on Falcetti et al. (2002)
polsystemrate	A measure of how the society rates the political system operative in the country (proxy for popular support for the constitution)	Author's calculations based on World Values Survey (1996/97, 1999–2002)
recovery	Dummy variable taking the value of 1 if real output is less than 70% of its value in 1990, and 0 – otherwise	Author's calculations based on World Bank (2013)

rights	Constitutional rights indicator reflecting the operative political rights and civil liberties	Author's calculations based on Freedom House (1990–2013)
trtime	Transition time beginning in 1989 for Poland and Hungary, 1990 – for other Central and Southeastern European countries (except Albania), 1991 – for Albania and the Baltic republics, and 1992 – for remaining former Soviet republics	-
trust	A measure of trust between individuals and in their relation with political institutions of the state (a proxy for civil society and the informal institutional framework within the state)	Author's calculations based on World Values Survey (1994–1999)

Appendix 4. Unit weights and predictor balance for the synthetic control study

Tables in this appendix accompany Figure 3. For each country we report:

a) the weights for the countries from the donor pool computed for the country's synthetic counterfactual,
b) the predictor balance, i.e. for each predictor used for constructing the counterfactual (except lagged dependent variables, which we do not report for the sake of clarity): the pre-treatment average for the treated country and the pre-treatment average for the synthetic country (for explanation of variable names see Appendix 3),
c) the root mean squared prediction error (RMSPE).

Country name: Albania

donor pool country name	unit weight
Armenia	0
Azerbeijan	0.158
Belarus	0
Bulgaria	0.416
Croatia	0
Estonia	0
Georgia	0
Hungary	0.127
Kazakhstan	0
Kyrgyzstan	0
Latvia	0
Lithuania	0
Macedonia	0
Moldova	0
Poland	0
Romania	0.118
Russia	0
Slovakia	0
Slovenia	0.181
Tajikistan	0
Turkmenistan	0
Ukraine	0
Uzbekistan	0

Country name: Armenia

donor pool country name	unit weight
Albania	0
Azerbeijan	0
Belarus	0
Bulgaria	0
Croatia	0
Estonia	0
Georgia	0
Hungary	0
Kazakhstan	0
Kyrgyzstan	0
Latvia	0
Lithuania	0
Macedonia	0
Moldova	0
Poland	0
Romania	0
Russia	0.105
Slovakia	0.313
Slovenia	0
Tajikistan	0.581
Turkmenistan	0
Ukraine	0
Uzbekistan	0

variable name	predictor balance	
	treated	synthetic
IC × trtime	8.400	6.050
IC × trtime^2	42.000	30.252
elections	3.000	3.142
RMSPE	0.042	

variable name	predictor balance	
	treated	synthetic
IC × trtime	−2.200	−1.600
IC × trtime^2	−5.133	−3.733
elections	4.000	2.257
RMSPE	0.042	

Country name: Azerbaijan

donor pool country name	unit weight
Albania	0
Armenia	0
Belarus	0
Bulgaria	0
Croatia	0
Estonia	0
Georgia	0
Hungary	0
Kazakhstan	0
Kyrgyzstan	0
Latvia	0
Lithuania	0
Macedonia	0
Moldova	0
Poland	0
Romania	0
Russia	0
Slovakia	0
Slovenia	0
Tajikistan	0.614
Turkmenistan	0.368
Ukraine	0
Uzbekistan	0.018

variable name	predictor balance	
	treated	synthetic
IC × trtime	-6.400	-6.164
IC × trtime^2	−14.933	−14.384
elections	0	1
RMSPE	0.054	

Country name: Belarus

donor pool country name	unit weight
Albania	0.039
Armenia	0.021
Azerbeijan	0.037
Bulgaria	0.037
Croatia	0.015
Estonia	0.027
Georgia	0.031
Hungary	0.026
Kazakhstan	0.028
Kyrgyzstan	0.019
Latvia	0.027
Lithuania	0.033
Macedonia	0.015
Moldova	0.021
Poland	0.021
Romania	0.084
Russia	0.008
Slovakia	0.015
Slovenia	0.119
Tajikistan	0.029
Turkmenistan	0.267
Ukraine	0.046
Uzbekistan	0.036

variable name	predictor balance	
	treated	synthetic
IC × trtime	-1.650	-0.9486
IC × trtime^2	-2.750	-1.581
elections	0	2.7
RMSPE	3.05×10^{-12}	

Country name: Bulgaria

donor pool country name	unit weight
Albania	0.032
Armenia	0.014
Azerbeijan	0.026
Belarus	0.028
Croatia	0.010
Estonia	0.021
Georgia	0.022
Hungary	0.021
Kazakhstan	0.021
Kyrgyzstan	0.014
Latvia	0.026
Lithuania	0.026
Macedonia	0.010
Moldova	0.015
Poland	0.022
Romania	0.199
Russia	0.006
Slovakia	0.010
Slovenia	0.199
Tajikistan	0.021
Turkmenistan	0.199
Ukraine	0.032
Uzbekistan	0.026

variable name	predictor balance	
	treated	synthetic
IC × *trtime*	2.100	0.021
IC × *trtime*^{2}	2.100	0.021
elections	3.000	1.167
RMSPE	1.31×10^{-12}	

Country name: Estonia

donor pool country name	unit weight
Albania	0.044
Armenia	0.040
Azerbeijan	0.038
Belarus	0.040
Bulgaria	0.045
Croatia	0.043
Georgia	0.039
Hungary	0.043
Kazakhstan	0.041
Kyrgyzstan	0.044
Latvia	0.050
Lithuania	0.043
Macedonia	0.043
Moldova	0.041
Poland	0.064
Romania	0.038
Russia	0.051
Slovakia	0.043
Slovenia	0.062
Tajikistan	0.038
Turkmenistan	0.035
Ukraine	0.037
Uzbekistan	0.039

variable name	predictor balance	
	treated	synthetic
IC × *trtime*	−0.600	0.070
IC × *trtime*^{2}	−1.000	0.117
elections	5.000	3.172
RMSPE	1.86×10^{-13}	

Country name: Georgia

donor pool country name	unit weight
Albania	0
Armenia	0.494
Azerbeijan	0
Belarus	0
Bulgaria	0
Croatia	0
Estonia	0.012
Hungary	0
Kazakhstan	0
Kyrgyzstan	0.037
Latvia	0
Lithuania	0
Macedonia	0
Moldova	0
Poland	0
Romania	0
Russia	0
Slovakia	0
Slovenia	0
Tajikistan	0
Turkmenistan	0.457
Ukraine	0
Uzbekistan	0

variable name	predictor balance	
	treated	synthetic
IC × trtime	−4.400	−4.374
IC × trtime^2	−10.267	−10.206
elections	3	2.604
RMSPE	0.101	

Country name: Kazakhstan

donor pool country name	unit weight
Albania	0
Armenia	0
Azerbeijan	0.51
Belarus	0.162
Bulgaria	0
Croatia	0
Estonia	0
Georgia	0
Hungary	0
Kyrgyzstan	0.273
Latvia	0
Lithuania	0
Macedonia	0
Moldova	0
Poland	0
Romania	0
Russia	0.055
Slovakia	0
Slovenia	0
Tajikistan	0
Turkmenistan	0
Ukraine	0
Uzbekistan	0

variable name	predictor balance	
	treated	synthetic
IC × trtime	−5.000	−4.997
IC × trtime^2	−11.667	−11.660
elections	1.000	1.039
RMSPE	0.030	

Country name: Kyrgyzstan (1993)

donor pool country name	unit weight
Albania	0.022
Armenia	0.050
Azerbeijan	0.026
Belarus	0.024
Bulgaria	0.022
Croatia	0.067
Estonia	0.034
Georgia	0.031
Hungary	0.034
Kazakhstan	0.034
Latvia	0.026
Lithuania	0.026
Macedonia	0.067
Moldova	0.047
Poland	0.031
Romania	0.016
Russia	0.262
Slovakia	0.067
Slovenia	0.016
Tajikistan	0.034
Turkmenistan	0.016
Ukraine	0.022
Uzbekistan	0.026

variable name	predictor balance	
	treated	synthetic
IC × *trtime*	-2.300	-0.047
IC × *trtime*^{2}	-2.300	-0.047
elections	3.000	3.475
RMSPE	1.31×10^{-14}	

Country name: Kyrgyzstan (2006)

donor pool country name	unit weight
Albania	0
Armenia	0.034
Azerbeijan	0
Belarus	0
Bulgaria	0
Croatia	0
Estonia	0.260
Georgia	0.055
Hungary	0
Kazakhstan	0.368
Latvia	0
Lithuania	0
Macedonia	0
Moldova	0
Poland	0
Romania	0
Russia	0.283
Slovakia	0
Slovenia	0
Tajikistan	0
Turkmenistan	0
Ukraine	0
Uzbekistan	0

variable name	predictor balance	
	treated	synthetic
IC × *trtime*	−17.250	−11.203
IC × *trtime*^{2}	−166.75	−108.293
elections	3.000	3.101
RMSPE	0.207	

Country name: Kyrgyzstan (2007)

donor pool country name	unit weight
Albania	0
Armenia	0
Azerbeijan	0
Belarus	0
Bulgaria	0
Croatia	0
Estonia	0.261
Georgia	0.057
Hungary	0
Kazakhstan	0.378
Latvia	0
Lithuania	0
Macedonia	0
Moldova	0
Poland	0
Romania	0
Russia	0.304
Slovakia	0
Slovenia	0
Tajikistan	0
Turkmenistan	0
Ukraine	0
Uzbekistan	0

variable name	predictor balance	
	treated	synthetic
IC × trtime	−18.400	−12.074
IC × trtime^2	−190.133	−124.761
elections	3.000	3.070
RMSPE	0.194	

Country name: Lithuania

donor pool country name	unit weight
Albania	0.046
Armenia	0.025
Azerbeijan	0.040
Belarus	0.042
Bulgaria	0.046
Croatia	0.020
Estonia	0.033
Georgia	0.035
Hungary	0.033
Kazakhstan	0.033
Kyrgyzstan	0.025
Latvia	0.040
Macedonia	0.020
Moldova	0.027
Poland	0.035
Romania	0.116
Russia	0.013
Slovakia	0.020
Slovenia	0.116
Tajikistan	0.033
Turkmenistan	0.116
Ukraine	0.046
Uzbekistan	0.040

variable name	predictor balance	
	treated	synthetic
IC × trtime	0.000	−0.084
IC × trtime^2	0.000	−0.084
elections	5.000	2.869
RMSPE	2.38×10^{-14}	

Country name: Macedonia

donor pool country name	unit weight
Albania	0.011
Armenia	0.036
Azerbeijan	0.015
Belarus	0.013
Bulgaria	0.011
Croatia	0.054
Estonia	0.021
Georgia	0.019
Hungary	0.021
Kazakhstan	0.021
Kyrgyzstan	0.036
Latvia	0.015
Lithuania	0.015
Moldova	0.033
Poland	0.019
Romania	0.006
Russia	0.541
Slovakia	0.054
Slovenia	0.006
Tajikistan	0.021
Turkmenistan	0.006
Ukraine	0.011
Uzbekistan	0.015

variable name	predictor balance	
	treated	synthetic
IC × trtime	2.500	−0.574
IC × trtime²	2.500	−0.574
elections	4.000	3.679
RMSPE	1.10×10^{-12}	

Country name: Moldova

donor pool country name	unit weight
Albania	0.013
Armenia	0.403
Azerbeijan	0.025
Belarus	0.019
Bulgaria	0.012
Croatia	0.058
Estonia	0.021
Georgia	0.026
Hungary	0.019
Kazakhstan	0.024
Kyrgyzstan	0.028
Latvia	0.011
Lithuania	0.017
Macedonia	0.058
Poland	0.010
Romania	0.016
Russia	0.081
Slovakia	0.058
Slovenia	0.007
Tajikistan	0.030
Turkmenistan	0.021
Ukraine	0.022
Uzbekistan	0.021

variable name	predictor balance	
	treated	synthetic
IC × trtime	−1.650	−0.624
IC × trtime²	−2.750	−1.041
elections	2.000	3.540
RMSPE	1.31×10^{-13}	

Country name: Poland

donor pool country name	unit weight
Albania	0
Armenia	0
Azerbeijan	0
Belarus	0
Bulgaria	0
Croatia	0.183
Estonia	0.024
Georgia	0
Hungary	0.266
Kazakhstan	0
Kyrgyzstan	0
Latvia	0.270
Lithuania	0.040
Macedonia	0
Moldova	0
Romania	0
Russia	0
Slovakia	0
Slovenia	0.217
Tajikistan	0
Turkmenistan	0
Ukraine	0
Uzbekistan	0

variable name	predictor balance	
	treated	synthetic
IC × trtime	8.550	8.555
IC × trtime^2	48.450	48.476
elections	5.000	5.000
RMSPE	0.160	

Country name: Romania

donor pool country name	unit weight
Albania	0
Armenia	0
Azerbeijan	0
Belarus	0
Bulgaria	0
Croatia	0
Estonia	0
Georgia	0
Hungary	0
Kazakhstan	0
Kyrgyzstan	0
Latvia	0
Lithuania	0
Macedonia	0
Moldova	0
Poland	0
Russia	0
Slovakia	0
Slovenia	0.578
Tajikistan	0
Turkmenistan	0.422
Ukraine	0
Uzbekistan	0

variable name	predictor balance	
	treated	synthetic
IC × trtime	1.700	0.241
IC × trtime^2	1.700	0.241
elections	3.000	3.312
RMSPE	5.56×10^{-7}	

Country name: Russia

donor pool country name	unit weight
Albania	0
Armenia	0
Azerbeijan	0
Belarus	0
Bulgaria	0
Croatia	0.333
Estonia	0
Georgia	0
Hungary	0
Kazakhstan	0
Kyrgyzstan	0
Latvia	0
Lithuania	0
Macedonia	0.333
Moldova	0
Poland	0
Romania	0
Slovakia	0.333
Slovenia	0
Tajikistan	0
Turkmenistan	0
Ukraine	0
Uzbekistan	0

variable name	predictor balance	
	treated	synthetic
IC × *trtime*	–1.100	2.731
IC × *trtime*^{2}	–1.100	2.731
elections	4.000	4.329
RMSPE	0.333	

Country name: Slovakia

donor pool country name	unit weight
Albania	0
Armenia	0
Azerbeijan	0
Belarus	0
Bulgaria	0.413
Croatia	0
Estonia	0
Georgia	0
Hungary	0
Kazakhstan	0
Kyrgyzstan	0
Latvia	0
Lithuania	0
Macedonia	0
Moldova	0
Poland	0.587
Romania	0
Russia	0
Slovenia	0
Tajikistan	0
Turkmenistan	0
Ukraine	0
Uzbekistan	0

variable name	predictor balance	
	treated	synthetic
IC × *trtime*	4.350	2.974
IC × *trtime*^{2}	7.250	4.957
elections	5.000	4.174
RMSPE	0.226	

Country name: Slovenia

donor pool country name	unit weight
Albania	0.011
Armenia	0.036
Azerbeijan	0.015
Belarus	0.013
Bulgaria	0.011
Croatia	0.054
Estonia	0.021
Georgia	0.019
Hungary	0.021
Kazakhstan	0.021
Kyrgyzstan	0.036
Latvia	0.015
Lithuania	0.015
Macedonia	0.054
Moldova	0.033
Poland	0.019
Romania	0.006
Russia	0.541
Slovakia	0.006
Tajikistan	0.021
Turkmenistan	0.006
Ukraine	0.011
Uzbekistan	0.015

variable name	predictor balance	
	treated	synthetic
IC × trtime	3.200	-6.113
IC × trtime^2	3.200	-6.113
elections	4.000	3.679
RMSPE	1.10×10^{-12}	

Country name: Tajikistan

donor pool country name	unit weight
Albania	0.008
Armenia	0.525
Azerbeijan	0.024
Belarus	0.012
Bulgaria	0.006
Croatia	0
Estonia	0.010
Georgia	0.019
Hungary	0.009
Kazakhstan	0.014
Kyrgyzstan	0.010
Latvia	0.005
Lithuania	0.009
Macedonia	0
Moldova	0.014
Poland	0.003
Romania	0.012
Russia	0.001
Slovakia	0
Slovenia	0.003
Turkmenistan	0.276
Ukraine	0.024
Uzbekistan	0.015

variable name	predictor balance	
	treated	synthetic
IC × trtime	–4.350	–2.563
IC × trtime^2	–7.250	–4.272
elections	1.000	2.845
RMSPE	3.49×10^{-13}	

Country name: Turkmenistan

donor pool country name	unit weight
Albania	0
Armenia	0
Azerbeijan	0
Belarus	1
Bulgaria	0
Croatia	0
Estonia	0
Georgia	0
Hungary	0
Kazakhstan	0
Kyrgyzstan	0
Latvia	0
Lithuania	0
Macedonia	0
Moldova	0
Poland	0
Romania	0
Russia	0
Slovakia	0
Slovenia	0
Tajikistan	0
Ukraine	0
Uzbekistan	0

variable name	predictor balance	
	treated	synthetic
IC × *trtime*	−28.900	−9.350
IC × *trtime*^{2}	−317.900	−102.850
elections	1.000	0.000
RMSPE	0.439	

Country name: Ukraine

donor pool country name	unit weight
Albania	0.008
Armenia	0.003
Azerbeijan	0.007
Belarus	0.044
Bulgaria	0.007
Croatia	0.002
Estonia	0.005
Georgia	0.006
Hungary	0.004
Kazakhstan	0.006
Kyrgyzstan	0.004
Latvia	0.006
Lithuania	0.007
Macedonia	0.002
Moldova	0.004
Poland	0.005
Romania	0.010
Russia	0.002
Slovakia	0.002
Slovenia	0.208
Tajikistan	0.006
Turkmenistan	0.223
Uzbekistan	0.429

variable name	predictor balance	
	treated	synthetic
IC × *trtime*	−3.500	−3.518
IC × *trtime*^{2}	−10.500	−10.555
elections	2	1.998
RMSPE	0.328	

List of Tables

Table 1: Selected empirical studies of economic effects of constitutional rules and their results 161

Table 2: Constitutions in post-socialist countries of Europe and Asia 43

Table 3: Systems of government in post-socialist countries 165

Table 4: Formal constitutional attributes determining the executive-legislature relationship in post-socialist constitutions 48

Table 5: Formal protection of rights and freedoms in post-socialist constitutions (as of 2013[a]) 52

Table 6: *De facto* protection of rights and freedoms in post-socialist constitutions 168

Table 7: Constitutional court independence in post-socialist countries 59

Table 8: Estimation results for specification (1), 1989–2012 (dependent variable: $econ\_reform_{it}$) 68

Table 9: Results of system estimations, 1989–2012 72

Table 10: Estimation results for country groups, 1989–2012 75

Table 11: Difference-in-difference estimates of the effect of constitutions 102

Table 12: Reform dividends (in %) 104

Table 13: Explaining the reform dividends – estimation results 106

Table 14: *De iure* mechanisms of direct democracy in post-socialist countries 122

Table 15: Estimation results for specification (1) including direct democracy, 1989–2012 125

Table 16: Estimation results for direct democracy in country groups, 1989–2012 127

Table 17: Direct democracy and reform dividends – estimation results 128

Table 18: Estimation results for specification (9), 1989–2012 133

List of Figures

Figure 1: Constitutional rules and post-socialist economic reforms – the theoretical nexus 37

Figure 2: Economic reforms in post-socialist countries as measured by EBRD's aggregated transition indicator, 1989–2012...................64

Figure 3: Baseline synthetic control estimates for subsequent post-socialist countries 170

Figure 4: Placebo tests results for subsequent post-socialist countries....... 174

Polish Studies in Economics

Edited by Ryszard Kokoszczyński

Volume 1 Wojciech Grabowski: Employee Stock Options, Payout Policy, and Stock Returns. Shareholders and Option Holders in Large U.S. Technology Corporations. 2012.

Volume 2 Jan Jakub Michałek / Michał Brzozowski / Andrzej Cieślik (eds.): The Relationship between Human Development, Exports and Foreign Direct Investments in Emerging Europe. 2013.

Volume 3 Tomasz Żylicz: The Economics of International Environmental Cooperation. 2015.

Volume 4 Juliusz Jabłecki / Ryszard Kokoszczynski / Paweł Sakowski / Robert Ślepaczuk / Piotr Wójcik: Volatility as an Asset Class. Obvious Benefits and Hidden Risks. 2015.

Volume 5 Janusz Kudła / Konrad Walczyk / Robert Kruszewski / Katarzyna Kopczewska / Agata Kocia: Modeling Fiscal Policy in the European Union. 2015.

Volume 6 Andrzej Cieślik / Jan Jakub Michałek (eds.): Liberalization of Transportation Services in the EU: the Polish Perspective. 2015.

Volume 7 Katarzyna Metelska-Szaniawska: Economic Effects of Post-Socialist Constitutions 25 Years from the Outset of Transition. The Constitutional Political Economy Approach. 2016.

www.peterlang.com

www.ingramcontent.com/pod-product-compliance
Ingram Content Group UK Ltd.
Pitfield, Milton Keynes, MK11 3LW, UK
UKHW021842100926
8556IPUK00019B/997

9 783631 669532